P9-DHH-173

BRANDES
ON VALUE
THE INDEPENDENT INVESTOR

CHARLES H. BRANDES

NEW YORK CHICAGO SAN FRANCISCO ATHENS LONDON
MADRID MEXICO CITY MILAN NEW DELHI
SINGAPORE SYDNEY TORONTO

Copyright © 2015 by Charles H. Brandes. All rights reserved. Printed in the United States of America. Except as permitted under the United States Copyright Act of 1976, no part of this publication may be reproduced or distributed in any form or by any means, or stored in a database or retrieval system, without the prior written permission of the publisher.

Portions of this book were previously published in *Value Investing Today, 3rd Edition,* by Charles Brandes

1 2 3 4 5 6 7 8 9 0   QFR/QFR   1 2 0 9 8 7 6 5 4

ISBN   978-0-07-184935-7
MHID   0-07-184935-1

e-ISBN   978-0-07-184936-4
e-MHID   0-07-184936-X

This publication is designed to provide accurate and authoritative information in regard to the subject matter covered. It is sold with the understanding that neither the author nor the publisher is engaged in rendering legal, accounting, securities trading, or other professional services. If legal advice or other expert assistance is required, the services of a competent professional person should be sought.

—*From a Declaration of Principles Jointly Adopted by a Committee of the American Bar Association and a Committee of Publishers and Associations*

Library of Congress Cataloging-in-Publication Data

Brandes, Charles H.
 Brandes on value : the independent investor / Charles Brandes. — 1 Edition.
   pages cm
 ISBN 978-0-07-184935-7 (hardback : alk. paper) — ISBN 0-07-184935-1 1. Value investing.
2. Stocks. I. Title.
 HG4521.B64633 2014
 332.63'22—dc23

                                                                                    2014036452

McGraw-Hill Education books are available at special quantity discounts to use as premiums and sales promotions or for use in corporate training programs. To contact a representative, please visit the Contact Us pages at www.mhprofessional.com.

To Tanya, with whom I have the greatest delights

Contents

Introduction

A dozen years flew by between the third edition of *Value Investing Today* and my preparation for its update. Considering the myriad industry changes in the interim, you would think that much more time had passed.

I began to extend the new edition's timeline to add my firm's experiences in these tumultuous years, and before long the new material outweighed the old. Like an axe that undergoes three handle replacements and two new heads since first purchased, you start to question if it's the same original tool. Clearly, it was time for a new book.

The heart of *Brandes on Value* is the same as its predecessor book: the Graham-and-Dodd principles of security analysis. Don't change a good thing, was my thinking there. Finding great companies priced cheaply can never go out of style. And the classic approach is especially relevant in a market so heavily influenced by speculation and uncertainty.

As you'll see, I didn't start off a value investor, but I embraced it early in my career and never looked back. My conversion was sparked by the father of value investing, Ben Graham, not only through his books on the topic but from his personal guidance. It was Ben who forged my value mindset and convinced me to start my own practice so that I could pursue it without boundaries.

You may also deduce from this book that value investing isn't for everyone. It requires patience, sometimes a lot more than most people have. Patience is something you can't easily glean from the pages of a book. But it can be fostered and strengthened through process and knowledge—two key components to value investing that are presented here.

Finally, you'll see that value investing also requires a natural, or strongly willed, propensity to take a different path than most. When everyone is herding to something shiny or new, value investors will most likely be among the few who are not. Many words describe this disposition: contrarian, emotionless, isolationist, even weird. I prefer the term *independent investor*.

As of this writing, my firm marks 40 years of independent value investing in companies around the world. All that time the market and investors took many directions, while we independent value investors chose the lesser-traveled roads toward opportunities.

In this context, *Brandes on Value* offers a combination of instruction and personal experiences to highlight the practicality and universal application of Graham-and-Dodd principles. Through historic performance and real-world examples, it explores why the value approach to money management has been very successful, with practical advice on how investors can develop the discipline and succeed with it.

Above all, I hope this book captures for you the essence of why I have been deeply committed to value investing for more than four decades and with no end in sight. I have seen its results; I know it works, and I'm confident it can build wealth for those who apply its principles. Now, I invite you to prepare your mind for a little exercise and a lot of fun as we begin to split the rails of value investing with the help of this totally new "axe" of a book.

Forging My Value Mindset and Grasping the Baton

I believe this is an excellent time to launch an enterprise of this sort.

—Benjamin Graham, in a personal letter to Charles Brandes, March 1, 1974

Fundamental Roots

It's difficult to describe in just a few words the sea change that the country was experiencing in 1968, the year I started in financial services. Suffice it to say that the American political, social, and economic scenes were all in a constant state of flux and uncertainty.

That was the last year of the "Go-Go Era," and the U.S. market then began a steady 36 percent descent over the next three years. From late 1968 to 1970 alone, the Dow fell 906 points to 753, some 45 percent. That was scary for everyone, let alone a newbie. To make matters worse, a one-two punch combination of high inflation and slow economic growth introduced a new word to our economic lexicon: stagflation. This environment, which lasted until around 1971, wasn't exactly the ideal environment for starting out as a broker/analyst. Yet, that's just what I did, because it was exactly what I wanted to do.

Why? I've always been a contrarian of sorts. I'm not exactly sure where this quality came from. I am among the approximately 13 percent of people who are left-handed, and a great deal has been written about the differences in the ways southpaws process ideas and motivations. In any event, always fitting in or going with the crowd has never been a big concern for me if my head and heart lay elsewhere. Admittedly, my inclination to stray from the pack didn't go over well with my drill sergeant. My armed forces stint offered many lessons, one of which was that if I was to be successful as an individual in whatever I chose to do, I would have to work, and think, independently.

Being a contrarian doesn't mean slighting fundamentals and orderliness. In fact, I've always felt more at home applying structure and process to disorder and randomness to solve problems. This is probably why mathematics appealed to me early in life. In due course, when college beckoned, I pursued an advanced math curriculum at Bucknell University in my native state of Pennsylvania. Within the first year, however, another topic caught my attention like a lightning bolt: economics. It became a new direction for me—one that clearly offered me more relevance and practicality than the esoteric theories that filled my math syllabus.

Fundamentals Meet the Markets

It was about this time, too, that my interest in stocks emerged. As I wrapped my head around classroom lessons in economic cycles and the like, I also began to understand how much impact these had on the equities markets and on company fundamentals. My sights were trained not just on the United States, but on international markets, too, as these were more intriguing to me than domestic markets. Adding to the excitement was witnessing the unprecedented number of new mutual funds that were being launched and the select "gurus" among them who seemed to be doing everything right. At the same time, a coterie of value investors was quietly carving its paths into history, among them Max Heine, Irving Kahn, and a young Warren Buffett, who spent part of the mid-1960s methodically absorbing a nondescript Massachusetts textile concern called Berkshire Hathaway.

When I was a college student, money was tight. Thus, along with my friends and classmates, I'd follow the markets mostly out of pure intellectual interest. Even without much skin in the game, it was a thrill to get things right, and, thankfully, it was financially painless when we got things wrong.

Returning to 1968, in my left hand was a bachelor of arts in economics and in my right, the day's *Wall Street Journal*. I was ready for my next chapter. The only question was where. Since I had finished my military obligations, I began exploring opportunities for advanced studies in business. I had a pretty good idea that I would eventually apply my passion for stocks to my chosen career. At the time, of course, most of the best investment jobs were concentrated in the heart of Wall Street. Although New York City is just a 300-mile trek from my alma mater's hometown of Lewisburg, Pennsylvania, I had just about made up my mind that I didn't want to work in the big city. I looked at a couple of schools and talked to a few brokerage houses around Manhattan, but these interviews just convinced me all the more that I wanted something other than a large, urban-based arrangement. It just wasn't for me.

Turn West on Wall Street; Continue for 3,000 Miles

If you've ever been to Lewisburg, I truly hope your visit was at any time but winter. The low-lying Allegheny Mountains are no shield when the Canadian cold snaps want to make themselves known to you. After a quarter century of winters in the Keystone State—and with my new freedom as a recent college graduate—I decided that enough winter cold was enough.

The seeds of relocation had been sown some time before. The emerging "California scene" was having a huge impact on the American psyche. California was in rapid growth mode, with roughly half of its population at the time having been born somewhere else. The appeal was strong, given its plentiful jobs, generous state-sponsored higher education, relatively cheap real estate, and, of course, mild climate. It didn't take much more than that to convince me that this was the time to head there and experience it for myself.

Probably because of my independent streak (again), I didn't naturally gravitate to Los Angeles or San Francisco the way most newcomers to the Golden State did. Those cities were either too densely crowded or too sprawling for what I wanted at the time. What I was looking for was a locale that was about the size of my hometown of Pittsburgh—a tightly knit city where you could get to know your neighbors and go from one end to the other with relative ease.

San Diego was just such a town. After a weeklong cross-continent drive in my Pontiac, my first sight of the cliffs at Torrey Pines told me that I was home.

San Diego was a growing yet very livable city with a rich history and a solid future. There wasn't a lot there in the way of financial services firms at the time. A few regional centers for big banks and branches of the larger national brokerage houses dotted the small downtown skyline. Nevertheless, I soon found one or two brokerages that were amenable to the idea of employing me while I picked away at graduate school at San Diego State.

Ready, Set, "Go-Go!"

Because of the limited finance-related opportunities in the San Diego area, I started as a broker/analyst. The more common term in that period was *stockbroker*, but there was much more to the role than just trading in and out of equities. In reality, that's exactly what I was doing at the beginning. The Go-Go Era bull market was still in full force, and I was swept up in it as I settled into my new job. Clients were indiscriminately throwing their money at a number of "genius" mutual fund companies that were using aggressive investing tactics that netted them 100 percent or more in annual returns. Initial public offerings were at record highs, too, and everyone wanted to get in on what was happening, no matter what it was.

For a starting broker/analyst, watching this unfold was exciting but somewhat uncomfortable. My mindset was different then. As it turned out, my brush with the Go-Go Era ended almost as quickly as it began. Suddenly, the phones went nearly silent, and the market began a trouble-filled three-year retreat. A lot of people were left without chairs when the music stopped.

It didn't require an economics degree to understand *how* the bust had occurred. But the question I wanted to answer was *why*? Looking for meaning in the mayhem, I couldn't attribute it to much more than basic human nature, especially investor greed. Would this ever change? I believed then (and I believe now) that it wouldn't. Yet, this early lesson confirmed my basic outlook. I began a universal shift in how I viewed the markets from broad to narrow, with a focus on fundamentals rather than fanfare. Although my eureka moment was still a few years off, I was erasing the word *speculation* from my professional vocabulary.

Value Emerges

As the bear market dragged on, I stayed focused on serving the few clients I had and applying any lessons that I learned on the job and in the classroom to my practice. The work was challenging, the hours long, and the environment competitive. Although I was practically starving, I loved researching and applying the basics of investing in the economy.

The inevitable wave of Wall Street firm consolidations and bankruptcies during 1969–1970 eventually had a direct impact on my own livelihood.

A change in employers gave me a solid opportunity as a broker/analyst in the La Jolla office of Hayden Stone, an early ancestor of today's Morgan Stanley Wealth Management. Although the market remained stifled, I was making a living doing what I had set out to do—working independently. Licensed broker/analysts literally had to run our book of business as if we were running our own company. Tabulating assets and liabilities, revenue projections, growth strategies, and merchandising were all part of our responsibilities, not to mention analyzing stocks and other investments for our clients. I liked it all, except maybe the marketing. More important, I was drawn to how all those elements fit together in an analytical snapshot of a business.

I enjoyed uncovering everything I could about a stock's issuer, which wasn't always easy. Younger readers may be surprised to learn that there wasn't much in-depth information that was immediately available on the vast majority of public stocks the way there is today. Everyone basically used the same Standard & Poor's Annual Stock Guide and its periodic supplement, which offered a little more information on a select number of issues and was updated more frequently. I enjoyed doing a lot of digging beyond these tomes. As I spent more time looking more deeply into fundamentals, I began to discover some large chasms between what the overall market thought it knew about various companies and what I could actually see. By definition, I knew that this bordered on value investing, which was one of many disciplines that had been broadly presented to me as part of my formal broker training. But to market-chasing investors, who by now were back at it with the "Nifty Fifty," value investing was boring, old school . . . over. So, as interesting as it was for me, value investing took a backseat in my practice until a routine workday changed everything.

Forever Changed by a Chance Meeting

There are two things that I know should be a rare sight: snow in San Diego and a brokerage office with a window sign that reads, "No Walk-Ins Welcome." I'm still waiting for both. While investment houses now have a wider range of channels through which to move their products, few of them will turn away an opportunity to sit down with someone who swings by unannounced. Back then, however, walk-ins were a much larger part of the sales model, and it was standard practice for broker/analysts to take turns keeping a sharp eye out for walk-in customers. After all, who could resist the impulse to buy a round lot of GE after popping into the nearby hardware store for a four-pack of its lightbulbs? These were interesting times. We made the most of them.

Although we were true to our signage, walk-in customers were rare. A day in the life of a broker/analyst was typically spent in preset appointments or in drumming up new business on the phone or around town. I talk to enough financial advisors today to know that things haven't changed much in that regard. Yet, on an unseasonably hot spring afternoon in 1971, I was taking my turn at the helm of our Prospect Street location when an elderly, unassuming man walked through the door.

At first glance, I was sure that he was just lost, so I dropped my slide rule and offered to help direct him to wherever in the neighborhood he had intended to be. As it eventually turned out, it was I who was temporarily off course, and he helped me find my way back.

He introduced himself as Ben and said that he wanted to open an account. By now you have probably figured out that my unexpected visitor was Benjamin Graham, whom many consider to be the father of value investing. He had retired many years earlier from running his investment partnership and teaching at Columbia University. To my delight, he told me that he was spending his winters in La Jolla. His mission at the moment was to purchase a particular stock. We set up an account and got to work.

His target was National Presto Industries, a midwestern maker of kitchen appliances that he had been tracking for months as a value stock example for a new book. He thought that the stock was undervalued, but he needed to check our S&P supplement to verify a few pieces of fundamental data that would buttress his case. The trade was processed in no time, but I asked him if he could hang around a while and talk more about investing and value stocks in particular. He was happy to do so.

My training as a broker had included only certain chapters in Graham and Dodd's *Security Analysis* and *The Intelligent Investor*. However, after that first encounter with Graham himself, I circled back and read both books from cover to cover.

Ben was a natural teacher and a pleasure to talk with about any investment topic. Nothing was taboo. Over the next several years, we became acquaintances, as we shared a mutual affinity for value investing and a dislike for the Nifty Fifty run-up, indexing, and the efficient frontier, among other things. Wherever the topic took us, though, he always managed to link it back to his core principles and his perspectives on value investing. It all made total sense to me. Between his sage advice and my own discoveries as I familiarized myself with the consistently superior track records of those who followed the Graham-and-Dodd investment principles, I was hooked. No other aspect of my education and training up to this point had had such a total, life-changing impact on me as getting to know Ben Graham face to face.

My First Lesson: Value Is Adaptable

What resonated most with me was his prescient view that value investing, while fundamentally sound, is not necessarily absolute. Its principles can be adapted in different ways based on one's own unique and independent way of looking at the world and at individual companies. He also more than hinted that where I was working and what I was doing there were not likely to provide me with the best opportunity to meaningfully apply my approach to value any time soon.

He was absolutely right. If I was going to devote myself to value investing, I needed to make a move. Fortunately, it didn't take long for the right opportunity to come along, or so it seemed. As I laid the plans for opening my own practice in late 1973, the markets were continuing a downward spiral that had started in January. When I opened my doors on March 1, 1974, the markets kept dropping. My only regret was that Ben Graham couldn't make it to the ceremony. Almost as good, however, he sent me a heartfelt letter congratulating me on my having taken the leap during what he called "an excellent time to launch a venture of this sort." His note is still preserved under glass and on central display at the firm's headquarters to help us all appreciate from whence we came and to inspire us to innovate and think differently when serving our clients.

While I got my bearings as the owner of a new business, some of our nation's darkest times conspired to push equities into a 45 percent free fall by the end of the year. It was a great time for established value investors, but it was a hostile climate in which to start a business. Building momentum took a lot of time and devotion. But I kept at it. I received a lot of criticism from my early clients when their short-term performance suffered, and I lost a few of these clients before long. Still, I was convinced then, as I am today, that the fundamentals of value investing made total practical sense for long-term investors. I had learned this from the experts, and I was ready and able to grasp the baton and apply their principles in my unique way.

Equities hit bottom nine months after our firm was founded. As things started to look better for the markets, investors began to recognize the strength of the companies that we owned. And, for the first time since I began my exclusive value investing journey, I held in my hands the *proof* of what I believed: value investing works.

Looking back over the years since then, value has fallen into and out of favor many times. For the long-term investor who is patient and objective, however, you'll see in the coming chapters how and why I have come to believe that value investing is a superior way to go.

A Priceless 'Good Luck' from the Father of Value Investing

BENJAMIN GRAHAM
LA JOLLA, CALIFORNIA 92037

March 1, 1974

Dear Mr. Brandes:

accomplishments

This is the day to wish all good future and
success to Branco Investors Ltd.. Naturally
I am complimented by your statement that the
new firm will be operated along "Graham principles." Actually I believe that this is an
excellent time to launch an enterprise of this
sort and I'm confident that your partners
will be well-pleased with the results.

I'm sorry to to say that my health is on the
poor side these days and I can't be sure that
I'll make my engagement for April 3rd. But
I'm hoping for the best.

Sincerely,

Ben Graham

PART I

WHY VALUE INVESTING?

L ike every book, this one has a beginning, although its featured topic—value investing—has no end. Value's never-ending story is no myth. Its principles are grounded in the simple reality that if you buy a company for less than its worth, you can improve economic efficiency and make money.

While its roots stretch back to the 1930s, value investing is as applicable as ever to the modern financial world. It is the efficient answer to an inefficient market fueled by ever-present irrational investor behavior. Bull and bear markets will come and go, but the principles of value investing are immovable, and their superior results have been clearly measurable.

Why value investing? It's reliable, repeatable, and, as you're about to see, relatively straightforward. *Successful* value investing, however, takes hard work, dedication, focus, and a lot of instinct and good judgment. But that's just part of the story, which begins on the next page. Here we go again.

CHAPTER 1

HERE WE GO AGAIN

The two most powerful warriors are patience and time.

—Leo Tolstoy

She was a soft-spoken senior auditor from the SEC making a routine visit to review my then 15-year-old asset management firm. Within minutes, she went into a frenetic panic.

"What is she yelling about?" asked an excited Glenn Carlson, the firm's lead portfolio manager. "Did she find something sketchy in our files? Who is she calling? Are we in trouble?"

Her horror had nothing to do with our recordkeeping, which turned out to be fine. It was about her investment portfolio. The guy on the other end of the phone was her boss in Los Angeles, and he seemed to have no time for or interest in talking to her because he was in his own world of hurt.

I'll never forget the way she looked or her gut-wrenching concern. She was just a few years from retirement, and visibly shaken by a genuine fear that by the end of the day, she could lose everything that she had saved for it.

Our attention suddenly turned to our phones, which were now ringing constantly as word of the dire trouble that was unfolding in New York City on that Monday, October 19, 1987, quickly spread. Clients wanted to know what was happening, but no one had a clue—not us, not our guest SEC auditor or her boss, and not our own brokers or the broadcast news media, which were the only immediate news sources at the time.

Thread together the handful of helpless global markets, scores of dumbfounded brokerage houses, millions of panicked investors, and billions in lost assets, and you have the wet blanket that was "Black Monday," an unprecedented 22 percent one-day market crash.[1] Everyone thought it was the end of the world as we knew it. For many of those who worked through it, even the 2008 meltdown couldn't surpass the 1987 crash in terms of heartfelt panic and the general feeling of sickness in their stomachs.

Early the next day, the market kept skidding while regulators and the media scrambled to untangle the mess. At our firm, a call came in from *Outstanding Investor Digest* editor Henry Emerson in New York. One of the more objective and balanced trade journalists, Emerson's sole focus that day was on the blood in the streets.

"I'm writing a story on how everyone is freaking out, and I thought I'd include what you're doing as a result of what happened yesterday," he began.

Unintentionally, I changed the entire angle of his story with my first word: "Nothing."

He began to pepper me with questions: "Nothing? What about your clients? Aren't they panicked? What are you telling them? How can you *not* be panicking?"

I told him that our clients were understandably concerned, and that we were reaching out to all of them with whatever information we had, which was still very little. Not to panic is our first order of business. Whatever the causes of Black Monday, I added, we needed to stay the course, especially because the market was undergoing what I viewed then as a long-needed correction.

With all due respect to the millions of investors who suffered that day, I felt that no matter what was behind the sudden tumble, the market would rebound. By that point, I had worked through 20 years of markets, and for 15 of those years, I had focused exclusively on value investing. My experience led me to believe that, while sudden and painful, these injuries would eventually heal. They did.

The Future Rhymes with the Past

October 19, 1987, is just another example of how I tend to be motivated by the markets in a different way from most people. I think that when the markets go south, it's time to keep a cool head and focus on basic fundamentals rather than just run for cover. This wasn't always the way I viewed the world. I came to it through a series of fortunate events soon after I entered the financial industry, all of them leading up to my profoundly life-changing encounter with Benjamin Graham that would help me see how my perspective could be put to constructive use.

So far, I have marked nearly a half century in the investment management business, most of that time serving as a steward of assets. It wasn't always a smooth ride, although I have absolutely no complaints. For more than 40 of those years, my experiences with "Mr. Market," to borrow Benjamin Graham's preferred sobriquet, have been dynamic.

With each ebb and flow, Mr. Market entices investors with the "quick and the new," leading them to believe that this time is very different, and that we've never seen the likes of this before. His pattern of tricks changes slightly each time, but usually only enough to mine the one constant: investor behavior. Why doesn't investor behavior change? We like to think it would, especially when you look at all the lessons of past markets. Short-term thinking, however, is human nature—it's in our DNA. It's how we are wired. We tend to process decisions relatively quickly based on what we see in front of us at the moment, or on what we believe others may be seeing. Such irrational behavior is ages old and is based on primal instincts like fear—we are afraid of either getting hurt or missing out. Many years later, this behavioralism was recognized as a key feature of value investing. This intricate world of behavioral finance is covered in depth later in the book, but I mention it briefly here to help establish some groundwork for why I embraced value investing and have never looked back.

Quick Brush with the "Go-Go Era"

In 1968, human nature in the form of short-term speculation ruled the day. It was the tail end of the Go-Go Era, and I had landed my first job as a broker/analyst just out of graduate school. The hype revolved around a select group of "star" mutual funds, such as Gerald Tsai's Manhattan Fund, and few people thought twice before handing over their money to these funds. Investors were chasing soaring returns, some of which went into triple digits—the by-product of a tidal wave of speculative investing. The fervor also sparked a rash of initial public offerings (IPOs) that fetched tremendous premiums. The returns were there, but so was the high risk.[2]

When I arrived on the scene, some 40 percent of American households owned stocks, either directly or through mutual funds,[3] and the stampede was still underway. It was an exciting but fleeting experience for me in my budding career, because it all deflated by 1969, sending the market into retreat and investors running for cover for the next few years.

Shift to the "Nifty Fifty"

Following the 1970 bear market, a group of about 50 companies soon captivated the market. First identified by Morgan Guaranty Trust (MGT) (later JPMorgan), these businesses were considered the go-to powerhouses, the most reliable and downright nifty companies. The name stuck, and the craze lionized the likes of Coca-Cola, IBM, and Polaroid (see Figure 1-1).[4] By 1971, right after the Go-Go Era ended badly, investors had caught the Nifty Fifty wave in droves. The logic at the time was that investors had learned their lessons from overspeculating on high-risk go-go funds, and it was time to play it safe with the perceived stalwart growth stocks.

In creating its list, MGT set investors on a course to believe that these companies had rock-solid business models and were surrounded by protective moats that market forces could never traverse to bear them harm. They bought these stocks in bulk, planning to hold them forever for the ride to the sky. Investors know better now (and supposedly knew better then, too); they know that nothing is impenetrable. The unjustifiable prices that these 50 stocks eventually hit would lead to their toppling by 1973. As so much of the overall market's run-up had been tied to them, their rapid sell-off was far-reaching and was felt for years throughout the world's major markets.

At the time, I didn't necessarily view the Go-Go and Nifty Fifty debacles as watershed events with important lessons. They did show me how dangerous it could be to engage in short-term speculation and herd mentality. As I saw it, the 50 companies involved weren't at fault. Most of them were excellent examples of well-run businesses, such as Dow Chemical and McDonald's, which, along with many others on the list, continued to perform well during and/or long after the meltdown. Instead, the mistake was the way investors hyped them well beyond their ability to deliver. While we hear many stories of how mismanaged companies can lead to poor market performance, the Nifty Fifty is a rare example of how good companies can be bad investments when investor behavior gets in the way.

"Nifty Fifty:" Some Survived and Thrived, Others Not So Much

Nifty Then & Still Strong
General Electric
Coca-Cola
Dow Chemical
Johnson & Johnson
McDonald's

Nifty Then & Now Gone
Digital Equipment Corporation (sold off to Compaq)
Heublein Spirits (sold off to R.J. Reynolds)
Burroughs Corporation (became Unisys)
Upjohn (acquired by Pfizer)
Schering-Plough Corporation (merged with Merck)

Source: Morgan Guaranty Trust Company.

Figure 1-1 That fact that there is no universal list of the actual "Nifty Fifty" is another testimonial to its nebulous nature. Those listed represent a small sampling of the more agreed-upon companies on the list in the late 1960s.

The resulting market collapse in 1973, combined with high inflation and other economic and political turmoil, conspired to reduce the supply of ready and willing investors. This gave me the time and a cause to reexamine and evaluate the long-lasting challenges that short-term investor behavior could create, especially for my nascent investment management practice. By 1974—months before the markets finished their worst downturn in 50 years—I had made a full commitment to value investing, a transition that would change the way I serve my clients forever.

Is Now a Good Time?

With the Dow Jones Industrial Average having slid nearly 45 percent, the world of equities looked very bleak in late 1974.[5] So much seemed to be working against investor psychology, such as a lingering energy crisis sparked by the 1973 OPEC oil embargo, rabid inflation, the divisive issue of U.S. involvement in Vietnam, and what economists called the "Nixon shock," which ranged from the political fallout from the Watergate scandal to his administration's decision to take the United States off the gold standard. The latter move shocked the global markets, because many developed nations' monetary policies had long been tied to the U.S. dollar based on the Bretton Woods system established in 1944. After the United States cut the golden cord, the pain was felt in markets throughout the world, with the worst being in the United Kingdom, where the London Stock Exchange, the FTSE 100, lost more than 70 percent of its quotational value.[6]

With such strong headwinds, one would think that this wasn't the best conditions in which to start an investment firm—not to mention land any potential clients. On the contrary, it was the perfect time to begin. With the market on its back, there were more opportunities for value investors than ever before. I just needed to have an environment where I could apply my convictions about researching and investing independently.

As you would expect, in the firm's early years, convincing people of the merits of fundamental value investing proved quite challenging, as most of what they were seeing in the short term constantly flew in its face. The market would soon pick up speed, and in 1975, not long after I founded my value-focused asset management firm, equities produced a double-digit uptick. Nixon had resigned the previous summer, our entanglement in Vietnam was over, and the economic data looked more hospitable. The following year, stocks produced another respectable gain, but they then gave it all back by the end of 1978. Although this was a little frustrating, it revealed that the market was sputtering back to life. Normal and expected gyrations returned, although investors did not. General hostility toward stocks still ran deep, and investors' reluctance to take the plunge stemmed from their lack of understanding and appreciation of what had burned them the last time. I remained optimistic as the 1980s approached. Then, with no warning, we were all invited to a requiem.

The Death of Equities

It still makes me smile how wrong *Business Week* got it in August 1979, when its cover story predicted that stocks were finished as the preeminent asset class (Figure 1-2). At the time, I was shocked. I was a half-decade into my new practice, and they were telling me not to bother. It was time to turn out the lights and go home.

Did They Get It Right?

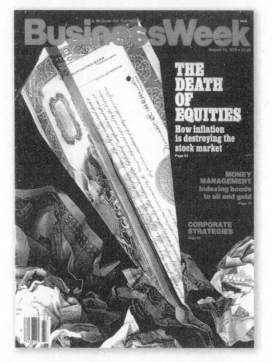

Used with permission of Bloomberg BusinessWeek copyright© 2014. All rights reserved.

Figure 1-2

I give the magazine's editors credit for their well-researched conclusions. They adroitly laid the groundwork for a systemic failure in the equity markets, ushered in by inflation's nagging toll on earnings, spiraling interest rates, and an apparently insurmountable 10-year drop-off in investor demand. There were 7 million fewer stock owners in 1979 than there had been in 1970, with most of the shrinkage being concentrated in the younger demographic (that is, the future).

Not helping, they argued, was a shift by institutional investors, such as pension plans, away from traditional equities and into more alternative-style asset classes such as commodity futures, real estate, and even precious metals and diamonds. Newer regulations, such as the Employee Retirement Income Security Act of 1974, now permitted plan administrators to do this.

The editors concluded that the inevitable death of equities was not something that "a stock market rally—however strong—will check." It all seemed rather dire, until I read a little further and was convinced otherwise.

What jumped off the page was a matter-of-fact statement that just floated there with little elaboration: "Even if the economic climate could be made right again for equity investment, it would take another massive promotional campaign to bring people back into the market," the editors forecasted. "Nor is it likely that Wall Street would ever again launch such a promotional campaign." In a nanosecond, I saw the opportunity.

Nothing attracts a crowd like a crowd, goes the adage. I can't imagine anything more effective as a "massive promotional campaign" for stocks than the one that they implemented for themselves—by just being equities—in the summer of 1982. Less than three years after their 1979 "passing," equities were resurrected and proceeded to clear a path to historic highs.

BusinessWeek had the facts. All its data made sense. Its conclusions seemed logical. However, for whatever reason, it dismissed one important fact that makes markets go up: the influence of economic growth, declining interest rates, and cheap starting prices.

Equities Resurrected

Economic and business cycles seemed to be in the right place at the right time starting in 1982, but investor psychology probably had the biggest role in the banner market uptick that unfurled over the subsequent five years. *BusinessWeek's* unattainable "massive promotional campaign" emerged—with a vengeance. Diversifying, thirsty business media, which now included CNN, CNBC, and Financial News Network, lapped it up. As in the Go-Go Era, stocks and the companies behind them as well as "star" fund managers were covered in more depth and woven ever more tightly into the daily news cycle. Investors watched from a distance at first, still shell-shocked, but they eventually got on board.

At the risk of sounding dismissive, I kept my distance and instead focused on how this would affect the all-important business cycles that make up such a large part of my value strategies. As the biggest bull market in history ran its course, I focused on what most people considered to be merely the sidebar components: the fundamentals of individual companies. As you'd expect, the market genie granted fewer new wishes for value companies, as everything rode upward; all the while, the lessons from the Go-Go and Nifty Fifty eras reminded me that he'd eventually return to his lamp. The only question was when.

A Case of the Mondays

The unforgettable fright exhibited by our visiting SEC auditor on October 19, 1987, was amplified by millions around the world that day.

Angry, confused, and even desperate, our clients called constantly to learn what we were doing about "it" at every moment. There wasn't a lot to share with them, because we just didn't know what "it" was or why "it" was happening. Information wasn't as readily available then as it is today. Our link to the ticker was via our external traders by telephone, and even they were in the dark and frustrated because the tape was delayed by more than two hours. The 24-hour news cycle had no presence in the workplace. The Internet was only a dream, and CNN was still something you watched when you got home. Radio provided little information, and TV news pretty much saved any depth for the evening broadcast. Most media then preferred to wait and report verified facts when they had them, rather than settling for parroting speculation by the minute. (I wish this were more true today.) Not helping public sentiment was President Ronald Reagan. In a hastily prepared, day-after press conference, Reagan intimated that the downward spiral was a logic-defying fluke because "the underlying economy remains sound." He wasn't wrong, although nothing that any world leader or media outlet offered that day could have stemmed the sell-off once that juggernaut started.

After our interview with *Outstanding Investor Digest* wrapped up, I went on practicing what I had just preached: do nothing rash. Stay calm. We responded or reached out to every client with a simple message: wait and see what is really happening before doing anything sudden.

Our portfolios certainly took their share of hits, especially the overseas holdings such as Australian banks and Dutch chemical and shipping companies, as those markets suffered even more than U.S. equities in the subsequent days and weeks.

Deep down, I still couldn't help being enthusiastic about the long-term opportunities this correction could offer our clients. To me, the fact that a hair-trigger event could cause such a stampede for the exit was proof that stock prices had become dangerously unmoored from business value. Until the time was right, I kept this opinion to myself out of professional and moral respect for those who were taking a tough hit in the near term.

What really happened on Black Monday had less to do with market fundamentals than with flawed computer programming—the first of its kind, but certainly not the last. When the dust settled, the blame went in many directions. The largest share went to a new kind of defendant: a technical glitch. The problem was program trading, particularly computer-based portfolio insurance programs used by institutional investors for hedging.[7] For the first time, the increasingly technical nature of trading, which had been growing exponentially behind the scenes, was forced to the surface. In theory, through its use of futures and options, program trading sounded like an effective safeguard against risk, but it caused more problems than it solved.

The software was written by people, who logically defined risk as a decline in price. If prices dropped, the software would automatically trigger a sell. If the price fell more, the software would sell more. The process became self-fulfilling in a blink. At the end of the day, it offered little protection for the portfolios it was supposed to be insuring, as everyone just blindly dumped their holdings.

After a cursory postmortem on program trading and index arbitrage, other culprits for the day's damage, the SEC quickly mandated circuit-breaker procedures to prevent similar trading snafus. Supposedly, all was well again. Given more recent similar events, such as the "flash crash" in 2010, apparently these solutions are not airtight.

Other reasons cited for the crash included overvaluation, illiquidity, and—my personal favorite—investor behavior. Talk about stating the obvious. These things are nice to know, but they are not things that lawmakers can realistically prevent from recurring.

Regardless of why Black Monday occurred, nearly $500 billion in value of wealth-producing businesses disappeared within a matter of hours.[8] How does one trust the markets after taking that sort of beating? Over the next few years, my firm suffered its share of the industrywide client exodus. We braced for the worst, which actually never came. The biggest fallout struck thousands of industry professionals who lost their jobs, but fears of a decade-long investor flight from the markets weren't realized. It took just a few years for investors to regain their confidence, which wasn't long compared to the wait-and-see periods after previous market setbacks.

Consequently, the market's natural course helped it regain its previous high-water mark within just two years. As the 1980s neared their penultimate year, 1989 placed a lasting dog-ear crease in a key page of my market lessons book: the savings and loan crisis. Known as the "S&L scandal," its roots stretched back to the 1970s, when soaring interest rates had convinced a wide swath of depositors to move their assets to money market funds. Protective rules tightly capped the yields that S&L institutions (a.k.a. "thrifts") were allowed to pay, so investors started to take their money elsewhere. Eventually, this spelled disaster for the thrifts.

Cincinnati Red S&L

Fast forward to the 1980s, when, after a period of aggressive lobbying by the thrift industry, lawmakers started to loosen the fetters. This may have helped S&Ls add more profitable products to their lineup in the short term. At the same time, however, it also reduced federal and state oversight, which opened the door to more "creative" yet risky investment ventures and, for some S&Ls, to pure chicanery. Although depositors started to return, the damage to many institutions had already been done. Real estate, a big portion of many S&Ls' "new and improved" business models, fell out from under them. First blood occurred in 1985 in Cincinnati, when it came out that Home State Savings Bank was so deeply in the red that it risked imminent collapse. Customers lined up outside every branch in the classic "bank run" fashion similarly captured in photos from the Great Depression. Withdrawals quickly drained Ohio's deposit insurance coffers, and the snowball effect took hold. Implosion at Maryland's Old Court Savings quickly followed, then many more, leading up to the two high-profile failures that would bring it all down: Silverado Savings and Loan and Lincoln Savings and Loan.

If this is all new territory for you, you're probably thinking that it didn't end well for anyone. You're right. It was a raw deal for most people, especially taxpayers, who ended up footing the nearly $125 billion bill for the cleanup.[9] My firm held some of the affected stocks, so it also was caught in the downdraft. For value investors in general, the years that followed would be deemed "nuclear winter." But there was a good side to this experience.

Suppose I told you that the challenging environment that it created actually helped some investors end on a high note. How? Through the basic value investing tenet that not all birds flock together. Without a doubt, the S&L crisis meant wholesale trouble for an iconic and tested institution that dates back to eighteenth-century British traditions. I prefer to try to look beyond such noise. Were all 3,000-plus thrift associations in dire straits? No. In fact, by the time it was all over, only about 750 had actually failed outright. Several smaller S&Ls caught our attention and played out well in the coming years. Taking a wider view, the market viewed the industry, meaning the *entire banking sector*, as a very bad bet. This offered tremendous value opportunities in some of the stronger commercial banks, whose prices were well below their intrinsic values. These were well-run businesses—otherwise untouched by the scandal—that had been hit by the market's stigma, and that now offered some of the largest margins of safety I had ever seen in my career. I discuss the significance of margin of safety in the next chapter.

Crossing the Ponds

It's been said many times that value strategies are beneficial only when most of the market is miserable.

This is true—but only some of the time. Value investors can, and do, take advantage of market downturns to invest in strong companies whose prices are being dragged down with the crowd (as I mentioned during the S&L crisis). On the other hand, value investors can be temporarily left out in the cold when the market party seems to be hopping along for everyone else.

There are those rare times when new investing paradigms seem to move everyone in the same direction simultaneously. One such occurrence was the major shift in investor attitudes toward a prevailing acceptance of international equities as viable investments. This began around 1990 as the last embers of the cold war faded, opening the door to a reunified Germany and access to other markets. It didn't take long to gel after a fury of free-trade agreements ensued, helped by the growing influence of the European Union and the 1995 formation of the World Trade Organization. While new international trade laws helped to remove many of the barriers to entry, the logistics of investing in foreign markets were made easier through the creation of more American Depository Receipts (ADRs) and other helpful bank instruments.

In my view, everyone was doing the right thing by adding more non-U.S.-based companies to their portfolios. I had been investing overseas since one of my first clients demanded it, and I had never backpedaled. In fact, it practically became my specialty. One of my earliest international investments (and my first emerging market stock) was Telmex, Mexico's primary telecommunications company, in the early 1980s. I examine the details of global investing in later chapters. For now, whether by the hands of value, growth, or other types of investors, the methodical expansion into markets beyond the United States was a collective win for us all. For someone like me, who needs to see everything add up correctly before I pursue it, international investing just made perfect sense, and it still does.

Value Has No Borders

The excitement and potential rewards of investing in companies around the world can also create distinctive drama. As investor interest in non-U.S. markets further widened throughout the 1990s, these markets began to be affected by a new crop of troublesome, rapid-fire events. Ironically, the farther the investment arena stretched, the more likely it was that problems from across the globe could reach our front doorstep practically overnight. Among many global challenges, the foremost and most influential to our firm's investors in the 1990s were those of Scandinavia, Mexico, and Asia—each a prime example of how value investors, who by nature focus on company fundamentals rather than macro events, just can't ignore the bigger picture sometimes.

The "Stockholm Solution"

A crisis can hit you in places that all the data suggest are the most stable on earth. In Sweden, a catastrophic real estate and financial bubble that burst in 1992 led to a fivefold jump in interest rates, massive unemployment, and failure of the financial system that nearly broke the government's back.[10] Practically overnight, Swedish authorities nationalized the country's banks to sort things out, leaving many investors, including my firm (which had holdings in Svenska Handelsbanken), with little more than a number to wait our turn for compensation. There was nothing we could do at that point except move on and chalk it up to an unpreventable bad experience. The most interesting aspect for me showed up years later, when I saw how the financial requirements imposed by the resulting "Stockholm solution" made Sweden's banks all but impervious to the financial crisis of 2008–2009.

The "Tequila Effect"

One of the largest untapped wells of international investing is literally right next door: Mexico. In 1994, the world was aghast when the Mexican peso went into a death spiral. The precursors of this tragedy are beyond the scope of this book. Let's just say that the economic impact on the world was far too important for the brotherhood of nations to just ride it out. The International Monetary Fund (IMF), the U.S. and Canadian governments, and various global agencies all combined to intervene. For the United States alone, the $20 billion in loan guarantees that it offered was its largest nonmilitary financial offering to a sovereign nation since the Marshall Plan.

As you can imagine, the crisis was impossible to ignore. Before the IMF stepped up, it had spread to Brazil and other areas of South America, and it was becoming a potential contagion to many other focal areas in our global strategies. Even during such times of duress, however, value investing requires a bottom-up view of the world. Our focus remained on our individual holdings throughout the crisis.

The "Asian Contagion"

Some 5,000 miles away from Mexico, what began as a Thai currency plunge mushroomed into a regional crisis that severely affected 10 nations and global markets for a very frightening month in the summer of 1997.

As with Mexico, it was disturbing to see the problems of one country—this time Thailand—spread so quickly to its neighbors, like Indonesia, the Philippines, and the region's economic anchor, South Korea. The latter's government all but went bankrupt in the process. As in 1994, the IMF and the world community rushed in to help get the affected nations through it. Nevertheless, the ramifications of the crisis were felt for many years, particularly as investors ceased to trust most of the affected local economies and those surrounding them. Even with the lessons learned from riding out the Mexico crisis just a few years earlier, it was still extremely challenging for us to ignore the Asian contagion. We still managed to lift the screen of confusion and saw little permanence in most of the problems.

Value investors often have to push through the fog to find the beacon of opportunity that the macroeconomic forces often leave lit for us. Then and today, all of these regions, from the Netherlands to the Asia-Pacific region and Latin America, provide some of the most productive veins of undervalued companies in the world.

Tulips Dot-Com

No discussion of historic market bubbles can overlook the tulip mania that reportedly spread throughout Holland until it unraveled in March of 1637. This myopic craze is usually considered to be the first documented speculative bubble. Since they were distinctive-looking flowers that were relatively new to this part of the continent at the time, tulips were quickly popularized as a status symbol. At one point, it is believed, one bulb fetched 10 times a worker's annual wages. It's a long story, well covered by Charles Mackay.[11] How could something with such low intrinsic value ever reach the meteoric price levels that are alleged? Does this sound practical or logical, or even believable? Yes. Being a longtime student of investor behavior, it would not surprise me that the tulip bubble happened exactly like that.

Some 350 years after tulip mania, we lived through a different market mania, equally narrow in focus, spawned not from seeds, but from silicon. Of course, I'm speaking of the technology bubble, whose bursting nearly devastated our economy beginning in March 2000. Also addressed later in the book, this bubble bears mention as another example of how frenetic speculation dwarfed basic fundamentals in grand style.

Investors couldn't get enough of Internet stocks. Companies of all shapes and sizes were sprouting up and going public, each vying for a position in the backbone of a "new economy" that would change the American business model forever. As in the Go-Go Era, IPOs soared as these ventures jockeyed for market presence and funding. As with the Nifty Fifty, price-to-earnings ratios and other key metrics for these start-ups were ridiculously unrealistic, but nobody cared. Finally, as in the mid-1980s, everybody wanted in—except that there was no wait-and-see first. The time to get in was yesterday.

In fact, the widespread adoption of the Internet was a resounding global game changer. In terms of its meaningful impact on humankind, social scientists liken its creation to Gutenberg's invention of movable type. However, this doesn't mean that you can't take a step or two back before you tether your investment strategy to anything with "dot-com" in its name. Although many investors may have thought of that, few followed the logic before jumping right in.

A Tangled Web

The flashy hype was omnipresent, creating an irresistible lure of the kind that speculators were born to chase. We watched and read everywhere about how "cool" these companies were, along with their celebrity-status entrepreneur founders—many of whom were made overnight millionaires (at least on paper). They were the wave of the future, and they simultaneously dominated the high-end advertising, pop culture, and news media scenes from 1996 to 2000. Investors were led to believe that if you didn't get it, it was because you were too "old-school" in your thinking. The feeling you were supposed to be left with was that if you didn't leap now, you'd miss your chance. Mr. Market had somehow uniquely combined youth and technology to make even experienced investors think that this time things were truly different.

Through it all, I saw a pattern in what was usually missing from all the hoopla. I couldn't get a true reading on how these businesses really worked or what their long-term business models looked like. No matter how we looked at them, we came to the same conclusion: there was little or no chance that their current price matched what their fundamentals told me they were actually worth. One buy-side analyst concluded that Amazon.com and AOL required a subscriber growth that would include every other planet in the solar system to justify their valuation. That is, even if all 6 billion people on earth signed up, it still wouldn't justify their multiples.

All that said, I could smell the tulips a mile away. When 33 percent of the S&P 500 Index's capitalization comes from one thing, technology, logic should tell you that something is about to break.[12] As you probably surmised, my firm did not participate one binary bit in the magnificent dot-com boom. Instead, we focused on the "boring" companies, solid businesses that the rest of the market was overlooking in the new gold rush. The closest we came to Internet stocks was telecommunications, which was still viewed as a traditional industry but was busily laying the physical infrastructure that would become the railroad tracks for high-speed access to the World Wide Web.

It was a lonely time to be a value investor, and it was often difficult to be taken seriously. In a national conference call in February 2000, just one month before the bubble burst, our portfolio managers were publicly scolded by the branch leader of a major brokerage firm, who said that we had "no chance in hell" of future success if we didn't start investing in tech. His vitriolic rant even went so far as to say that we were nearly in breach of our fiduciary duty by *not* chasing the pack. We took a lot of heat during those years. We also graciously took the praise and appreciation from our clients when the floor eventually caved in far from where they were standing.

Investing should be grounded in basic fundamentals. If you rely on speculation, it will fail you every time. Reliance on fundamentals means looking past the hype and right into the heart and soul of a company. This will get you a lot further down the road to your goals, or at least give you more than a fighting chance when the market takes a swing at you.

Financial Crisis of 2008–2009

Although they were still nursing their burns from the tech bubble, investors were right back in the fire soon enough. From 2002 to 2007, a strong recovery and its usual sidekick, excess, made themselves heard. This time, overenthusiasm and major speculative trends in the mortgage industry took over. Most people knew that this would bring problems, but few saw what was really coming, including me.

The culprit this time was leverage, which was a new behavior *pattern*, but one that was still based on the same classic human motivators: greed and a herd mentality. The term was carefully labeled in ledgers and annual reports as if to homogenize it for acceptance into the world of large and, as we soon discovered, tenuous financial institutions. However, leverage can lead to risky borrowing to allow you to invest money that you don't have. At the same time, banks were hedging against their own subprime loans through credit default swaps, marking the first time that they actually began betting against their own customers. In basic economics, if consumers owe more than they make, it will eventually lead to a slowdown in spending to let them catch up. When institutions overextend themselves, it spells trouble, but the problems are survivable with a little capital and time, as we saw in Sweden in the early 1990s. In this case, consumers and institutions the world over were up to their ears in debt, again unmooring prices from value and creating a whole new breed of disaster that changed the financial landscape for a very long time. This is the essence of the 2008 economic collapse. Foremost, it was a crisis of credit, a lack of capital, an implosion of mortgage pools, and recurring errors in mark-to-market and other accounting practices, all rolled into one insurmountable force. Speculative excesses—albeit under new wraps—came home to roost once again. In Chapter 10, I dive deeper into the financial crisis of 2008–2009 and its important takeaways that we try to apply to value stock selection going forward.

Old Approaches in New Wrappings

Now, fast-forward a few years and Bill Gross, the former West Coast–based manager of the largest bond mutual fund in the world, is predicting that "the cult of equity is dying."[13] He and other pundits predicted the death of equities all over again, seeing them as being bested by the more enticing returns and supposedly lower risk of alternative-style fixed-income products. Walk a little further, and fixed income begins to show its proverbial slip against the headwinds of rising rates. Outflows from traditional bond mutual funds were setting new records by 2013 as rate-starved investors woke up to the fact that bonds, like any other asset class, offer their own variety of risks.[14]

Today, some 45 years removed from the Go-Go Era, investor reactions to the markets have not changed, but the new "shiny" distraction has: risk. Risk has now been popularly redefined as the impact of short-term volatility, not as what it really is, which is the permanent loss of capital. In my more than 40-year career, I have never seen risk as misunderstood yet as overemphasized as it is today, especially in the institutional world. Many people are fixated on reducing short-term volatility, not positioning for long-term growth. In this process, indexing is now taking a front seat, whether because of its perceived cost benefits, its supposed lower risk profile, or someone's viral idea that active investing just doesn't get the job done over the long run. We'll visit all this later in the book as well.

So it will continue, this overemphasis on short-term considerations and the constant chase for the shiny new thing. Long/short strategies, hedge funds, commodity futures, and other alternatives keep coming and going, offering little more than a zero-sum game. Old, "fishy" approaches continue to arrive in new wrappings. The *new* new thing may have been tried in the past, yet it keeps coming around again, repackaged by the crafty hands of Mr. Market to distract investors from their long-term goals.

All the while, the real long-term producers of wealth, individual businesses, continue to hum along, with many of the best of them often being overlooked by the markets as a whole. Is it really worth sacrificing the long-term returns that these opportunities can provide for short-term speculation or the illusion of "risk" reduction? I believe not.

Having just shared a comprehensive synopsis of what led me to believe this, permit me now to show why I think I'm right.

2

FUNDAMENTALS: WHAT IS VALUE INVESTING?

The value investing philosophy eschews short-term considerations and gets you thinking most about fundamentals, as if you actually owned the business itself, not just its stock.

—Charles Brandes, in an interview with Bloomberg Radio, October 2013

H ave you ever walked out of a cinema or a theater wondering whether what you just watched was worth the cost of your ticket? The answer basically depends on whether you enjoyed the experience, which can involve more than just the feature you watched; it includes such things as the seating environment, whether you could find easy parking, and the like. In other words, what sort of value did you get for your money?

To avoid oversimplifying, I'll quickly connect the dots: investing in companies can work the same way. The price you pay for something—whether it's movie tickets or stocks—is relevant only as it relates to its underlying value.

This is the essence of value investing, that is, purchasing shares of a company at a *price* that is substantially lower than the company's underlying *value*.

Some people think that there is no difference between share price and a business's worth; they believe that a $30 share price means that the stock is worth $30 a share. Among these faithful are the ever-present efficient market theory advocates, who believe that you can't beat the market because stock prices reflect all available and relevant information at all times. Looking at the successes of some of the greatest investors of the modern age—Benjamin Graham, Warren Buffett, Sir John Templeton, Peter Lynch—it's fair to say that this theory has a few holes in it. I believe that you can beat the market, because price is only what you pay, while value is what you actually *get*.

Applying this value investing philosophy can be straightforward. First, find companies with measurable worth. Then, when their stock is selling at a price that is below that worth, buy them. In time, as others recognize their value, their prices are likely to rise. When that happens, sell them and redeploy the proceeds into the stocks of other undervalued companies. This isn't easy, mind you. On paper, buying low and selling high sounds like something that anyone can do. Not really. It takes a team of trained professionals or a very disciplined and effective individual to get it right on a regular basis. There are many considerations on an analytical level, more than just market price relative to intrinsic value. Well beyond the numbers, there is also a great deal to be said about the advantages of experience and applying lessons learned from years of repetition, trial, error, and success. Yet adherence to the value approach has produced solid results over the long run. I'll elaborate on and document the success of this strategy in greater detail in Chapter 3. For now, we begin with the basic concept known as the *margin of safety*.

The Margin of Safety

Benjamin Graham challenged himself to "distill the secret of sound investment into three words" when he wrote *The Intelligent Investor*, first published in 1949: "margin of safety."[1]

The margin of safety represents the difference between a company's stock price and the value of the underlying company, often called its *intrinsic value*. Generally, value investors are not interested in stocks that trade at a *slight* discount to their underlying value. Rather, we seek a *substantial* discrepancy, because we are looking for solid companies whose stocks are selling at large discounts compared with the intrinsic value of the businesses they represent. A large margin of safety provides higher return potential and a greater degree of protection over the long term.

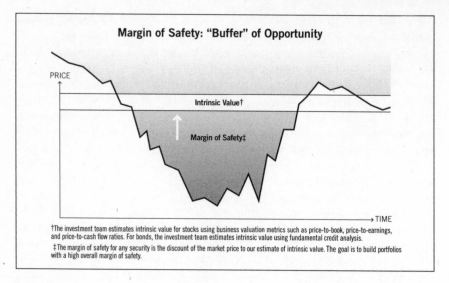

Margin of Safety: "Buffer" of Opportunity

PRICE

Intrinsic Value†

Margin of Safety‡

TIME

†The investment team estimates intrinsic value for stocks using business valuation metrics such as price-to-book, price-to-earnings, and price-to-cash flow ratios. For bonds, the investment team estimates intrinsic value using fundamental credit analysis.

‡The margin of safety for any security is the discount of the market price to our estimate of intrinsic value. The goal is to build portfolios with a high overall margin of safety.

Figure 2-1

Figure 2-1 helps you to visualize how the margin of safety works. The logic of this approach may appear obvious: buy stocks at a bargain price and sell them after the price has gone up. However, investment decisions are not made in theory. They are honed in an ever-changing environment where logic can be overshadowed by emotion. I'll address this point in greater detail later, and explain how investors can help protect themselves by maintaining a strict adherence to the value investment principle.

Often, it takes a great deal of conviction to stick to value investment disciplines, especially when a company's stock price declines while you own it. For those who focus only on price, share price declines can be devastating emotionally. Even worse, they can lead to bad decisions, such as selling out just because the price is down. Some market participants focus only on how much money they are losing in the short term. However, for long-term investors who evaluate share price in relation to business value, price declines can represent a tremendous opportunity in the form of discounts. Discounts are the building blocks of value.

To me, serious investors are those who have the confidence and patience to back their judgment by buying stocks that they are prepared to hold for five years or more if necessary. Value investors do not focus on day-to-day oscillations in share price. They adopt and maintain a disciplined approach to evaluating business value. They are confident in their research and analysis and patient in implementing their strategy.

Not all investors choose this route, such as those who pursue a growth-oriented strategy.

Value Versus Growth: Is There a Difference?

In recent years, it's become popular to classify investors' approaches as being either "value" or "growth." These have come to be accepted as being polar opposites, almost like taking sides in a sports team or political rivalry: Do you support "value" or "growth"? You may not be surprised that I reject this popular approach to classifying investment styles. Value and growth are not enemies, nor are they based on incompatible beliefs. For investors (in contrast with speculators), company fundamentals are an important element of either a value or a growth approach to selecting stocks. I believe that value investing is the more profitable discipline in the long term, but there are many fundamental growth investors who are successful. However, most speculators consider themselves "growth investors," and it's among this group that we expect to see a high failure rate. After all, as speculators, aren't they primarily being reactive and short-sighted, and, essentially, relying on luck? They may get wins in spots, but when they have little more than their gut to guide them, their failures will overwhelm their successes over the long run.

Even at the stock level, classifying stocks as value or growth is not always cut and dried. Often, such generalizations reflect guidelines imposed by index sponsors or buy-side analysts and have little or nothing to do with fundamental analysis at the individual company level. I have researched companies in every sector and every industry all over the world with the goal of uncovering investment opportunities that offer the greatest margin of safety. This search has led me to undervalued businesses in areas that many people may perceive to be growth industries, such as technology and pharmaceuticals.

A business reporter once summed up value investing as "buying stock in companies which make things that rust." I encourage you to discard any such preconceptions you may have regarding value investing. It's not a purely defensive tactic that should be applied only in bear markets. Its focus is not so much on backward-looking businesses in dying industries, but on forward-thinking, strong businesses in *any* industry or country.

Growth companies are believed to be those that are on the fast track to success, regardless of their stock price. They can be successful, well-managed companies with solid products and services and, yes, a great future. Value companies are designed for future growth as well, only with more absolute and unflinching attention to what that future is costing the investor today. Compared to growth investors, value investors want a buffer between what they pay and what they think the company is worth on an intrinsic level. The market doesn't always see the real value of a company. As bad news, temporary hurdles, or other short-term issues unmoor a company's stock price from its value, this disconnect is the all-important margin of safety for which the diligent value investor searches.

In their own way, growth stocks offer promise, but the value investor wants that promise with a little more wiggle room for potential setbacks. I often see promising businesses behind what many people call growth stocks. However, I often have to turn them away, as their stock prices far exceed the worth of their underlying businesses, even though they are fantastic companies.

For a real-world example of this disconnect, let's turn again to my experiences during the tech bubble that I mentioned in Chapter 1. Near the peak of the Internet stock mania in early 2000, share prices for various dot-com or "new economy" companies (many of which were neither solid nor established and offered unproven products or services), were leaping to successive record highs. At the same time, share prices for "old economy" companies in industries such as insurance, utilities, and manufacturing were languishing. At that point, some market participants mistakenly believed that new economy growth stocks were stocks that went up, while old economy value stocks were those that went down.

Returns for value and growth stock indexes appeared to support this notion. By the end of March 2000—even as technology stocks began their retreat—the Nasdaq 100, a measure of returns of the 100 largest companies in the technology-heavy Nasdaq Composite, had gained 108.7 percent in the previous 12 months versus only 13.3 percent for the venerable Dow Jones Industrial Average (DJIA). Technology stocks, spurred by the shares of start-up Internet firms, were soaring while it seemed that the rest of the market was being left behind, some said for good.

In fact, many of the best-performing stocks at the time were initial public offerings, or IPOs—companies that had never issued stock before. Of the 486 IPOs in 1999, about half were Internet-related companies that gained, on average, 147 percent their first *day* of trading. Figure 2-2 illustrates the divergent paths of technology growth stocks, as measured by the Nasdaq 100, and the broader market, as measured by the S&P 500 Index.

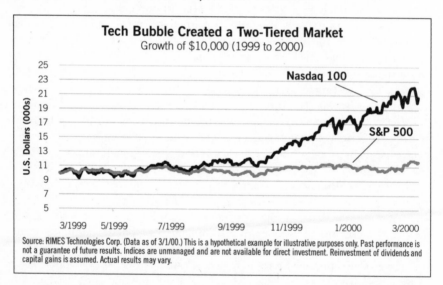

Source: RIMES Technologies Corp. (Data as of 3/1/00.) This is a hypothetical example for illustrative purposes only. Past performance is not a guarantee of future results. Indices are unmanaged and are not available for direct investment. Reinvestment of dividends and capital gains is assumed. Actual results may vary.

Figure 2-2 At the height of the tech bubble, the growth of stocks in the technology-heavy Nasdaq 100 handily outpaced the boring old economy stocks in the S&P 500, which is exactly where select value opportunities were getting exciting.

At that time, I believed that the divergent paths taken by growth and value stocks represented the biggest two-tiered market bubble that I had ever seen in my career. I didn't believe that the gains of the growth stocks were sustainable because the prices of so many of these stocks had climbed to ridiculous heights—levels that were well beyond the intrinsic values of the underlying companies. Many of these high-flying dot-com companies had zero earnings as well. While I was scratching my head over the market's ridiculous excesses, my firm was taking advantage of this environment to add solid businesses that were trading at extremely attractive prices to our portfolios. I was more excited about the opportunities available for value investors, especially in the United States, than I had been in nearly 20 years. Select companies in utilities, construction materials, auto manufacturing, and telecom were among those that we targeted especially.

When the bubble burst in March 2000, the majority of the dot-com stocks offered no margin of safety. In the wake of huge losses, market participants returned their attention to fundamental strengths, and the out-of-favor stocks that we had purchased during the Internet stock run-up were once again in favor. Their share prices generally rose, while the prices of many of the highly touted new economy stocks declined substantially.

The Internet bubble illustrated one important difference between growth stocks and value stocks: growth stocks tend to be accompanied by expectations for future earnings that are far greater than the average shown in the past. Such stocks are often in exciting new industries, about which there is a great deal of promise and optimism.

However, when it comes to future earnings growth, it is extremely difficult to project it with a high degree of confidence. Additionally, the farther out the prediction, the more likely it is that it's going to be off-target. Building long-term forecasts of well-above-average earnings growth for companies is particularly questionable, as unforeseen competition will almost certainly arise to wrest away some of these hyperprofits, making such predictions very unreliable. Value investors believe that the best approach is to focus on the current state of the business: what it would be worth now to someone who wanted to buy the whole company. Not only is this more prudent, but it's more grounded in sanity because you're not trying to outforecast other investors.

Are We Rich Yet?

In today's fast-paced world, patience is often thin. On every level, time is limited, and we see many more investors, over and over, who are driven by the expectation that they will make lots of money in very little time.

There is no end to the parade of get-rich-quick investment schemes. Back in the 1960s, visions of boundless wealth floated before investors with the advent of a new magic formula called *synergy*. By combining companies, synergy would enable management to make more profits, as the combined companies would work together to increase revenue while cutting shared costs. This became the driving force behind the craze to create conglomerates—large companies composed of a variety of often-unrelated smaller companies. In theory, synergy meant that under astute corporate management, 2 plus 2 could indeed equal 5. It worked for a while, at least in terms of the stock price, and at least until it became apparent to investors that the eventual total might not in fact be 5, but might even be heading for 3.

Synergy was neither the first nor the last of such maneuvers. Indeed, like most fashions, such enthusiasms cycle back every so often. Most recently, we saw the same craze with hedge funds, alternative investment products, and the real estate run-up of the early 2000s. A little further back, there was the popularity of momentum investing, as in the tech bubble, and the notion of buying stocks simply because they were going up. The epitome of this was the day trader; this was hailed as a new profession in the late 1990s, and, to my mind, it was the exact opposite of everything that investing should represent. And let's not forget about my first professional encounter with such a phenomenon: the "Go-Go Era" stocks, high-turnover performance game, market timing, and momentum investing of the late 1960s.

What all of these tend to have in common are an obsession with short-term results, a disregard for fundamental business values, and the ability to cause major losses to speculators who jump on the bandwagon.

Sophisticated investors who are responsible for investing billions of dollars on behalf of others and individual investors managing their own portfolios have proved to be equally susceptible to the crowd mentality. Both types of investors are prone to short-term thinking. Many pension funds, for example, hire professional money managers and measure their performance on a quarterly basis, leading to short-term "hire and fire" decisions. Inevitably, this encourages managers to chase what's hot and disregard sound investment principles. In fact, the IPO bubble of the late 1990s was as much a product of institutional excesses as it was of the mistakes of individual investors.

Some pension funds, insurance companies, and other institutional investors seem to be in synch with hired asset managers who have abandoned the practice of doing an in-depth analysis of the companies they buy. Almost uniformly, a variety of strategies have been adopted that may differ in some respects, but that have one horrendous defect in common: they all reject the need for or feasibility of making company-by-company judgments about price and value and the need to examine time horizons and other factors that relate to the basic fundamentals necessary for long-term investing. This also results in a misallocation of capital in a free-enterprise economy, which is discussed later in the book.

The combination of the age-old desire to get rich quick with the speed of today's 24/7 news cycle means that we have become increasingly preoccupied with short-term events and fast results. To borrow a few words from Sir John Templeton, a respected pioneer in global money management, "There is too much emphasis now on everything yesterday."

As I see it, we are no longer as thrifty as we should be, and this is leading to more speculation, more danger, and more risk. Investors are bombarded by data from an escalating number of sources, such as 24-hours-a-day financial news on cable television, the Internet, broadcast and satellite radio, and a good but shrinking number of capable print media. As our appetites for information and our expectations have increased, our ability to wait and anticipate has decreased.

Hold, Please

Most people recognize that stocks are a good long-term investment, yet most people don't hold them for long. Why? It starts with basic human nature and the emotive tendencies that drive our decision making. One catalyst could be the mixed messages that investors receive from professionals and the financial media. In one breath, investors are advised to stay the course and to hang on for the long haul. In the next breath, they are given a road map to short-term riches and reasonable-sounding guides to switch paths and chase the latest fad.

Evidence suggests that most people are doing the latter, according to a Quantitative Analysis of Investor Behavior (QAIB) study by DALBAR, Inc.[2] Although the study focuses on mutual fund investors only, it has strong implications for the behavior of most market participants. DALBAR describes its annual study as an examination of the real returns from equity, fixed-income, and money market mutual funds from January 1984 through December 2013. First released in 1994, the QAIB study investigates how mutual fund investors' behavior affects the returns they actually earn.

Each year the results produce the same pattern: mutual fund investors do not have a long-term perspective, and this adversely affects their results compared to the market. The 2014 study showed that the average equity fund retention—how long someone stayed invested in a particular fund—was 4.1 years in 2013. This is up from 2.6 years in 2000, which saw the tech bubble burst, and 1.7 years following the 1987 market crash. Even at four years, is this really long-term investing?

When compared to the corresponding indexes, the lack of a buy-and-hold strategy appears to hurt investor returns:

- The average equity fund investor experienced a 24.54 percent return in 2013, compared to 32.41 percent for the S&P 500 Index.

- The average fixed-income investor lost 3.66 percent for the year, compared to a 2.02 percent drop for the Barclays Aggregate Bond Index.

The disadvantage is even more significant over longer time frames:

- For the 20-year period, the average equity fund investor earned 5.02 percent, versus 9.22 percent for the S&P 500 Index.

- For the 10-year period, the results were 5.88 percent for the investor and 7.40 percent for the index.

While 2013's steady run-up in the markets gave equity investors their best gains in many years, they could have done even better had they not tried to time their investments. In the 30 years that DALBAR has published this study, not once have average investors stayed put long enough to fully benefit from the market's performance.

The DALBAR study also provides a key lesson in terms of investors' tendency to buy high and sell low. Rising market prices lure investors back with confidence, but they're buying as prices move upward. Conversely, emotions typically get the better of them as prices drop, so they begin to sell. Short-term thinking is one thing, but it also leads to paying too much for stocks, and this affects returns, too.

If investors are to make money consistently, they must return to farsighted, long-term investing. This is the only strategy that promises rational investors the greatest potential for economic rewards over the long haul.

Investing Versus Speculation

What's the difference between investing and speculation? What do we mean when we use each term? Why is this important?

Benjamin Graham addressed the differences between investing and speculation on the very first page of his book *The Intelligent Investor:* "An investment operation is one which, upon thorough analysis, promises safety of principal and an adequate return. Operations not meeting these requirements are speculative."[3]

This still rings true today. Yet, with my contemporary perspective, I add two more criteria that define speculation:

- Any contemplated holding period shorter than a normal business cycle (typically three to five years)
- Any purchase based solely on anticipated market movements

Today, the media often refer to "investors" taking profits, bargain hunting, or driving prices higher or lower on a particular day. I attribute these actions to speculators—not investors.

Investors and speculators approach their tasks differently. Investors want to know what a business is worth and imagine themselves as owning the business as a whole. Unlike speculators, investors maintain a long-term perspective—at least three to five years. They look at a company as if they were its owners. This means that they're interested in factors such as competitive positioning, corporate governance, and succession issues that may affect a company's future and its ability to create wealth for years to come. Investors may use their voting rights to assist in enhancing company value over the long term.

On the other hand, speculators are less interested in what a business is actually worth and more concerned with what a third party will pay to own shares on a given day. They may be concerned only with short-term changes in a stock's price, not with the underlying value of the company itself.

Why Not Just Guess?

The problem with speculation is simple: no one can predict what a third party will pay for shares today or at any time in the future. Market prices typically swing between extremes, stoked by the irrational emotions of fear and greed.

These market swings have become more pronounced since the late 1990s. For example, between 1990 and 1997, the S&P 500 Index moved 3 percent in either direction in a single day only eight times. This happened nine times in 1998 alone, and it has hovered around this number for each subsequent year through 2013.

Such dramatic price fluctuations on a day-to-day basis can test long-term investors' mettle in maintaining their focus on business value. Refer back to the margin of safety figure and the tendency for business values to remain relatively stable. Daily price changes should hold little interest for the long-term investor, unless a price has fallen to a "buying level" that represents a sizable margin of safety for a stock. But that's often difficult to remember when headlines, news anchors, friends, and coworkers are lamenting or lauding the market's most recent lurch forward or back.

With a clearer understanding of what we mean by *value investing*—what it is and how it works—we turn our attention in Chapter 3 to *why* it works.

CHAPTER 3

THE VALUE PEDIGREE AND THE REWARDS OF VALUE INVESTING

An extreme focus on the principles of value investing is the reason I was successful and am still in this business. I was able to focus, despite the noise all around me, because I knew and saw how value comes out better in the end.

—Charles Brandes, in an interview with *The Edge Singapore*, March 2014

In the whirl of Wall Street, there are strong winners and big losers, and the majority of participants are stuck in a perpetual toggle between the two camps. Meanwhile, over the last half-century, a relatively quiet group of like-minded investors has been achieving superior results, watching its portfolios grow, taking some profits, and working to manage risk over the long term.

How did these investors do this? Not by happenstance or accident, or by listening to the innumerable prophets that spring up now and again with "new" strategies, advice, and magic bullets.

Nor, for that matter, was it done by employing complicated theories, such as market timing, technical analysis, the efficient market hypothesis, or the intricate tools of academics, market technicians, and algorithm writers.

These successful investors accomplished their goals the old-fashioned way: through fundamental, classic value investing. In a well-cited white paper, the highly respected and always plain-spoken value investor James Montier likened the advent of ever more complicated investment management products to "old snake oil in new bottles."[1]

"One of the myths perpetuated by our industry," Montier wrote, "is that there are lots of ways to generate good long-run real returns, but there is really only one: buying cheap assets." I could have written 1,000 more words to support his sentiments; instead, I'll just say that he managed to summarize perfectly in two brief sentences what I've known to be true for more than 40 years.

The purpose of this chapter is to review the rewards of value investing. To make my case, I'll cite objective studies, benchmark returns, and actual track records of professional money managers. Keep in mind that value investing is not a get-rich-quick scheme or an investment panacea. Don't expect riches overnight. Nor is it easy to do. By carefully following value principles, however, prudent, rational investors may obtain several significant advantages: capital preservation, lower volatility, reduced trading costs, and favorable long-term results.

Three Benefits of Value Investing

The first benefit of value investing is that by buying into companies at discounted prices, you lower your risk, especially compared to growth investing and other strategies. I define risk as losing money over the long term, because value investing has generally been synonymous with a relatively higher capacity for capital preservation.

The second benefit from value investing is slightly lower volatility, defined as fluctuations in returns from month to month or quarter to quarter. I understand that it can be difficult to tolerate swift, short-term changes in portfolio value, but volatility is not necessarily bad. In fact, the chapters ahead will demonstrate why short-term volatility really should not concern most investors.

The third benefit is reduced trading costs, since value proponents tend to hold securities longer than growth investors. Fewer trades means lower costs, over time, with a potentially large cost savings for the patient investor.

Beyond these benefits is the proverbial pot of gold—value investing has delivered superior results over the long term, the proof of which is in the data I'm about to show you.

A Matter of Style

There are many variations of investment management, but two general styles predominate: value and growth. Expanding on Chapter 2, where I outlined these styles, let's delve a bit deeper into the similarities and differences between them. The distinctions between the two styles of investing can be confusing because both strategies seek *growth of principal* as a primary objective.

Growth-oriented investors tend to buy stocks of companies whose profits are expected to increase rapidly, either because of the individual business's own actions or because of a general rising tide. Value-oriented managers buy at a discount and wait for the mispriced stock to revert to its true value as determined by fundamental gauges such as earnings, dividends, book value, or cash flow.

Historically, value investing has delivered better long-term returns than growth investing because misplaced sentiment can distort what investors are willing to pay to own a stock. We especially saw this as the dust settled after the tech bubble burst in 2000–2001, when traditional "old economy" companies that had been overlooked during the Internet stock craze fared very well after the dot-com bust.

The aggregate holdings of a growth-style manager typically have an above-average price-to-earnings ratio and a below-average dividend yield. Growth portfolios also tend to be expensive relative to aggregate book value and cash flow. Graham called this zone the "dangerous fields of anticipated growth"[2] that tend to attract a lot of attention, but eventually usually disappoint. It is easy to see that the further out people try to predict a company's growth potential, the more likely they are to be wrong.

Why the hefty price tag on growth stocks in general? In effect, growth investors pay extra because of the expectation that a company will grow its earnings rapidly. But high expectations are difficult to meet and sustain. Historically, stocks haven't maintained lofty price-to-earnings (P/E) ratios for extended periods. One of two things tends to happen: earnings rise dramatically to justify the prices, or the prices decline to come into line with earnings. With that in mind, doesn't it make more sense to estimate a company's current value based on conservative estimates of future growth, pay less than what it's worth, and anticipate that the stock price will eventually revert to the mean? To me, this approach makes more sense, and the data support its long-term advantage.

The Data Breakthrough

In 1994—the sixtieth anniversary of *Security Analysis*—another breakthrough in the value investing world emerged. The *Journal of Finance* published a study by professors Josef Lakonishok, Andrei Shleifer, and Robert W. Vishny (a trio often referred to collectively as LSV) that quantified the long-term outperformance of value stocks over growth stocks (which they called "glamour" in their study).[3] A number of researchers had previously published research exploring the relationship between value and growth stocks, but LSV's work was received as a landmark study, and it still is.

LSV tracked U.S. stocks between 1968 and 1994, segmenting them into 10 groups (deciles) based on fundamental traits such as price/book and price-to-earnings ratios. They found what everyone had had a hunch was true, but hadn't had the proof yet. For example, LSV showed that the stocks with the lowest valuations relative to earnings and book value, or the *most* attractive valuations (most *under*valued), delivered average annual five-year returns of 19.8 percent, well over the 9.3 percent return delivered by those with the *least* attractive valuations (most *over*valued).[4] In Chapter 12, I discuss this study in greater detail and explain how my firm expanded it to include global investing.

Price Versus Value

Value stocks are priced differently from others. By definition, value stocks sell for below-average prices relative to their normalized fundamentals. Investors' expectations for these companies are generally low, and their stocks are priced to reflect their supposedly more modest prospects. Not all such companies are good investments, of course, but skilled value investors can uncover overlooked gems. The value investor sells when the overlooked gem is no longer overlooked and the newfound attention has driven its price to where it equals or overstates the company's true potential. The value investor exploits this "sentimental journey" from undervalued to fairly valued.

The value investor doesn't try to forecast exactly *when* that transformation in sentiment will take place—doing so would be speculating. But the value investor does believe that free markets will price businesses appropriately over time. And when they do, a company's price and value will once again become linked as investors come looking for shares. This is the process called *reversion to the mean*.

The Dollars and Sense of Value Investing

Seeing is believing. What better way is there to appreciate what value investing can accomplish than to scrutinize historical results for value strategies, as measured by objective, third-party studies *and* the track records of some of value investing's most notable practitioners?

Returns from indexes compiled by Russell Investment Group also reveal the long-term superiority of value stocks. A $100,000 investment in the Russell 3000 Value Index in 1979 would have grown to roughly $6,353,135 by year-end 2013. This is about $2,452,523 more than an equal-sized investment in the Russell 3000 Growth Index.[5]

Proof in Results

Even better, the actual returns posted by many value investing practitioners also underscore the benefits of the value approach. Many of the value investment managers shown in Figure 3-1 are direct students of Graham-and-Dodd–style investing, like me, while others take a somewhat different approach. As Ben Graham reminded me some 40 years ago, value investing is not absolute.

While I recognize that mutual funds do not share the same structures, fees, or expenses, I believe that a comparison of their respective returns does shed light on value investing's long-term potential for success.

Forty Years of Value Fund Performance			
	Annualized Return 1973–2013	Number of Negative Years	Number of Underperformance Years vs. S&P 500
Pioneer A	11.05%	9	18
Vanguard Windsor™	13.13%	8	17
Dodge & Cox Stock	12.73%	8	16
Fidelity® Equity-Income	12.58%	8	17
Sequoia	16.08%	6	16
Valley Forge	9.91%	6	27
S&P 500	10.98%	9	—

As of 12/31/2013. Source: Morningstar Direct. Past performance is not a guarantee of future results. Indices are unmanaged and are not available for direct investment.

Figure 3-1

There are at least two valuable lessons that emerge from the track records of the acclaimed value strategies shown in Figure 3-1:

- Investing is a marathon, not a sprint.

- Value investing strategies can differ from one another, sometimes significantly.

- Even the best long-term investors will experience periods of short-term underperformance.

Each of these value investors posted negative absolute returns in at least six of the 40 years that we tracked. But the fact that they achieved superior overall results despite an occasional short-term stumble highlights the importance of adopting and maintaining a long-term horizon.

Many value investment managers can also shift or alter course, often unintentionally, toward a blend, a growth, or even an indexlike strategy (closet indexers), depending on their stock picks and turnover rate. This so-called style drift occurs more frequently than you would think, given the tendency of asset owners to place many short-term demands on their portfolio managers.

Skill—Not Luck

Critics might argue that the extraordinary track records compiled by these value investors are the result of simple chance, or an accident. Borrowing from Warren Buffett, if you could get one million monkeys to sit in front of typewriters for a million years and bang on the keys, one result, through some quirk of chance, might produce something akin to Shakespeare's *Hamlet*. But none of those one million monkeys would have set out to create a finished work comparable to Shakespeare's masterful tragedy.

The results achieved by these value investors were no accident. They were identified as value investors before their track records were developed. And, each followed a unique approach to the Graham-and-Dodd principles and delivered solid long-term results.

You may wonder whether these superior returns were the result of each manager's magic touch. Can the average value investor expect to do as well? Certainly some portfolio managers are more skilled than others. Not all investors will achieve the same results, even if they apply the same selection criteria. As in any profession, skill levels among practitioners vary.

Evidence suggests that value investors have the benefit of a superior approach to portfolio management. In other words, given the same level of expertise, the value investor tends to win big over the long haul. Let's go back to the LSV study, which concluded that certain value strategies outperform glamour strategies by 8 percent per year.

"In the very best months, the value strategy significantly outperforms the glamour strategy and the [market] index, but not by as much as it does when the market falls sharply," the study said. "Overall, the value strategy appears to do somewhat better than the glamour strategy in all [economic] states and significantly better in some states."

More Return, Less Volatility?

Earlier, I cited lower volatility as a key advantage of value investing. The LSV study, as well as returns and volatility statistics for the Russell 3000 Index, suggests that value stocks have delivered exceptional returns—with less volatility. As we showed, returns for the Russell 3000 Value Index outpaced gains for the Russell 3000 Growth Index between 1979 and 2013. In addition to better performance, the Russell 3000 Value Index had a lower standard deviation of quarterly returns: 15.91 percent versus 19.36 percent for the Russell 3000 Growth Index over the same period, reflecting lower volatility.

Higher returns *and* lower risk? That sounds too good to be true. First, it's important to recognize that the terms *volatility* and *risk* are often used synonymously, yet they can have quite different connotations. In Chapter 17, I'll delve deeper into common misperceptions regarding volatility and risk. For now, I will adopt the common vernacular for the purposes of this discussion.

We've all heard the investing maxim, "The only way to achieve higher returns is to take more risk." That statement is true if the assets you are investing in are all priced efficiently (that is, if price equals intrinsic value). But if our view that stocks get *mispriced* regularly is correct, then you indeed may be able to achieve *higher* returns with *less* risk if the margin of safety is effectively intact. On the topic of value and growth strategy comparisons, the LSV study states: "We also look at the betas and standard deviations of value and glamour strategies. We find little, if any, support for the view that value strategies are fundamentally riskier."

On his website, Dartmouth College finance professor Kenneth French compiles historical value versus growth stock returns. French uses price/book ratios to separate value from growth stocks.[6] Analysis of these data for the 50-year period ended December 31, 2013, yield compelling results that show some solid benefits of value investing (see Figure 3-2).

Better Returns Aren't Always More Risky

	Annualized Return 1963-2013	Annualized Standard Deviation 1963-2013	1973-1974 Return	2008 Return	Worst 12-Month Loss
Small Growth	8.6%	28.0%	-63.3%	-39.4%	-50.5%
Large Growth	9.6%	18.4%	-45.0%	-33.5%	-46.0%
Small Value	16.9%	23.9%	-40.8%	-32.0%	-47.3%
Large Value	12.5%	18.4%	-26.3%	-39.1%	-53.3%

Source: As of 12/31/2013. Source: Brandes Investment Partners, Kenneth French.
(http://mba.tuck.dartmouth.edu/pages/faculty/ken.french/index.html) Past performance is not a guarantee of future results.
For simplicity, the table above only includes the value and growth portfolios formed on the ratio of book equity to market equity (i.e., not the "neutral" portfolio of companies falling between the 30th and 70th NYSE percentiles). The portfolios include all NYSE, AMEX, and NASDAQ stocks for which the study authors have market equity data for the periods shown.

Figure 3-2 Kenneth French, along with professor Eugene Fama of the University of Chicago's Booth School of Business, spent years studying the relative success of value and growth strategies. The pair found that value outperformed growth over the entire period without any added volatility (as measured by standard deviation). With the exception of large-cap value's underperformance in two extreme periods (the financial crisis of 2008–2009 and one other 12-month period), large- and small-cap value strategies have outperformed large- and small-cap growth strategies, respectively, over the long term with equal or less short-term volatility.

Higher Return Without Higher Risk—How Can That Be?

Efficient market theory (EMT) contends that risk and reward go hand in hand. As a result, EMT suggests that value stocks have delivered greater long-term returns than growth stocks only because they are inherently riskier investments. Using standard deviation as a measure of risk, the Fama and French data just cited show that value strategies have delivered the best of both worlds: higher return *and* lower risk. But how can that be? How can value stocks deliver better returns with *less* risk?

One plausible hypothesis is that value stocks are consistently underpriced compared to their actual risk/return characteristics; that is, their inherent discount tends to lower the investor's base price or starting point. Most value investors would probably agree that their strategies produce favorable returns because they counter the often-irrational strategies followed by other market participants. The latter strategies often contain one or more of the inherent biases we address in Chapter 4. In essence, investors apparently get excessively excited about glamorous growth stocks and drive up their prices.

Similarly, they often overreact and sell stocks that are the subject of bad news, causing these stocks to become unpopular and underpriced.

By underpriced, we are referring to the difference or gap between the value investor's estimation of a company's true worth and its stock price, which we have defined as the margin of safety. Prices for growth stocks may be dependent upon the companies living up to lofty expectations. When actual performance fails to meet those expectations, the company's stock price can be especially vulnerable.

Safety First

Value stocks, because of their margin of safety, are generally not as susceptible to sharp and painful downturns. By their nature, they are selling at a discount. Essentially, when growth companies stumble, their profit estimates often tumble along with their valuation multiples, resulting in steep stock price declines. By their nature, they are selling at a premium, and people soon enough discover that they are paying too much for them. Not only does the price-to-earnings ratio come down sharply because of the market's disappointment, but the estimated future earnings number is also reduced. (This is sometimes referred to by the highly technical name of "the double whammy.") For value stocks, future profit expectations may decline, but typically not as drastically as the inflated ones associated with glamour stocks. More important, the already low multiples for value stocks often tend to insulate them from significant further stock price declines, as little in the way of growth expectations was built into them.

Ironically, glamour stocks often may appear to be the more "prudent" investments. Because of growth stocks' popularity, investors may feel that there is safety in numbers. By their nature, value stocks are not popular. But popular doesn't necessarily mean prudent. Professional portfolio managers, just like individual investors, can be fooled into thinking that they are making a conservative investment when, in fact, they are merely being conventional.

Even if they personally believe in value principles, portfolio managers may find it hard to present clients or their superiors with unpopular stock holdings. Often, the value manager must be willing to look out of touch, sometimes even foolish, to his or her clients, at least over the short term. For example, in a meeting with clients, it is often easier to point to a portfolio of popular blue chip holdings than to explain why a portfolio resembles a kennel crammed with underperforming, out-of-favor "dogs."

Narrowing Views

Another possible reason that a number of market participants continue to prefer growth stocks—and continue to underperform value strategies—is the short-term time horizon of many investors. This can also be true for professional investors. Anchoring on an index for comparison and framing their evaluation of performance within a narrow time interval, professional investors may simply lose patience before a value strategy can succeed. Value strategies take time to pay off optimally, but professional portfolio managers often cannot afford to underperform an index, even for a short time. They are frequently measured every three months, which is really a trivial amount of time to a true value investor. Even two years is short term to us. Value needs time to work its charm.

Competing Interests

Underperformance can have significant career consequences for investment professionals: an underperforming manager or analyst can miss a bonus payment, be passed over for promotion, or even lose his or her job. Thus, a value strategy that takes three to five years to show meaningful results might be too risky for a portfolio manager from the standpoint of career security. LSV stated, "The career concerns of money managers and employees of their institutional clients may cause money managers to tilt towards 'glamour' stocks." Even for those who are brave enough to defy the herd instinct personally, their employer or their clients may lose patience and overrule (or fire) them, often making the switch back to the herd approach just as the herd approaches the edge of the investment cliff. To get the best long-term results, everyone—the manager, the firm, and the client—must be aligned in accepting that value investing can involve some short-term pain.

Scientific evidence shows that people who are under the influence of a bias are reluctant to give it up, even when they become fully aware of its existence. Despite the availability of the data, it is not surprising that glamour strategies continue to draw investors' attention. Everyone wants to own a piece of a company whose future seems bright. This focus on business prospects, however, overshadows a crucial element of security analysis: price. The data support the view that value strategies produce higher returns, at least in part, because they avoid the high prices that are attached to stocks about which the market is intensely optimistic. On the contrary, value strategies typically invest in stocks about which the market is severely pessimistic. As value investor David Dreman wrote, "If one had to speculate about the future, it probably would be safer to project a continuation of investors' psychological reactions than to predict the exact financial performance of companies themselves."[7] Again, the combination of *rational* fundamental analysis and *irrational* market prices creates opportunity for value investors.

Does Value Still Work?

If you're still skeptical and unconvinced, the impressive performance statistics may help. But you still could question whether the investment world has become far different since pioneers such as Sir John Templeton, Irving Kahn, and Warren Buffett first started their distinct approaches to value investing amidst the markets of the 1940s, 1950s, 1960s, and 1970s. It has.

Financial markets have changed, but in ways that can make value investing even more profitable. The two dominant trends of the last more than 40 years—the growing importance of professional investors and the shrinking of investment time horizons—have increased stock price volatility and pushed share prices to even more irrational levels, playing into the hands of the patient value investor. Combine this with my earlier point on how investor behavior has remained largely the same, and the persistent human biases that impair rational decision making can create opportunities for disciplined value investors.

The LSV study contends that, "Many individuals look for stocks that will earn them abnormally high returns for a few months. . . . Institutional money managers often have even shorter time horizons. When both individuals and institutional money managers prefer glamour [growth] and avoid value strategies, value stocks will be cheap and earn a higher average return."[8] In other words, the trend toward instant financial gratification rewards the value investor by keeping a segment of stock prices cheap.

Yes, But Can Value Stocks Be Found?

As to whether attractive value investment candidates can be identified, efficient market theorists would probably answer resoundingly: "No. The market can't be beaten. There are too many smart analysts that know too much about too many companies." I disagree. Diligent value investors have been uncovering promising opportunities for decades. A recent example helps support my conviction on finding great values.

Microsoft

Microsoft Corporation is the largest computer software maker in the world based on sales. Its long and influential reach in the IT universe is undeniable. As a key component of the Nasdaq, and with more than $350 billion in market capitalization as of 2014, Microsoft is one of the most closely followed stocks among financial analysts any day of the week.[9]

In 2006, several perceived missteps in its consumer products business led to a 22 percent slide in its stock price. It started with poor reception of Microsoft's first new Windows operating system in five years, Vista, as well as its Windows mobile product, both of which played large roles in the market's sudden change of heart, which lasted for some time. Not helping matters was investors' growing fondness for Silicon Valley's latest darlings, Apple and Google, which were quickly benefiting by filling the innovation-starved technology consumer's needs with game-changing cell phones and computer tablets. Suddenly, Microsoft—which had once been synonymous with the computer revolution itself—was seen as mature, stagnant, or, worse, very boring.

The astute value investor, however, could look beyond the sudden distractions of the negative headlines to see that the market was overemphasizing Microsoft's consumer business. In reality, nearly 80 percent of its earnings stemmed from enterprise software designed to serve businesses, government agencies, and other organizations. While the market was focusing on the short-term setback to a small part of the company's business, value investors were paying attention to Microsoft's strong returns and attractive valuations. It never stopped being a great business, and it only got better as it helped lead the mass transition to cloud computing. By its nature, enterprise software benefits from a "sticky" base of customers who rarely jump ship to competitors because of the time and cost burdens of the transition process. In other words, it's a cash cow. After riding out the downdraft of the financial crisis of 2008–2009, Microsoft's stock price more than doubled between 2009 and 2013, and rose some 30 percent between 2012 and 2013 alone.[10]

For those who believe that value investing focuses only on companies that no one else bothers with, Microsoft is a great example of why that's not entirely true. Value opportunities can be hidden in plain sight.

A Look Ahead

The charm of value investing—its commonsensical simplicity—permits investors to apply its fundamental strategies if they dig deep, remain disciplined, and are willing to be patient. Throughout Part I, I highlighted the key elements of value investing over the last 40 years and observed the superior results that help to reinforce my belief that it works. In the next few chapters, I tackle the universe of investor behavioral biases and share my own real-world approach to identifying value companies and building and monitoring a portfolio of value stocks.

PART II

VALUE INVESTING IN THE REAL WORLD

Human psychology can make life interesting and surreal. However, when it spills over into the markets and irrational behavior takes over, value opportunities become very real.

Natural biases tend to bring out the worst in investors, but they can create the best opportunities for value investing. Knowing where to look for value stocks is the first step in finding them. It's a global journey that follows a path winding through developed and emerging markets alike, one company at a time.

Undaunted by waves of short-term media prattle and other distractions, the value investor is securely moored to the margin of safety. To be sure, political unrest, accounting scandals, economic malaise, and other aspects of the wider picture can have a major influence on the bigger world around us. Yet, the real-world test of a company's potential for success begins and ends in a narrower universe—the health of its ledger, the quality of the people who lead it, and whatever else you can research within it.

At the end of the day, value is perhaps more reality based than any other investment approach. By the time you finish Part II of this book, I hope you agree.

CHAPTER 4

BEHAVIORAL BIASES: WHY VALUE INVESTING WORKS

People in both fields operate with beliefs and biases. To the extent you can eliminate both and replace them with data, you gain a clear advantage.

—John Henry, Boston Red Sox owner and renowned former commodities trader[1]

One of the attractions of watching sports is its ability to give you clear-cut results that are based primarily on merit. Baseball is especially interesting because it involves so much more strategy than what appears on the field. Hits and runs are exciting, but I find that I am just as interested in what it takes to get them. Some time ago I had the pleasure of meeting bestselling author Michael Lewis, who knows a thing or two about the game. Lewis had just captured perfectly the true story of how rigorous data analysis built a competitive major league ball club. You may recall the book, and later the hit movie, *Moneyball*. It was a great read for me, because it said as much about value stock investing as it did about the player engineering behind the Oakland Athletics' 2002 roster.

The takeaways from *Moneyball* were very relevant to value investing on two levels. First, the more you know about what you are purchasing—a rookie ball player, for instance—the greater your chances of success. Second, behavioral biases and the collective "wisdom" of the crowd, represented by owners, scouts, coaches, and the front offices, can lead to flawed and misjudged valuations of those players. With an objective and somewhat unique view of certain metrics—not to mention the third-lowest payroll in the league—the Oakland As turned to value investing, and it paid off. Anti-*Moneyball* traditionalists notwithstanding, general manager Billy Beane's trailblazing value approach seemed to work.

I'll get further into information gathering and analysis for value investing later. First, let's look at the other major component of the value investor's arsenal: investor behavior, which drives the erratic folly that creates value opportunities for those who know how and where to look for them.

The Self-Designated *Good* Driver

In framing human behavior, psychologists often cite an example that begins with a simple question: How good a driver are you? Think of the other drivers you encounter on the road and estimate your driving ability on a scale of 1 to 10 (with 10 being best). Include everything about yourself in your criteria—reaction time, years of experience, driving record, adherence to traffic rules, courtesy, maneuvering, and so on. After weighing these factors, what number did you assign yourself?

If you rated yourself a 7 or better, you are typical. If you ranked your driving skill as greater than 5, you are among the overwhelming majority. Regardless of your actual driving ability, it is highly unlikely that your self-appraisal was 4 or less. That's because when researchers pose this question to virtually any group, the average answer is generally around 8 or 9. Think about that: on a scale of 1 to 10, the *average* answer is 8 or 9. In other words, a majority of drivers believe that they are substantially above average—which, of course, is statistically impossible.

This example illustrates one of many systematic errors of judgment that impede daily decision making.[2] Psychologists have studied these biases for decades to better understand human behavior.

Resistance Is Useful

Right about now, you are probably asking, "What does this have to do with value investing?"

Despite theories that the markets are efficient (which I'll address later in this chapter), I believe that most people make investment decisions based on these psychological biases without even realizing it. These biases influence a substantial proportion of market participants to go in the same direction, contributing to the short-term irrationality of stock prices that value investors see as opportunities. But value investors can benefit only if they are able to resist the biases that are influencing everyone else. That means that they must be aware of these influences, and they must set up their own investment disciplines to make sure they don't fall victim to them.

Let's take a closer look at a few of these behavioral biases. Studies of investor psychology have led to the development of *behavioral finance*. Research in this area reveals that flaws such as faulty intuition, extrapolation, overoptimism, anchoring, and hindsight make investors susceptible to surprises or disappointments. And when a surprise or disappointment occurs, investors tend to overreact, resulting in poor decisions.[3] To counter such biases, investors must follow a disciplined approach that stresses a preestablished rational process rather than personal preferences or out-of-context judgments.

Human nature is far more predictable over time than the day-to-day swings of the stock market. By understanding the lessons of behavioral finance, investors can apply a rational approach in a market crowded with irrational participants, and expect much improved results.

Value investing—essentially buying and holding inexpensive, out-of-favor common stocks and bonds—seeks to combine company-specific fundamental research with an objective, unbiased strategy that exploits innate human shortcomings. This approach has proved its merit for more than 80 years since the depths of the Great Depression, and it certainly dates back long before behavioral finance became a topic of formal study. As you read on, you'll see that many aspects of investor psychology have been part of the value investor's discipline all along. But now we're able to understand in more detail why these disciplines work. I learned very early in my career that you're always better off understanding why something works than just applying a process in the dark. Knowing the "why" improves both your confidence and your judgment within the framework of the discipline.

This is also where professional guidance may have a significant positive influence. Financial advisors (FAs) may help prevent investors from succumbing to behavioral biases. Later in the book, I share ideas about this important relationship, including a disciplined approach that, as mentioned earlier, stresses a preestablished rational process. In the meantime, though, let's look at some basic human flaws that FAs can cite to help introduce or discuss behavioral finance with their clients and prospects—and how understanding such flaws may help better position investors to take advantage of this knowledge.

The Laws of Flaws

In Part I, returns data showed that value investing has historically outperformed other styles, particularly growth investing. Now, let's explore one primary reason why value investing has delivered such solid results: human behavioral flaws. I hope that with a clearer understanding and examples of these tendencies, you can guard against their potential adverse influence.

Faulty Intuition: Making Misguided Predictions

Suppose we conducted two experiments. In the first, we flipped a coin nine times and recorded the outcome of each toss. The results—heads (H) or tails (T)—were:

T-T-H-T-H-H-H-T-H-T

In the second experiment, we took the same coin and flipped it the same number of times. The results were:

T-T-T-H-H-H-H-H-H

Which of these do you believe is a more probable outcome? If we did this experiment 1,000 times, which pattern would repeat more frequently—the first or the second?

When most people see these two results, they believe that the first pattern is more likely to occur. Is that the one you picked? The first result *seems* more likely to them, even though they may have no definitive evidence to support their belief. It just feels right, and the second pattern seems too contrived to recur with any frequency.

The answer: the two outcomes are *equally* probable. The results in the first experiment are no more likely to occur than the results in the second.

If we extend the first experiment and flip the coin a tenth time, most people will say that it's virtually impossible to predict the results of the next flip. Yet, in the second experiment, many people will still make a prediction. They might predict heads as a continuation of the trend or tails for a trend reversal. Either way, they believe that they can see a pattern in these random outcomes and make an accurate prediction of the future. This misperception is the essence of faulty intuition.

The cognitive error—seeing a pattern of predictability in random, short-term events—is so common and so embedded in stock market analysis that it is almost taken for granted. An entire school of investment thought called *technical analysis* is devoted to finding patterns in the short-term movement of stock prices. The market participants (I can't call them investors) using this approach study patterns and trends in past stock prices in order to predict future price movements. They may look for tricky patterns in the charts, such as a *head and shoulders* or *ascending triangles*, or spend a lot of time on trend interpretation. I don't recognize this as investing. To me, it is speculation using fancy software and has about as much chance of long-term success as consistently predicting the results of coin flips or where the roulette wheel ball will drop.

Extrapolation: Misshaping the Present into the Future

Attempting to establish patterns to explain random events with the hope of predicting the future can lead to yet another important behavioral bias: extrapolation.

For example, when you're sitting in a traffic jam, maybe you've thought, "It took me 30 minutes to go 1 mile. At this pace, I'll get home tomorrow afternoon."

Or, when you're golfing, maybe you've made a birdie putt on the thirteenth hole and thought, "If I keep this up, I'll shoot a 33 on the back nine."

These are simple examples of extrapolation—basing a longer-term forecast on an emotional reaction to short-term developments. Over the years at my firm, my colleagues and I have repeatedly seen the dangerous effects of extrapolation. Market participants often look at negative short-term performance and think, "If this continues, I'll lose all my money in three weeks." Or if performance is good, they may say, "At this rate, I'll quadruple my money in six months!"

From the tulip bulb craze in Holland during the seventeenth century to the real estate collapse of 2008, history is full of examples of the dangerous effects of extrapolation. Whether we are inside a market bubble, stuck in traffic, or on the links, the results are rarely as good or as bad as we envision at the moment. We often set ourselves up for disappointment or surprises when reality differs from our expectations. It's a quirk of human nature—and one that has consistently surfaced in the investment industry.

The most prominent example is market analysts' projections of trends much too far ahead. They forecast sales, earnings, stock prices, and many other statistics for years or decades, despite evidence that all of these are inherently impossible to predict with any accuracy. In forecasting the future growth of rapidly expanding companies, analysts' expectations are often tied to the recent past, even though growth rates usually revert toward an average. Remember two things about market analysts' predictions. First, analysts are rewarded for doing a "thorough job," and in today's world of computerized spreadsheets, extending a growth rate projection for a few more years is a very easy way of looking impressively thorough. Second, and even more important, you need to be especially wary of any projection that extends beyond the time that the analyst expects to be in that job! To sum up this point, I share successful value investor David Dreman's sage advice: "Take advantage of the high rate of analyst forecast error simply by investing in out-of-favor stocks."

Knowing this, it's easy to see how our natural tendency toward extrapolation is a big part of investor behavior in the markets. Go-Go Era stocks, the Nifty Fifty, and later the tech bubble and the real estate collapses were all founded on one extrapolated notion: that there was no place to go but up. Overvaluations, excessive leverage, and similar more relevant facts were overlooked or underestimated.

Streaming Extrapolation

One very recent example of extrapolation is the case of Netflix, one of the most popular providers of web-based on-demand streaming media. As its online subscriber base grew rapidly, the market took this as a solid long-term trend, mistaking it for profitability. So, although the stock price soared from $50 to nearly $300 from 2010 into the first half of 2011, it was eventually revealed

(continued)

that the company's profits were actually suffering from what some analysts considered convoluted and expensive program licensing agreements.[4] In 2012, Netflix tumbled in dramatic style when customer growth rates slowed as a result of a growing perception that the company lacked appealing content. It was trading at around $50 again by the summer of that year.[5] As if one painful lesson in extrapolation wasn't enough, however, the market was right back at it with Netflix in 2013. That year, the company introduced the first of some well-received original programming, coincident with a seemingly smart move to expand its customer base outside the United States. The market ran the stock price right back up to over $470, despite the fact that the company's global expansion and new programming were both unproven.[6] The decline wasn't as significant this time, but the company's valuation still borders on the outrageous, with even the most conservative estimates hovering at a price-to-earnings ratio of 128.

Overoptimism: Putting On the Ritz

We tend to think of optimism as a desirable trait in our lives, and it should be. But in investing, dispassionate analysis often proves more profitable. Decisions should be based on the relationship between business value and stock price. Be wary of becoming too optimistic, as the desire to win on Wall Street may have quite the opposite effect. In addition to guarding against personal overoptimism, be careful not to adopt others' overoptimistic views on particular companies, even if those others are professional analysts. This is no easy feat, because the system is typically designed to reinforce overoptimistic views wherever you turn.

Why should analysts be systematically overly optimistic? A 2002 study shows that Wall Street analysts get paid more if they are. Research by Harrison Hong, an associate professor at Stanford Business School, and Jeffrey Kubik of Syracuse University found that analysts who deliver optimistic earnings forecasts (not necessarily *accurate* ones) are more likely to be promoted.[7] This is yet another reason to be cautious when analyzing businesses and acting on information provided by "experts."

Anchoring: Grasping at Nonrelevant, Counterproductive Information

It's human nature to want to keep things relatable. Anchoring is a natural extension of this desire. It is the tendency to use information that really has little or no relevance to a given issue to draw conclusions or make decisions about that issue.

As an everyday example, if a dealer gives the list price of an SUV as $20,000, you may be very happy to pay $19,000 for it. Why? Your mind is anchored to the $20,000 list price. If your goal is to get the most value out of the purchase, however, would you still think the list price is relevant if you know that the vehicle is worth just $18,000? Not anymore, because now you know that you paid too much. The most relevant information was the $18,000 value, not the $20,000 list price on which you were anchored.

One of the most interesting experiments on the topic was done in 1974. It involved a rotating wheel with the numbers 1 to 100. Each participant spun the wheel and after it rested on a number was asked to estimate the percentage of African countries that are represented in the United Nations. "The obviously irrelevant random number generated from the wheel-of-fortune generates systematic bias in the estimations," the study's authors concluded. "For example, the average estimate from subjects who observed the number 10 was 25 percent. In contrast, the average estimate from subjects who observed the number 65 was 45 percent."[8]

Hindsight: Succeeding at What Has Already Happened

I will spare you the stereotypical adages about hindsight. But as a bias behavior, it bears mentioning because the markets are as unpredictable as ever. The chances are really good that market participants won't see something coming until it happens. We like to think that we got it right, though. It's only natural, because from an early age, we're conditioned to be judged and validated. Medical checkups, school report cards, job performance reviews, and other life "checkpoints" are all reminders that we have to verify how we're doing all the time. Hindsight bias is just another way of revalidating the facts—after the fact.

Of the millions of people who lost their houses, or came close to doing so, in the financial crisis of 2008–2009, how many do you honestly believe saw it coming? After the bottom fell out, all you heard was, "I knew that was going to happen, what with all the predatory lending and adjustable mortgages with the option to pick your payment amount. Of course it would all come down." Because it's focused on the past, hindsight tends to rank low on the "impact" scale. But I think it represents a troubling pattern of thinking that keeps getting market participants into the same trouble. Extreme hindsight bias prevails, as many investors are still looking for—and protecting against—a repeat of the 2008 decline.

Can Predictions Hurt Performance?

Evaluating driving skills, getting stuck in traffic, analyzing golf scores, and buying an SUV can be fun stories to share with friends or to help illustrate fundamentals of behavioral finance. What about objective facts? Is there any broad statistical evidence that really illustrates that "doing what is not popular on Wall Street" pays off in better long-term performance? There is.

The notion of investor expectations prompted my firm to further investigate a related angle in the "value versus glamour" framework that I discussed in Chapter 3. This time, rather than examine stock returns based on *reported* earnings, we studied returns based on *forecasted* earnings. Here too, the stocks in the most attractively valued deciles had the lowest current prices relative to their earnings forecasts.

Figure 4-1 shows the median expected earnings growth rates for the companies in the study ranked by valuation deciles. The study included about 3,000 companies from 23 developed markets worldwide between 1990 and 2009. The stocks in decile 1 had the highest expected growth rates and the highest forecasted price-to-earnings ratios.

After grouping stocks into valuation-based deciles, analysts tracked their returns over time. The results were very similar to those of the original study, with value stocks outperforming glamour stocks by a significant margin on both a one-year and a five-year basis. Just as interesting were the returns for value and glamour stocks that beat and missed their earnings' targets. Prices for both glamour and value stocks that *beat* expectations climbed over the subsequent 12 months—with value stocks outpacing glamour stocks (Figure 4-2).

But look at the returns for both groups when they *missed* their earnings targets. It's perhaps not surprising that the glamour stocks were punished. These stocks are often priced for perfection—and when reality doesn't match the expectations, stock prices have tended to tumble. But look at the returns for value stocks in deciles 7, 8, 9, and 10. Even though they *missed* their earnings forecasts, their returns over the subsequent 12 months were positive.

I believe this reflects behavioral biases among investors, who overestimate the likelihood of problems for value stocks, then recalibrate their views when business reality doesn't necessarily align with their poor perceptions. In fact, a Brandes Institute research study shows that perceptions (and prices) for these value stocks often began to shift even *before* the business fundamentals improved.

Buying stocks at low prices relative to their business values doesn't guarantee success, but studies like this show that it can greatly improve your chances. The Institute's complete study was published in the *Journal of Behavioral Finance* in 2011.

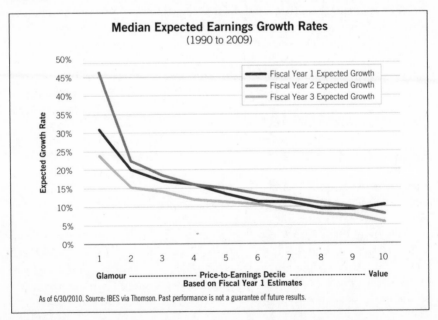

Figure 4-1

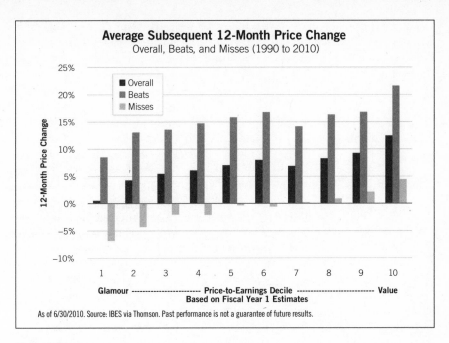

Average Subsequent 12-Month Price Change
Overall, Beats, and Misses (1990 to 2010)

- Overall
- Beats
- Misses

Glamour -------------------- **Price-to-Earnings Decile** -------------------- Value
Based on Fiscal Year 1 Estimates

As of 6/30/2010. Source: IBES via Thomson. Past performance is not a guarantee of future results.

Figure 4-2

Faulty intuition, extrapolation, overoptimism, and other behavioral flaws can set the stage for overconfidence and subsequent overreaction. While overconfidence in intuitive models can lead to losses, it may also cause investors to miss opportunities for gains. For example, an incorrect model analysis might lead to the belief that a poorly performing business will never recover. In the late 1970s, expectations of continued "stagflation" led to a general negative overreaction by investors. This is what prompted the 1979 *BusinessWeek* article "The Death of Equities" that I referred to in Chapter 1. You know how that story ends, too: in 1982, stocks began the greatest bull market in history.

Value investors recognize such tendencies and, as stated earlier, establish predetermined processes based on objective analysis rather than personal preferences or out-of-context judgments to guide their investment decisions. In Chapter 5, I explore the benefits of following investment processes as part of a discussion on how I apply value investing to manage portfolios.

Exploiting Market Behavior

Investors who strictly adhere to value disciplines have achieved favorable performance results with limited risk over the long term because they seize opportunities created by flaws that are inherent in human nature. These emotional biases often cause stock prices to fluctuate much more than the intrinsic value of businesses in the short term. These exaggerated price movements create opportunities for astute investors. Virtually by definition, value investors run counter to popular trends. When many market participants are selling, value investors are often buying, and vice versa. Value investors realize that achieving better-than-average returns depends on thinking and acting differently from the average investor.

Sanofi

Extrapolation can sometimes work in your favor. For example, Paris-based Sanofi S.A. is among the five largest global pharmaceutical companies, based on prescription sales. Its diversified portfolio includes prescription and generic drugs, vaccines, animal health products, and consumer care products. Among its most popular products are the allergy medication Allegra, the prescription insulin Lantus, and Plavix, which helps to prevent blood clots.

Pharmaceutical companies are generally considered defensive investments, companies whose offerings are usually in demand regardless of the current economic climate or business cycle. But they are not immune to market forces, a fact that hit close to home for Sanofi starting in 2007. That year, the company approached what analysts call a "patent cliff," an expected sharp decline in revenues as patents for several of its marquee drugs expire and competition from peers and generics begins to swarm.

The market's reaction to patent cliffs can sometimes be right on target when the companies that they affect have little else in their product pipelines to offset them. But a careful and patient value stock picker can frequently spot the opportunity beyond the nervous hype. In the Sanofi situation, value investors saw beyond the potential drop-off and into the heart of a company with a strong business model and a substantial R&D pipeline.

As Sanofi was facing its patent cliff, the market was giving the company's pharmaceutical pipeline very little or no credit. Sanofi had more than 100 drugs in development, with regulatory approvals imminent for some of them. Moreover, the majority of Sanofi's market value could be attributed to its currently marketed pharmaceutical products, which were fairly well diversified; Sanofi's top five drugs represented about one-third of its sales, and its other profitable core products, such as vaccines and animal health medicines, were not at risk.

The company continued to generate attractive cash flow and return on capital, which also led to solid dividends of more than 3 percent. At the end of the day, value investors believed that the market was unjustified in its pricing of Sanofi, and the most conservative estimates had Sanofi trading at a discount of around 10 times earnings.

Sanofi represents a classic situation of market extrapolation, the tendency for investors to draw conclusions based on a narrow and limited view of one or two things. With a wider, long-term view, value investors were able to see an opportunity despite the short-term headwinds, and were able to purchase an attractive business with a well-diversified product portfolio.

Value investment strategies tend to work because the majority of investors remain captive to judgmental errors, emotional biases, and short-term thinking that adversely influence their decisions. Even when objective facts contradict their biased views, investors often continue to overreact, sending market prices to extreme highs or lows. Human behavior is not always dictated by rational thought. But it's predictable. How good a driver are you? From time to time, ask people you know and keep track of their responses. Now that you're armed with a little more background on human behavior, their answers probably won't surprise you.

Applying the same principles to the stock market can limit your vulnerability to overreacting to short-term developments. The key is to adhere to investment policies and procedures that circumvent bias and reflect sustained objectivity. As a value investor, you don't want to fall victim to the very behaviors you are seeking to exploit.

Put simply, the reason a value approach works is not because investors benefit from predicting fluctuations in interest rates or economic output. The success of value investing isn't predicated upon the strength of corporate earnings or which political party holds the upper hand in Washington. Value investors just think of buying the business, not the stock. This works because it reflects a consistent focus on the relationship between value and price, and it takes advantage of innate human foibles.

I hope I haven't made this sound too easy, because it isn't. "To achieve satisfactory investment results is easier than most people realize," wrote Ben Graham. "To achieve superior results is harder than it looks."[9]

Accepting that these ideas make sense doesn't mean they are simple to apply in the financial markets. If you've ever been on a diet, you know how easy it is to decide that you'll eat less tomorrow, especially after you've just had dinner. But the next time you're offered a piece of chocolate cake, you usually find some excuse to deviate from your diet plan: you don't want to offend your host, or it's just *so* tempting. The effects of temptation on human behavior are well ingrained in all of us. Culturally, we want to please others. Going with the flow is generally rewarded. So, it's difficult to keep temptations in check. In Part III of the book, I will review some of the specific disciplines that we apply, as well as lessons learned, that have helped keep my firm on the value investing path.

Efficient Market Theory—and Reality

Many academics, observers, and pundits argue that the stock market acts efficiently without anyone or anything's help. This is portfolio-speak for the theory that stock prices always accurately reflect everything that is known about a company's prospects. According to this view, studying fundamentals such as earnings and book values is as useless and unreliable as reading tarot cards or tea leaves. The reason? Undervalued stocks—or so it is claimed—don't actually exist, because security analysts and other market participants have already harvested all available information and thereby ensured that prices are unfailingly appropriate. In other words, you can't beat the market because stock prices are assumed to always be equal to business values.

Proponents have embellished their belief with jazzy computer printouts and a three-letter acronym, EMT (efficient market theory) or EMH (efficient market hypothesis). EMT is divided into three camps: weak, semistrong, and strong.

Weak: Premised on Past and Future Price Disconnects

The weak version of the efficient market theory holds that past prices have no bearing on future prices. In other words, what investors will pay to own shares of a company in the future is essentially independent of their past actions; ergo, price patterns over the long haul are completely random.

Generally, value investors have no quarrel with the weak form of EMT. Technical analysis of just price behavior, or forecasting future returns based on the study of past price movements, has not served as an adequate substitute for fundamental company-specific analysis. Studies have revealed that a weak link between past and future prices may exist, but it's not strong enough to generate trading profits after you consider transaction costs.

Semistrong: Information Access Levels the Field, Somewhat

The semistrong form states that markets are efficient because of the rapid way in which knowledge is dispersed in the Information Age. As information about companies, industries, and the economy enters the marketplace, prices quickly reflect the assimilation of the new data.

However, fast information doesn't guarantee the accuracy of the conclusions drawn from it. It may suggest a certain outlook, but a significantly different picture may emerge as the ideas are interpreted over time.

Strong: Everyone Knows Everything at All Times

This version of the efficient market theory holds that at any given moment, security prices already accurately reflect all knowable public and private information. In other words, there can never be a difference between the value of the underlying business and the stock price. Therefore, the margin of safety, the gap between a company's intrinsic value and its share price that creates a bargain-priced stock, is an illusion. No amount of skilled interpretation of available public data can enable any investor to profit from discrepancies between business value and stock price. In this view, the efforts of security analysts to identify mispricings have a stronger role in creating market efficiency.

Reality Trumps Theory

EMT is predicated on a world in which every investor has all the knowledge that's available, understands it, and is able to act logically on it. But markets aren't orderly or logical. The Internet stock bubble of the late 1990s provides more than a few examples of real-world opportunities created by the worst market illogic we've seen in decades. Excessive optimism and greed pushed the prices of dot-com companies well beyond their underlying values. Many investors assumed that the Internet would have a major impact on *every* business, and dot-com companies appeared to be best positioned to benefit. Accordingly, investors clamored for Internet-related stocks and shunned much of the rest of the market.

In this environment, prices of old economy companies, such as the U.S. consumer product–based firms Heinz and Sara Lee, fell well below their intrinsic values, creating opportunities for value investors who were looking for high-quality businesses. In early 2000, a value investor could have purchased shares of Heinz and Sara Lee for $29 and $15, respectively. Two years later, Heinz had climbed to $37, and Sara Lee's stock price had reached $21.

This trend wasn't limited to consumer goods, and in some industries the opportunities were amplified. Premier automaker BMW, for example, was also largely unappreciated in the late 1990s, as it was perceived as a staid company that lacked the tremendous growth potential of the day's more glamorous firms. Its Rover subsidiary was also bleeding cash; this, along with some management shake-ups, sparked concerns about the erosion of the entire company's value. Not true. BMW never lost its defendable competitive advantage, prestigious brand image, and highly profitable auto-financing unit. An astute value investor could have bought shares in 1999 at $12 to $17. By 2002, the company's staid business was attracting more attention than the new economy stocks, most of which had hit the skids. As a result, BMW topped $30 by 2002. While its stock price backslid along with the entire industry during the financial crisis of 2008–2009, it's now trading at around $90.[10] BMW represents another example of the rewards available to investors who think and act differently from the crowds.

Regarding the flaws associated with EMT, Clifford F. Pratten of the University of Cambridge wrote just after the 1987 crash,[11] "When the S&P Index fell by 30.7 percent in 6 days, [it] gave a new impetus and direction to tests of EMT and added credibility to tests which contradicted the hypothesis, because such a large and swift fall was not compatible with changes in stock market prices being determined by new information concerning fundamentals alone."

One of the foremost value investing academics was Robert A. Haugen, who was an economist and professor of finance at the University of California–Irvine, and also studied EMT throughout the 1990s and found it lacking: "We now see a market that is highly inefficient and over reactive; a market literally turned upside down—where the highest risk-adjusted stocks can be expected to produce the lowest returns and the lowest-risk stocks, the highest returns."[12]

Both of these esteemed academics found that emotions play an important role in stock prices. Haugen wrote: "Overwhelming evidence is piling up that investors overreact to the past performance of stocks, pricing growth stocks—those expected to grow faster than average—too low. Subsequent to these overreactions, growth stocks produce low returns for the investors who buy them at high prices, and similarly, value stocks produce high returns for their investors."[13]

In the real world, where emotions such as fear and greed abound, logic is often scarce. This situation is rewarding for the value investor, as long as the gap between price and value caused by such inefficiency can be successfully exploited. Next, I'll describe for you just how I have done that.

CHAPTER 5

THE SEARCH
FOR VALUE

Your method of operation has to differ from the majority of investors. If you're not different in the way you think from the majority, it's harder to be successful.

—Charles Brandes, in an interview with the *Business Times*, Singapore, March 2014

For me, the most exciting difference between value investing and other strategies, such as growth investing and indexing, is that value investing places a more deliberate focus on the process. The general direction of many investment styles may overlap in the short term, but the uniqueness of the hands-on methodology behind value investing still motivates me when I go to work every day. Why? Because I believe that the many steps you take toward your goal are as important as the results themselves. In the value investing world, you can't assume growth or outperformance without first applying the process—not if you expect to get results with any likelihood of repeatability.

To help illustrate the point of goals versus process, I share an old story of two men working at opposite ends of an onion field. After a few hours, one of them suddenly notices that the other has stopped plowing and has taken up a shovel and started digging in a far corner.

"Why are you digging a hole?" he shouted.

"I'm not digging a hole," was the reply, and the second man kept at it.

"You're digging a hole. I can clearly see that," the first man insisted.

Pausing, the second man assured the first, "What you clearly *see* is a man digging the *dirt*. What you're *assuming* is that I want to leave a hole in it."

Of course, the hole was his objective. But the process—the tedious act of digging—represents the necessary steps to reach his goal. Two different views; same general outcome. In our world, value investing is all about the digging process. In a market filled with shortsighted goals and assumptions about what to expect, identifying companies that qualify as value stocks is about first knowing what to look for and how to look for it. And you have to be willing to dig for them.

Value Is Everywhere

Value opportunities can be found in companies in practically every industry, in all shapes and sizes and, most important, in just about any country. Regardless of where or what they are, attractively valued companies all tend to share some key characteristics. Here are some of the ones that are most important to me:

1. *Understandable products and services.* If you have a solid understanding of a business's products and services—what it sells to earn money—you can effectively evaluate its strengths and weaknesses and its intrinsic value. My firm looks for companies whose products and services can be clearly understood. Comprehension paves the way for an in-depth analysis of investment opportunities as well as proper monitoring of existing holdings. Knowledge also provides an important measure of self-defense. Understanding a business diminishes the likelihood that you'll be swayed by media hype that could adversely influence your investment decisions over the short term.

2. *Consistent earnings generation.* Earnings records for value companies typically show lengthy, relatively stable histories of income creation. Intermittent losses don't rule out a potential investment opportunity; on the contrary, the negative sentiment that frequently accompanies temporary earnings downturns sometimes pushes a company's stock price down to attractive levels. However, value investors believe that, although past results do not guarantee future success, a consistent long-term earnings record can be a strong foundation on which to build long-term wealth creation.

3. *Strong financial health.* By generally focusing on companies with low debt levels, value investors help ensure that their holdings will be able to manage through the inevitable headwinds. The next chapter reviews specific measures that are useful for conducting financial health checkups.

The Starting Point

The oft-heard saying, "Let's begin at the top and work our way down," doesn't cut it for me or my firm. From the day I opened my business in 1974, I have always been a bottom-up manager. Ben Graham purposely chose to make the title of his seminal book *Security Analysis* singular because he truly believed that it needs to be done one investment at a time to be effective.

Exclusively top-down investors, by contrast, start broadly and then conduct their search for individual stocks based on a number of macroeconomic-based assumptions. For example, before looking at company-specific traits, top-down investors gauge the strength of a certain country or region. They may study forecasts of economic growth, business sentiment, or the recent performance of stocks in that area. If they are pleased with the prospects for a region or a country, they may then seek what they believe are the most promising sectors or industries within that area, perhaps drawing on sales projections or the profit potential of new products or services.

In addition, top-down investors may factor in expectations for interest-rate moves, changes in the political climate, or shifts in broad economic trends. Eventually, they get around to pinpointing specific stocks, but they are certainly less interested in the business and more in the external factors that drive it. But there are far too many variables beyond my control in top-down investing for me to get comfortable with it.

To me, it makes better sense to start at the street level—with an individual company. We evaluate thousands of individual businesses each year, researching and analyzing companies that by their nature represent different industries, sectors, and countries. We look for the most attractive candidates we can find, regardless of where they are located, and we pay less attention to macroeconomic factors such as interest rates or unemployment or gross domestic product. We don't have to forecast which sectors or industries will be the top performers in the short term; we are principally focused on the prospects for individual companies.

With the help of technology, my firm's team of global research professionals is dedicated to evaluating businesses all over the world every day. I can appreciate that individual investors may not have the time and resources to conduct such extensive, company-specific evaluations. With that in mind, I'll still offer a few essential techniques for searching for value companies. With dedication, commitment, and patience, I'm confident that you can achieve solid long-term results. In my opinion, your success largely depends on two things: stock selection and adherence to value principles.

Where and When to Find Value

Although it always comes down to the merits of each company, value invest-ing does have some favorite search zones and seasons that are most reliable for select opportunities.

Out-of-Favor Industries

Value investors frequently search for bargains among companies or sectors that have been relegated to the scrap heap by the public. Recall the examples from Chapter 1, such as when the stresses on the financial system from the savings and loan crisis and the subsequent 1990–1991 recession resulted in tremendous bargains in the banking sector. Many banks were selling for below book value. As the economy recovered, regional and money-center banks staged a powerful rally. Similarly, the Internet stock bubble, which turned the market's attention away from traditional or "old economy" stocks like manufacturing, retail, and utilities, offered the most undervalued companies in over a decade.

Geographic Hard Times

The value strategy's practitioners can also look for problems that are unique to a particular geographic region. The goal is to benefit from the investing public's overly emotional reaction to a temporary situation.

Just a few examples include:

- *Texas and Oklahoma (mid-1980s).* The collapse of oil prices temporarily depressed economies in the oil patch of Texas and Oklahoma; pockets of strong but undervalued businesses that were unrelated to energy persevered.

- *California (early 1990s).* Federal budget cuts in the defense sector hurt the California economy; more defensive industries such as consumer goods, food and retail, and healthcare continued to offer opportunities.

- *Southeast Asia (summer of 1997).* Economic woes and the threat of currency devaluation weighed on sentiment and dragged down share prices for a number of otherwise very solid businesses there.

- *Egypt (spring of 2011).* While emerging markets are home to many successful companies, they also face political, social, and other risks that can create periods of investor biases.

- *Russia (2014).* Political tensions and sanctions against this country, stemming from the Ukraine conflict, had little long-term impact on some of Russia's premier industries, including oil and gas companies.

New Lows

Another source of potential bargains is the newspaper or online stock listings that contain information on companies whose stock prices have fallen to new lows. Influential news media like the *Wall Street Journal*, Bloomberg, Reuters, and *Investor's Business Daily* regularly list companies that have just fallen to new 12-month lows. Such stocks certainly qualify as out of favor and could warrant further investigation. But whether they also pass the basic tests of financial health, earnings generation, and understandable businesses is another story.

Value Portfolios

You also might study the portfolios of value investors who have put together lengthy and outstanding track records. For example, a review of the equity holdings of value-based fund groups such as Longleaf Partners, Third Avenue Funds, or Tweedy, Browne could point to potential investment opportunities. A fund's shareholder report, which lists its recent holdings, can usually be viewed online, or print versions can be requested by e-mail or telephone. But don't buy a stock just because a highly touted professional investor has done so. You should understand and have confidence in the logic behind the decision to avoid buying or selling at the wrong time or for the wrong reason.

Media

For something that was considered "fuddy duddy" and "old hat" just a few years ago, value investing seems like hot news these days. Its renewed popularity, too, seems almost bottom-up in nature and may prove lasting; more graduate students, for example, are immersing themselves in classroom-based value fundamentals, fostering new generations who are interested in the pursuit of fresh analysis, thought leadership, and white papers on myriad topics in the value space.

Lots of news on or around the core value philosophy could be good or bad for value investors, depending on the source of the information and how you process it. For reliability, I generally turn to the print and online versions of *Barron's*, the *Wall Street Journal*, the *New York Times*, *Investor's Business Daily*, or the *Financial Times* for good value-based ideas. These are the opinion-leading media with the most "street cred" for me, and they can offer rosy commentaries—and some that are not so rosy—about companies that Wall Street already loves. Occasionally, I can glean a few strong leads when they feature companies that meet certain value criteria, such as having undervalued assets. They're a great starting point for now, but we'll see what happens to them in the coming years. As the electronic age dramatically changes the business models for major news media, eliminating some of the better ones, I truly hope this batch remains unscathed.

"The more I learn, the more I realize how much I don't know," goes the self-effacing barb from Albert Einstein. I'm not positive, but I think he was probably referring to academic and theoretical breakthroughs, not the mundane occurrences of everyday life. Regardless, Einstein lived in an era in which access to information meant everything, but it took considerable time and effort to locate and acquire it. Fast-forward less than a century to today, a time when information is easy to get and available on a 24/7 basis, but making sense of it all is the hard part. Are we living in an age of too much information? I don't think so, but the potential overload poses some risk for investors.

Ironically, the easier access to and higher volume of investment-related information offered through the Internet may actually do more harm than good. News travels fast and certain, even when it's not really news. The race to be the first to post a story, for example, has significantly compromised the overall quality of news in terms of content and accuracy. As users, our expectations have dropped as well. Technology journalist Nicholas Carr has spent considerable time on the topic of user habits in several articles and books, arguing that consumers are losing the seriousness of sustained attention to the frantic superficiality of the Internet. "Once I was a scuba diver in the sea of words," Carr laments. "Now I zip along the surface like a guy on a Jet Ski." Basically, we have been conditioned to be "scanners," not "readers."[1]

On a consumer level, there are many web- and smartphone-based calculators, stock screeners, and financial planning portals, all designed to help you better understand your options and make educated investment decisions. Many of these are sponsored by nonprofit groups and government agencies, such as the Social Security Administration and public universities. Finally, if you have a personal brokerage account through some of the leading firms, it probably offers additional resources and tools to help you along, either as part of your account or for additional charges. These are all viable sources of useful information.

However, the sundry financial "advice" pundits of the Internet and the financial cable networks tend to make matters worse for many investors. Is the advice objective, or are they pushing you toward or away from certain stocks for personal reasons? Even for the professional investor, it can be hard to tell sometimes.

I don't discard all of them. There are many knowledgeable and objective financial news sources that devote time and resources to covering topics of interest, although the landscape is continually changing. PBS's *Nightly Business Report*, for example, stands out for me as one of television's most comprehensive business news formats ever presented. It's been going strong for 35 years (Alan Greenspan got his start there), but while its editorial integrity remains intact, its viewership, unfortunately, continues to fall.

Free Advice Could Cost You

My problem is with the so-called free advice websites, blogs, and discussion forums that come with few checks and balances. They answer to no content governance or oversight entity, which can be troublesome for those people who have little time to filter out fact from fiction. With so much opinion, discourse, and direction, the web, as a tool of convenience, can literally be like the Wild West—extremely dangerous if you're not careful to protect yourself.

As you absorb financial news, try not to pay too much attention to one of the media's favorite topics: short-term movements in the price level of the overall market. There are many hidden dangers in not understanding the potential impact of "stock pundit'" recommendations on your investment strategy. And, the expanding universes of microblogging can be a lot of fun, but how meaningful or helpful can 140 characters be to hopeful followers? (For Twitter fans, that question was 140 characters.) The same thing goes for seemingly objective economists, such as those from the International Monetary Fund. Are they really in the know when it comes to what's going on at the company level? I don't think so.

Remember, true value investors focus on a bottom-up, company-by-company search for large discrepancies between a stock's price and its fair value. Accordingly, the broad market's day-to-day fluctuations are usually of no significance. Don't hesitate to click the "no thanks" button from time to time.

IPOs in the Value Investing World

Few investment strategies more embody the seemingly opposing acts of making the unpredictable more predictable than the initial public offering (IPO). As we have seen in recent high-profile examples, IPOs can be unreliable and inconsistent. As a general rule, IPOs are not recommended for the average value investor.

Consider the conflict of interest associated with the sale of IPO shares. The private owners are seeking to sell shares at the *highest* price possible, while value investors are seeking the *lowest* possible price. Be especially wary of IPOs when the stock market is surging to successive record highs. The hype that usually accompanies IPOs during a bull market tends to push their valuations beyond the range that would interest a value investor. Price/earnings ratios for IPOs, for example, can reach double or triple that of the overall market, with some of the hotter new offerings selling on nothing more than a wing and a prayer.

With expectations set so high, the odds of disappointment are often too great. A value approach to stock selection requires that investors pay only for what is seen, not for what is hoped.

A recent example of the unpredictability of IPOs is Zynga. The social gaming company founded in 2007 had millions of devoted players of its flagship product FarmVille, so it seemed ripe for an IPO in 2011. Its near-exclusive tether to Facebook was also expected to boost its image. What could go wrong? As it turned out, just enough went south at the last minute to tip the needle the other way. Hard-core, well-followed gaming critics judged Zynga's offerings to be "unchallenging," while nascent intellectual-property controversies and litigation bubbled up as the IPO drew near. The newly issued stock opened at $10, but dropped 5 percent on its first day. While that doesn't sound so bad, consider that the underwriters initially valued Zynga at $10 per share To make matters worse, by 2012 the stock had sunk to about $2.25 as a result of weak earnings and the drag from Facebook, which generates most of Zynga's revenues and had suffered its own IPO stumble that year.[2]

However, despite challenges like Zynga, young public companies shouldn't be dismissed out of hand. There is a time to look at them, but in most cases it's after the stock has traded for a period and the initial fanfare has faded. Problems may have arisen in the young company's fortunes: either management can't handle growth, fails at diversification, and expands too rapidly; or competition becomes more intense.

Several scenarios might occur. The stock may be richly priced at the time of the offering, rise for a while, then fall back as earnings difficulties arise. The company's stock may be overpriced to begin with and immediately fall below the initial offering price. Of course, there is always the *potential* for the company to do well and end up being a good investment.

Bargains are there for the asking in the post-IPO market if you have the patience to look and wait. You should determine, however, whether any problems with a young company are only temporary and will be rectified in a reasonable time.

Keep in mind that the absence of a lengthy operating history means that many IPO opportunities don't deserve a value investor's time. Sometimes, however, companies with stable operating histories spin off divisions as IPOs. In other cases, a private company with a long-term track record may raise capital through an IPO. These special cases may present opportunities for value investors. Again, always evaluate the value of the underlying business against its stock price.

What's Good About It?

Is a good company the same as a good investment? Not necessarily. An established firm with high revenue levels and a stable, strong earnings record, for instance, certainly sounds like a good company. But like any business, that firm is a good opportunity in the eyes of a value investor only if it can be purchased at a favorable price.

For example, in 2013, few would have considered either Amazon.com or Facebook to be anything other than a good *company* with an excellent future. Despite their success, however, most value investors stopped short of calling them good *investments*, as shown in Figure 5-1.

Companies to Be Careful About

No matter where value investors search for opportunity, they'll undoubtedly encounter dozens of potential investments that can be ruled out after a cursory review. How can undesirable businesses be spotted? The following guidelines explore several easy-to-recognize warning signs. These guidelines are not necessarily universal. Experienced value investors might recognize opportunity in a company that is priced well below its true value, even if it falls short in one or more of the following areas. In fact, although the negative qualities shown here

Is a Good Company Always a Good Investment?

Company	Market Cap*	2013 Revenue*	2013 Net Income*
Amazon.com Inc.	$154,481	$74,452	$274
Facebook, Inc.	$154,449	$7,872	$1,500
	$308,930	**$82,324**	**$1,774**
Corning Inc.	$28,957	$7,819	$1,961
Seagate Technology Public Limited Company	$18,463	$13,968	$1,619
Nissan Motor Co., Ltd.	$37,456	$96,558	$3,653
Honda Motor Co., Ltd.	$63,619	$109,274	$4,559
Marks & Spencer Group PLC	$12,218	$16,921	$831
British Sky Broadcasting Group PLC	$23,637	$12,357	$1,496
Ericsson	$42,813	$35,368	$1,867
Chesapeake Energy Corporation	$16,725	$17,506	$724
Swiss Re Ltd.	$31,725	$36,925	$4,511
The Bank of New York Mellon Corporation	$40,117	$15,018	$2,111
	$315,730	**$361,713**	**$23,333**

*($ Millions)
As of 12/31/2013. Source: CapitalIQ. Past performance is not a guarantee of future results.

Figure 5-1 Amazon.com and Facebook, Inc., are good companies, but to value investors, their stock prices translated into astronomical market capitalizations in 2013: nearly one-third of a trillion dollars combined. This figure dwarfs their revenue and net income numbers, a situation that most value investors avoid. Contrast these with significantly lower market capitalizations for the other companies shown, which had just as solid revenues and earnings. These were considered good *companies* that also could be good *investments* at the time.

can pose risks, they can also occasionally lead to value investing opportunities for those who are willing and able to dig deeper into the companies. Discerning the good and bad among them, however, usually takes more work and experience than most individual investors have.

High Debt

Avoid businesses that are loaded with debt. A good rule is, "businesses should have no more debt than they have equity." (Of course, that's not true in all cases. For example, the rule doesn't apply to financial companies, whose lines of business often require high levels of debt relative to equity.)

Disproportionate Payrolls and Perks

Run from corporate managers who seem concerned with perks, golden parachutes, bonuses, and excessively high salaries in relation to the return to shareholders. How does the value investor get answers to these concerns? Simply thumb through a company's SEC-required filings, such as the 10-K report, the notice of shareholders' meeting, and the proxy statement. Also take a quick glance at industry reports, which provide benchmarks for executive compensation in a particular type of business.

Creative Accountants

Don't invest in businesses that generate money through accounting cleverness rather than real cash. Such businesses require more investment as sales grow, resulting in a further buildup of working capital. Look at cash flow figures; a healthy free cash flow indicates that a company can pay all its bills with enough left over to buy back its shares, pay a larger dividend, or invest. I address more aspects of what we call *corporate governance*, including accounting practices and executive salaries, in Chapter 9.

Chameleons

Detour around companies that change character every time a hot idea appears on the horizon. Many defense contractors, for example, promote sweeping and risky new programs just to stay in business. Other managers assume so much risk that this is literally a "bet your company" situation.

Pricing Constraints

Stay away from companies that are committed to providing services or commodities at fixed prices for a long time in the future. Rising inflation could wreak havoc here.

High-Cost Enterprises

Bypass capital-intensive companies. Often the cash flow of such companies is insufficient to provide a satisfactory return while still maintaining a plant at competitive levels. These companies must borrow or issue stock regularly to stay in business.

Highly Regulated Companies

Be particularly cautious about businesses that are subject to government regulation. These firms generally don't make good long-term investments, since their rates of return are limited by law.

Complicated Share Structures

Watch out for companies with different classes of stock. Shareholders may be disenfranchised through the issuance of limited or nonvoting stock. Also be careful to avoid foreign companies that issue different classes of stock for non-domestic shareholders. These shares may trade at substantially different levels from those of stocks owned by domestic investors.

Nip and Tuck Remedies

Pass by companies with managements that only occasionally initiate cost-reduction programs. Cost reduction should be an ongoing way of doing business.

Dilutions of Grandeur

Avoid companies that continually issue additional shares. Each subsequent equity offering dilutes the ownership value of existing shareholders. The dilution also lowers a company's earnings per share, an important factor in determining a stock's fair value. Be especially cautious if the proceeds from a secondary stock offering are used to invest in businesses with lower rates of return, or those that management seems ill prepared to deal with. Remember, a bigger pie is not always a better pie.

The Growth Factor

Business growth is essential, even in the value investor's domain. At the same time, before I'll invest, I need to ensure that growth is creating value, not destroying it.

Value-destructive growth occurs when a company's investments generate returns that are below its cost of capital, which can occur regardless of sales or earnings per share growth. In other words, the opportunity costs of growing the business exceed the income that the business generates. This value-impairing growth can occur organically, such as when a company becomes overly aggressive in its pricing to win new business, or externally, when a company overpays for acquisitions.

Growth is a key attribute for value companies, as long as it has a positive influence on the company's wealth-creation potential. Although there are no hard and fast definitions of what makes a value company, low debt, consistent earnings, and comprehensible business activities tend to be most characteristic of the equities that value investors prefer. Along with these characteristics, price is the ultimate factor to be considered. Effective value investing comes down to the price you pay for a company. That being said, you may appreciate more why I avoided the shares of fast-growing dot-com companies during the Internet bubble of the late 1990s, even at the risk of appearing out of touch at that time.

This chapter addressed the general techniques, information sources, and potential hurdles of value investing. Next, we'll examine other opportunities such as "net-net" and define key metrics like the price-to-earnings ratio and book value, as well as the sources and tools that help determine a straightforward and often reliable measure of a company's intrinsic value.

CHAPTER 6

BY THE NUMBERS

In God we trust, all others must bring data.

—W. Edwards Deming[1]

To set the tone for a chapter on gathering company data, I thought it very appropriate to share the sentiments of one of the twentieth century's most influential statisticians. W. Edwards Deming all but invented the U.S. Census process and almost single-handedly designed the efficient production and quality control models that revolutionized Japan's global manufacturing capabilities in the 1970s. He achieved all this and more through a disciplined appreciation for what the numbers told him. Like Deming, value investors know that little can be accomplished without solid, reliable data.

Narrowing Your Focus

So far, we have identified typical characteristics of value stocks and set out some qualitative rules for pinpointing investment opportunities. So, how can an investor apply these criteria to a company that makes it through the initial screen? What sources yield clues to a company's strengths and weaknesses, and where can numbers such as shareholders' equity and earnings per share be found?

At my firm, we begin company analysis by asking a pair of simple questions: Would a rational investor want to own this business? And, if so, at what price? To answer these questions, of course, you need lots of facts, including adequate information about a company's history, type of business, and potential for cyclical highs and lows. The information-gathering process can be time consuming, but the cold, hard facts it generates often make the difference between a successful investment and one that underperforms.

Valuation Methods

Ben Graham's well-known method of valuation focused on three pieces of data: earnings yield, dividend yield, and balance sheet debt. A stock that was attractive on all three measures, Graham believed, qualified as a true bargain.

Earnings Yield

Earnings yield is calculated by dividing a company's earnings per share (EPS) by its stock price. If XYZ Co., for example, has recently reported $3 in EPS and has a stock price of $20, its earnings yield is 0.15, or 15 percent. An alternative way to calculate earnings yield is to take the inverse of a company's price-to-earnings ratio—that is, to divide 1 by the company's P/E. We'll talk more about P/E later in this chapter.

Generally, Graham believed that by comparing earnings yield to the long-term (20-year) yield on AAA bonds, investors can begin to gauge a stock's investment potential. A bargain stock's earnings yield needed to be at least double the long-term AAA bond yield to qualify as attractive.

Dividend Yield

Dividend yield is another screen. Similar to earnings yield, dividend yield is calculated by dividing all dividends per share paid in the last year by the current stock price. If XYZ Co. paid $1 in dividends and traded at $20, for example, the stock's dividend yield would equal 0.05 or 5 percent.

Again, one would compare dividend yield to the yield on long-term AAA bonds. Based on traditional Graham-and-Dodd approaches, a bargain stock's dividend yield must be no less than two-thirds of the long-term AAA bond yield. With long-term AAA bonds yielding 6 percent, XYZ Co. would meet this threshold: the company's dividend yield of 5 percent exceeds 4 percent, which is two-thirds of the AAA rate.

Balance Sheet Debt

The final data point is balance sheet debt. From the beginning, Graham considered high debt levels to be troubling because they typically lead to heavy, asset-draining interest expense. As a result, investing in debt-burdened companies means that you could be gambling that future earnings will be high enough to meet the debt service. To Graham, investors were better off scouting for companies with low debt.

How much is *too* much? The general rule was that companies should owe no more than they are worth. More formally stated, a company's total debt should not exceed its shareholders' equity. This means that a bargain stock's debt-to-equity ratio should be less than 1.0.

However, evaluation of a company's debt level also depends on the nature of the company and its business. Banks, for example, depend on funds borrowed via savings and checking accounts to make profit-generating loans. As a result, banking companies with debt-to-equity ratios much higher than 1.0 are often well financed and may be sound investments.

In general, however, a high level of debt is dangerous, and I think my aversion to firms with debt-to-equity ratios greater than 1.0 is realistic and prudent. Taken together, the combination of the debt-to-equity rule and the requirements for earnings yield and dividend yield forms a solid foundation for the analysis of most investment opportunities.

The Net-Net Method

Net-net's doubled-up name is just a short way to describe what it captures: *net* working capital, *net* of all other liabilities. Designed by Ben Graham, the method calculates a company's value by subtracting all its liabilities—the total amount of money owed to creditors—from its current assets, which essentially represent the company's cash or near cash (such as receivables and inventories) on hand.

In other words, a company with positive net-net current assets theoretically could pay off all its debtholders' claims using its cash on hand and still have cash left over. To Graham, one of history's most finicky investors, if a stock's price is less than two-thirds of net-net current assets per share, and if the company is currently profitable, investors need no other yardstick: the stock is a buy. The reasoning behind this rule is straightforward. When the share price is less than two-thirds of net-net current assets, investors can effectively buy this excess cash for less than 67 cents on the dollar—and get a full claim on the company's fixed assets for free. In Graham's eyes, this would indicate an extremely attractive investment, as long as the company was currently generating profits. I think this rule still applies today, but times have changed, and with them the dynamics of profitability. For many years, one of the more fruitful areas of the world for finding net-net value investment opportunities was Japan—another interesting value proposition discussed in detail in Chapter 11.

Does Profitability Matter in Net-Net?

Yes. In one of my one-on-one mentoring sessions with Graham, I asked him, "What if a company qualified using net-net, except for its recent profitability?" In his usual Socratic manner, he answered with a question: "Do you think a company's losses would have an impact on its assets or its capacity to gather more assets?" he asked. I didn't even have to really think about the answer to that, and he knew that it registered almost immediately. In fact, regardless of their net-net position, unprofitable companies are dangerously situated. Graham believed that losses could rapidly burn up corporate assets and subsequently endanger the potential payoff of an investment. In other words, profits are essential in applying the net-net measure to the decision-making process.

Admittedly, even during Graham's lifetime, few companies met his stringent net-net criteria, except when the market was at the bottom of a major decline. More recently, high valuations—especially in the United States throughout 2013 and 2014—and increased investor vigilance have made it nearly impossible to find a profitable company selling at a one-third discount to its net-net current assets. A quick search of the Internet can find you some of the more prominent websites that feature a net-net screen tool.

Bargain-Hunting Techniques

Companies and their structures have certainly come a long way since 1934, the beginning of the Graham era, but his value and safety tests still have considerable currency in today's equities world. Tests for value focus on income and income-generating assets, while safety tests put the spotlight on risk factors like debt levels and earnings stability. If a stock satisfied at least one of the criteria on each list, Graham believed, it probably qualified as a good bargain.

I use these tests every day as starting points, but I know that they are certainly not all-inclusive in a modern investment arena that is more riddled than ever with exceptions, special situations, and the occasional unexpected catastrophe.

Graham-and-Dodd Evaluation Guidelines

Value

1. Earnings yield is at least twice the yield on long-term AAA bonds.
2. The P/E ratio falls among the lowest 10 percent of P/Es in the universe.
3. Dividend yield is at least two-thirds the yield on long-term AAA bonds.
4. The stock price is less than two-thirds of tangible book value (total book value minus goodwill) per share.
5. The stock price is less than two-thirds of net current assets (current assets minus current liabilities).

Safety

1. The debt-to-equity ratio is less than 1.0.

2. Current assets are at least twice current liabilities.

3. Total debt is less than twice net current assets.

4. Annual earnings growth is at least 7 percent over the previous decade.

5. There have been no more than two year-to-year earnings declines of more than 5 percent during the previous decade.

Expanding on Graham and Dodd

Drawing on Graham's teachings and my own experience, I've condensed the most significant precepts of the value philosophy into a four-step test that you can quickly apply to any company that catches your eye. A stock that measures up to each of the four criteria given here probably qualifies as a true value stock. If the issue falls short in one or more areas, I recommend proceeding with caution:

1. No losses were sustained within the past five years.

2. Total debt is less than 100 percent of total tangible equity.

3. Share price is less than book value per share.

4. Earnings yield is at least twice the yield on long-term (20-year) AAA bonds.

These guidelines seem strict, but there is some wiggle room. Yet, be careful not to let yourself rationalize taking on too much risk. Within the parameters of sound judgment, value investors might possibly ignore one or more of the criteria, but only if compelling and well-researched reasons exist for doing so. For example, the second test might be overlooked if a company's debt has a low interest rate, or if a company's earnings are especially strong and stable. Or, the third test could be ignored if the company has sustained high rates of return on book value. If that analysis proves too tricky, however, it may be safer to follow the precise guidelines.

Measuring a Company's Value

The value approach places strong emphasis on three crucial factors. The first is earnings strength, a quality that is measured by a variety of criteria, including consistency of annual earnings per share and freedom from periods of net losses. The second is financial strength, which is typically evaluated using metrics like debt-to-equity ratios. The third is low price, a factor accounted for in ratios such as the price-to-book ratio and earnings yield.

All three of these factors are also integral to another key value investing approach: purchasing companies at substantial discounts to their intrinsic value. But what is intrinsic value, exactly? And how is it calculated in practice?

Inside Intrinsic Value

First, what is intrinsic value? I'll share one definition of it given by Warren Buffett at the 2007 Berkshire Hathaway annual meeting of shareholders: "The intrinsic value of Berkshire, like any other business, is based on the future amount of cash that can be delivered between now and Judgment Day, discounted back at the proper rate."[2] In other words, a company's intrinsic value is equal to the value today of all of the money it will deliver well into the future. Figure 6-1 shows how the value process works in conjunction with intrinsic value and margin of safety.

So how is intrinsic value calculated? Unfortunately, the answer to this question is not so simple. As Buffett's definition suggests, one path to estimating a company's intrinsic value involves very long-term projections regarding its future cash generation. Of course, for even the most stable companies, the future is filled with uncertainty.

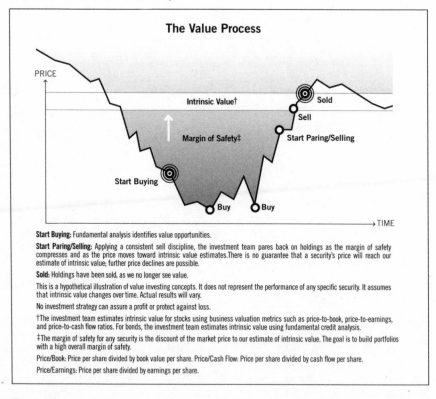

The Value Process

PRICE

Intrinsic Value†

Sold

Sell

Margin of Safety‡

Start Paring/Selling

Start Buying

Buy

Buy

TIME

Start Buying: Fundamental analysis identifies value opportunities.

Start Paring/Selling: Applying a consistent sell discipline, the investment team pares back on holdings as the margin of safety compresses and as the price moves toward intrinsic value estimates. There is no guarantee that a security's price will reach our estimate of intrinsic value; further price declines are possible.

Sold: Holdings have been sold, as we no longer see value.

This is a hypothetical illustration of value investing concepts. It does not represent the performance of any specific security. It assumes that intrinsic value changes over time. Actual results will vary.

No investment strategy can assure a profit or protect against loss.

†The investment team estimates intrinsic value for stocks using business valuation metrics such as price-to-book, price-to-earnings, and price-to-cash flow ratios. For bonds, the investment team estimates intrinsic value using fundamental credit analysis.

‡The margin of safety for any security is the discount of the market price to our estimate of intrinsic value. The goal is to build portfolios with a high overall margin of safety.

Price/Book: Price per share divided by book value per share. Price/Cash Flow: Price per share divided by cash flow per share.

Price/Earnings: Price per share divided by earnings per share.

Figure 6-1

Accordingly, the value strategy's adherents tend to place significant emphasis on insights gained from a thorough analysis of a company's past and present. This is where the three key factors come into play. To calculate intrinsic value, we rigorously examine such qualities as financial strength and earnings strength in the context of the company's past results, its current operations, and its future prospects. Once calculated, this value is divided by the number of shares outstanding to arrive at an estimate of intrinsic value per share. Then, this per share intrinsic value is compared with the company's stock price. If the stock price is low enough to offer a significant discount to intrinsic value, we buy the stock.

An estimated intrinsic value *range* is often just as useful as a precise number in evaluating the suitability of a potential investment. Likewise, a ballpark estimate of intrinsic value can sometimes be enough to discern an investment opportunity if a stock is trading at a much lower price.

Value investors don't expect to be able to come up with intrinsic value estimates for every stock in the market. Firms operating in nascent industries with rapidly changing dynamics are often surrounded by levels of uncertainty that make any estimates of their underlying worth dubious. In cases like these, value investors recognize the limits of their abilities and move on to evaluate other companies.

My firm analyzes thousands of stocks of all sizes and industries from all over the world. A clothing manufacturer in China operates much differently from an energy provider in Russia or a specialty food retailer in Greece, and so on. It stands to reason, also, that we often apply different angles to valuing various types of companies. For example, the methodology used to value a utility would look somewhat different from that used to value a technology company. Utilities, which are usually buffered from economic influences, may allow a little more leniency on the debt-to-equity or annual earnings growth tests, while for a potentially more volatile technology-based business, these would be two must-pass criteria before we would even consider it.

The P/E Ratio: Simple But Important

Overall, the process of calculating intrinsic value may involve as much art as science. At the same time, the familiar factors of earnings strength, financial strength, and low price stand out as key themes. A focus on these qualities— applied within the realm of one's expertise—is critical to the value investor's approach.

The P/E ratio is a popular metric that, despite its simplicity, can help greatly in the evaluation of investment opportunities. In its most basic form, the P/E ratio is calculated by dividing a company's share price by its EPS. Remember our XYZ Co. example earlier? We imagined that the firm was trading at $20 and had recently reported $3 in EPS. The company's P/E ratio would then equal 20 divided by 3, or about 6.7.

So what does that 6.7 mean? A useful way to think of the P/E ratio is to view it as a price tag on $1 of earnings. XYZ's P/E of 6.7 means that a buyer of the stock is paying $6.70 for every $1 the company earned in the most recent year. From this perspective, you can begin to harness the power of the P/E ratio as an evaluation metric.

By comparing XYZ's P/E ratio to the P/E ratio of the overall market, for example, you can get a quick idea of the company's relative price. A P/E of 15 for the S&P 500, for instance, means that the going rate on $1 of earnings from the average company in the index is $15. XYZ would seem inexpensive by comparison and might warrant further investigation. The current and historical P/E ratios for major market indexes can frequently be found on each index provider's website. Bloomberg.com, Yahoo! Finance, and other web portals also offer index-related performance.

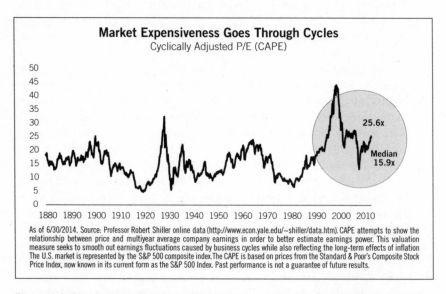

Market Expensiveness Goes Through Cycles
Cyclically Adjusted P/E (CAPE)

As of 6/30/2014. Source: Professor Robert Shiller online data (http://www.econ.yale.edu/~shiller/data.htm). CAPE attempts to show the relationship between price and multiyear average company earnings in order to better estimate earnings power. This valuation measure seeks to smooth out earnings fluctuations caused by business cycles while also reflecting the long-term effects of inflation The U.S. market is represented by the S&P 500 composite index. The CAPE is based on prices from the Standard & Poor's Composite Stock Price Index, now known in its current form as the S&P 500 Index. Past performance is not a guarantee of future results.

Figure 6-2 Data going back to the 1880s reveal a median cyclically adjusted price-to-earnings (CAPE) ratio of 15.9 times for the S&P 500. The higher CAPE in the later years shown suggests an expensive U.S. market that may not offer as many value opportunities as there were in the past.

P/E ratios are also useful for stock-by-stock comparisons. Imagine a firm called QRS, with a current price of $24 and EPS of $2. The P/E ratio for QRS would come in at 12; in other words, with QRS, investors must pay $12 for $1 of earnings. By comparison, XYZ's P/E of 6.7 strikes me as a better deal—probably.

Probably? With a P/E ratio of 6.7, how could QRS be anything but a better deal? The answer is that not all P/E ratios are created equal. Let's look at some examples of how P/E-to-P/E comparisons can drift into "apples and oranges" territory—and how you can make sure your analysis stays strictly apples to apples.

The main limitation on the power of the P/E is the fact that the E in the equation equals earnings per share from just one year. What if QRS, our company with a P/E of 12, was coming off an unusually difficult period that saw its EPS take a one-time dip? Perhaps in a normal year, QRS would have delivered

EPS of closer to $4. With that in mind, does XYZ still look as compelling in comparison? Maybe not. Remember our discussion of extrapolation, which is the bias we want to avoid of drawing large conclusions based on small amounts of information.

Sustainable EPS

A good way to account for the year-to-year fluctuations in EPS is to look at "sustainable EPS." A nonscientific but useful way to calculate sustainable EPS is to simply average a company's EPS figures over the last several years. I recommend reaching back 5 to 18 years of inflation-adjusted earnings in your calculation; usually, that's enough history to smooth out any unusual events and variations in the company's business cycle. Of course, any analysis based on estimates of sustainable earnings estimates must incorporate any doubts concerning the true sustainability of the company's earnings power in the future.

Another P/E option involves estimated EPS. Many publicly traded firms are monitored by Wall Street analysts, who frequently publish estimates of the company's EPS for both the current year and the year ahead. These earnings estimates often ignore unusual items, so P/E ratios with estimated EPS in the denominator can help keep company-to-company comparisons legitimate. However, earnings estimates must be used with extreme care, as reality frequently diverges from Wall Street's projections. Consensus earnings estimates are calculated and offered by many free and subscription online sources.

Before I dive into a company's numbers, I also like to have a general understanding of the firm's history, its current lines of business, and any significant recent events that may have affected its stock price. Thanks to the Internet, much of this information is just a few mouse clicks away.

One site that may prove useful to an investor who is aiming to evaluate an investment opportunity is Hoover's (owned by Dun & Bradstreet) at www.hoovers.com, which provides free and subscriber-only data tiers. Hoover's offers company profiles on hundreds of publicly traded firms. With content ranging from timelines of company history to consensus estimates of future earnings, the profiles are structured to help you quickly get up to speed on a given firm. Additional in-depth research is available with registration.

Another web-based resource that is worth adding to your toolbox is Value Line Investment Survey at www.valueline.com. This site's features include a comprehensive, company-by-company archive of recent news as well as interactive price charts, where investors can compare a stock's price performance with those of other equities and even market indexes. Subscribers gain access to Value Line's company reports, which contain buckets of important financial data in a compact, easy-to-read format.

Value Screens

Web technology lends itself nicely to screening, and many sites offer tools that can quickly sift through reams of data to spotlight stocks that meet user-specified qualifications. Kiplinger (www.kiplinger.com), for example, features an easy-to-use Stock Screener that filters thousands of stocks based on customizable criteria such as market capitalization, annual revenue, P/E ratios, and debt-to-equity levels. Lead generators like Stock Screener can be quite useful to value investors in the early stages of a hunt for investment ideas.

While Hoover's, Value Line, and Kiplinger tend to focus on U.S.-based firms, JPMorgan's adr.com (www.adr.com) offers similar content with an international emphasis. ADRs, or American Depository Receipts, are essentially securities created to allow larger non-U.S. firms to be traded in the United States. At adr.com, JPMorgan provides a wide range of firm-by-firm information for hundreds of non-U.S. companies with ADRs in circulation. I'll take a closer look at international equities in Chapters 7 and 8.

It's helpful to explore widely, of course, but always absorb critically. Keeping a keen eye on the company information offered helps you develop your own particular viewpoint. As I mentioned in the context of general financial news in Chapter 5, these sources of detailed company information are not necessarily free from bias—a fact that value investors need to keep in mind.

One more resource in the quest for company information is the website managed by the company itself. If a company is publicly listed, it probably has an online presence, which can contain insights into the firm's business activities, albeit in the company's own words. On pages dedicated to communicating with investors, usually labeled "investor relations," you'll typically find e-mail addresses and phone numbers of key staff members that you can contact with questions or information requests. Usually, the sites also offer direct links leading to the real goods: annual reports and SEC filings containing the company's financial statements. [SEC filings and forms can also be accessed and downloaded freely via EDGAR (the SEC's Electronic Data Gathering, Analysis, and Retrieval system) at www.sec.gov/edgar.shtml.]

The Big Three: Financial Statements

Once you've gained a broad familiarity with a company's history and its current operations, it's time to move on to the all-important triumvirate of investment information: the balance sheet, the income statement, and the statement of cash flows.

In this section, I'll examine the fundamental contents of the three major financial statements. This examination is by no means a complete review; thick textbooks and in-depth college courses are devoted to understanding and analyzing financial statements, and the following discussion is not intended to serve as a substitute. At the same time, a broad familiarity with the financial statements should help you begin to make sense of the vast amount of data they contain.

The Balance Sheet

Also called a statement of financial position, the balance sheet reports on the levels of three distinct items at a specific point in time:

- Assets, which are resources owned or controlled by the firm

- Liabilities, or external claims on assets

- Shareholders' equity, which is capital either contributed by owners or generated internally

The interrelationship of these three items is governed by a simple equation:

$$\text{Assets} = \text{liabilities} + \text{shareholders' equity}$$

Rearranging this equation leads to an alternative definition of shareholders' equity:

$$\text{Shareholders' equity} = \text{assets} - \text{liabilities}$$

Shareholders' Equity

Shareholders' equity—also known as book value—is one of the most important data items on the balance sheet. Investors can't take the number at face value, however. The listed value of assets like property, equipment, and inventory, for example, must be reviewed for appropriateness. If any of these values are overstated or understated, shareholders' equity must be reduced or increased accordingly.

Assets and Liabilities

Other important balance sheet categories include current assets—the portion of its assets that the company could convert to cash quickly—and both short-term and long-term debt. Many of these items can be used in combination to begin evaluating the health of the company.

Total debt, for instance, is calculated by adding short-term debt and long-term debt. Dividing the resulting value by shareholders' equity leads to the firm's debt-to-equity ratio, a central indicator of financial fitness.

Hidden liabilities can also impact a company's value, and are not always easy to see. These can include below market–rate loans, festering environmental problems, unsolved tax issues, and pending litigation.

Fishing for Hidden Assets

Flexibility in accounting rules means that firms have leeway in calculating some of the balance sheet items. Inventory is a good example, as generally accepted accounting principles (GAAP) allow for more than one approach to inventory valuation. If one widget manufacturer uses the LIFO (last-in, first-out) technique and a second uses an alternative called FIFO (first-in, first-out), the two companies could report dramatically different inventory values—*even if they have an identical number of widgets in their respective warehouses*. Value investors must be aware of such subtleties and make adjustments accordingly.

Hidden or undervalued assets can be one of the value investor's best friends. Corporate assets are sometimes not reflected on balance sheets. Real estate, for instance, frequently falls into the undervalued asset category, since land is carried at cost and buildings at *depreciated* cost. What if land prices go up? When that happens, the actual market value of real estate can be considerably higher than the value shown on the firm's books.

Additional balance sheet items of note include goodwill and other intangible assets. Goodwill is the difference between the amount paid for an acquired firm and the fair market value of its net assets at the time of acquisition. In essence, this difference represents a premium paid for the acquired firm's profitability. Other intangibles are identifiable nonmonetary resources such as licenses, leasehold rights, copyrights, patents, and brand names.

While goodwill and other intangible assets lack physical substance, they sometimes generate significant revenues and can represent an important portion of a firm's value. In addition, some investments that accounting rules consider expenses—such as those associated with research and development—might be more accurately classified as assets for analytical purposes. As a result, investors should keep an eye on each of these items and fine-tune their analysis as necessary.

The Income Statement

Whereas the balance sheet reflects company information *as of* a particular *date*, the income statement reports the firm's performance *over* a particular *period*, such as a quarter or a year.

Like the balance sheet, the income statement has three primary components:

- Revenues, also known as sales

- Expenses, the costs of producing goods and rendering services

- Net income, which equals revenues less expenses

These items are calculated based on the accrual accounting method, which holds that revenues should be recognized when a firm delivers goods, rather than when it collects cash for those goods. Similarly, expenses should be recorded as the firm incurs costs, not necessarily when it makes payment for the goods and services that it uses. By matching a period's proper revenues with its related expenses, the income statement measures the period's appropriate net income.

Typical expenses include cost of goods sold, depreciation, interest, and taxes. These cost-of-doing-business indicators are useful in comparing a company with its competition. For example, if a company is paying taxes at a rate that is considerably lower than the corporate tax rate, an investor needs to understand why. The answer may reveal that the company will face a tax-rate boost in the future, which could negatively affect earnings over the long term.

Net income is synonymous with earnings, the data item that, on a per share basis, forms the denominator of the P/E ratio. When working with this figure, investors must watch out for "managed" earnings. Some companies may try to give earnings a one-time boost through maneuvers such as property sales or the disposal of investments in subsidiaries. Profits from such activity should be excluded from the calculation of true earnings for at least one year.

Because net income tends to fluctuate from year to year, it's also important to avoid placing too much emphasis on a company's earnings during any one period. As I mentioned earlier, calculating "sustainable" or "normalized" earnings can shed light on a company's true earnings power by smoothing out income swings. Again, this calculation involves averaging net income numbers over the last several years.

The Statement of Cash Flows

The use of accrual accounting in the income statement means that it doesn't tell investors about a crucial detail: how much cold, hard cash came into and flowed out of the company during the period under review. This information is found in the statement of cash flows, where the company classifies all of its cash receipts and payments into one of three categories:

- Operating cash flows
- Investing cash flows
- Financing cash flows

Operating cash flows involve cash generated or used by the firm in the course of its production and sales of goods and services. Funds generated internally can be used to pay dividends, repay loans, replace existing capacity, or invest for future growth. For most firms, positive operating cash flows are essential for long-term survival, although negative cash flows from operations are expected in some circumstances, such as rapid expansion.

Investing cash flows involve purchases of property and equipment, the creation of subsidiaries or business segments, and investments in other firms. These purchases allow a company to maintain its current operating capacity and to create new capacity for growth. Cash flows from investing also include receipts from the disposal of business segments or assets.

Financing cash flows relate to the debt and equity that the firm uses to raise capital. The issuance or retirement of debt, along with outflows for interest payments, are reported in this section. Similarly, cash flows from financing include the issuance or repurchase of shares of stock and dividend payments to shareholders.

Broadly speaking, the statement of cash flows is designed to shed light on a company's ability to sustain and increase its cash generated from current operations. When professionals read these documents, the items they focus on include the strength of cash generation from operations and the cash consequences of investing and financing decisions. In general, a strong, positive cash flow usually bodes well for a company's long-term health. Temporarily losing money—in an accounting sense, at least—is acceptable. Even so, beware of chronic negative cash flow.

The information provided in the financial statements is typically accompanied by footnotes and other disclosures. These sections contain data on subjects such as off-balance-sheet obligations, business segments, and the company's retirement plans. A careful review of all supplementary materials is critical to an evaluation of the firm.

Even after reading every inch of fine print, the investor must realize that the financial statements can't provide a complete picture of 100 percent of a company's situation. Unfortunately, there is no way for the average investor to learn a corporation's innermost secrets, or to look into a crystal ball and see the company's future. Despite their limitations, however, the financial statements are a key resource in the quest for information, and their contents help answer many of the questions that a value investor should ask.

Reliability of Company Data

High-profile accounting scandals over the years have left many investors wondering whether company financial data and corporate governance in general can be trusted at all. In my opinion, these concerns are overstated, but constant vigilance and constructive skepticism can't hurt. While the wounds from powerfully destructive scandals like Enron (2001), WorldCom (2002), and AIG (2004) have somewhat healed, investors are right to wonder whether such things could happen again on such a grand scale.

The use of "creative accounting" is always a possibility, but I believe that the financial statements for the vast majority of publicly traded companies reflect integrity and accuracy. One reason is that company boards are now held more accountable on a fiduciary level—the product of such laws as the Companies Act of 2006 in the United Kingdom, for instance. However, one way to protect yourself is to pay close attention to the auditors' letter, found at the end of audited financial statements. Such letters can be "clean," that is, presented without qualification. If, however, the letters are "subject to" certain conditions, the investor should give the preceding data special scrutiny.

Simply put, there is always company-specific risk associated with investing in stocks. The old adage about not "putting all your eggs in one basket" remains sound advice to reduce this risk. Based on my experience, I believe that a focus on creating portfolios comprising a number of securities that offer a reasonable margin of safety mitigates some of this risk and creates a good opportunity for favorable performance results over the long term.

One more piece of insight: take a look at a company's proxy statement disclosures for clues regarding management's propensity for self-indulgence. In these pages, investors can examine executive compensation, read up on insider borrowings and ownership, and look for any other sweetheart transactions between management and the company it serves.

As harmful as the likes of Enron and WorldCom were to investor trust, these watershed scandals actually ushered in stricter accounting standards in the United States in the form of the Sarbanes-Oxley Act of 2002. Some people argue, interestingly enough, that by holding U.S. companies and their auditors more accountable to these new standards, this act has put American companies at a competitive disadvantage relative to international businesses that are not held to the same code. This is still a hotly debated topic, and I address it as part of a look at accounting standards in the global investing arena in the coming chapters.

CHAPTER 7

WHY GO OVERSEAS?

If you seek peace, if you seek prosperity for the Soviet Union and Eastern Europe, if you seek liberalization, come here to this gate. Mr. Gorbachev, open this gate. Mr. Gorbachev, tear down this wall!

—U.S. President Ronald Reagan, in a speech at the former Berlin Wall, June 12, 1987

Regardless of their feelings toward the 40th president—whether based on history's account or on personal memories from the Reagan years—most people agree that he was a speechmaker for the ages. His Berlin Wall oration is still ranked by *Time* as among history's 10 most impactful.

I'll spare you the long political backstory, but as far back as I can remember, I believed that the Berlin Wall represented more than a lethally enforced physical barrier between ideologies and their citizenry; it was a killer of ideas and opportunities on both sides of the fence. While it was primarily ceremonial, to me, Reagan's challenge to the Soviet premier marked the beginning of a major shift in how average investors would begin to view the world.

About three years later, the official Berlin Wall razing was a touchstone for Reagan's successor, George H. W. Bush, in his 1990 address to a joint session of Congress: "A new partnership of nations has begun, and we stand today at a unique and extraordinary moment. [A] new world order can emerge: an era in which the nations of the world, east and west, north and south, can prosper and live in harmony."

As if on cue, East and West Germany were soon unified into a single nation for the first time since World War II, forging what is today's economic powerhouse on the continent. Soon after, 12 individual republics were formed from the dismantled Soviet Union. New governments, infrastructure, and enterprises were sprouting up all over, fostering new markets, businesses, companies, and, of course, stocks. Although I had already been investing overseas for decades, by 1990 it was time to get even more serious about it; in that year, my firm introduced our flagship international (non-U.S.) focused value investment strategy, something that was very new to the industry and as yet untested. It's still going strong today.

Home Country Bias

We've all heard the term "home field advantage." In the sports world, it's supposed to be a big plus. In the investment world, a similar attitude can actually work against you.

Investing abroad is much more acceptable now, but it isn't as prevalent or as well understood as one might think. I can appreciate that investors, regardless of where they live, may take an overly provincial approach to where they put their money. It's natural. Usually, we prefer to stay close to home, as human nature drives us to stay within known boundaries. In investing, this tendency is known as *home country bias*. It basically is a reluctance to trust markets or companies located in countries with which we are not completely familiar. It creates a narrow focus on domestic markets and businesses that are based there. The result is missed opportunities—clearly not an advantage when it comes to long-term investing.

Although there have been some improvements in the past 10 years, home country bias is still particularly strong among Americans, and it shows up among individual and institutional investors alike. For example, domestic stocks and bonds make up an average of 68 percent of all U.S. pension plans. Compare this to Australia, where only 38 percent of that country's pension assets are those of home-grown companies. Similarly, 47 percent of the assets of Canadian plans and 52 percent of those of Japanese plans are composed of domestic stocks and bonds, according to Callan Associates Inc.[1] When you consider that the Australian, Canadian, and Japanese markets represent such a small percentage of the global stock arena, having large weightings in them amplifies the potential for missed opportunities elsewhere.

The low percentage for U.S. investors seems a little odd, considering that we're so much more globally interlaced these days. But, no matter where they reside, investors may simply not know enough about opportunities beyond their borders to want or be able to invest with any confidence. Still, if they knew where to start—at the company level rather than the country level—perhaps their comfort level would improve.

Value Knows No Boundaries

In 1974, when I started my firm, my first client was a Canadian resident who wanted a portfolio of companies from all over the world, including the United States. I obliged him, and over a period of time identified some excellent overseas companies that met my value criteria and complemented the portfolio. It wasn't long before it became clear that not only could I find more opportunities when I looked around the world, but frequently those companies were better performers than those in the United States.

This was another milestone in my application of the Graham-and-Dodd principles. That is, besides applying the basic value fundamentals to stock selection, I was now using my knowledge and experience to search for value all over the world, especially in corners where even my value investor peers weren't looking. The best part is that it isn't necessary to know everything about every company and every country in which they are based. This is why screening is important. You just have to know *enough* to find the opportunities, evaluate them, and then move in with the same value filter you would apply to a company in your backyard.

Why Leave Home?

There are two overriding reasons for holding a significant level of overseas stocks in a diversified portfolio. First, no matter what country you live in, most of the world's businesses are located outside your home market. This is just basic math. Second, investing around the world can deliver diversification benefits, such as a reduction in overall portfolio risk, at least as measured by fluctuation in short-term returns.

Let's take a closer look at the opportunities and the diversification benefits of international investing.

Vast Universe

World markets have expanded over the last few decades, more so overseas than in North America. This is due to a combination of stock price movements and the substantial amount of new capital being raised by existing and new companies. At the same time, much of the world's population lives in countries that have recently moved toward free-market economies and that have an expanding middle class. Among these are Brazil, Chile, China, the Czech Republic, Hungary, India, Indonesia, Mexico, Poland, the Philippines, Russia, and Turkey.

Just consider how large the non-U.S. market presence has grown in the last few decades. Non-U.S. markets represent about half of the global total. This compares to only 34 percent in 1970.[2] It also represents about $45 trillion in stocks of companies based outside the United States. Those who claim that investing outside the United States is not worthwhile are basically claiming that none of that $45 trillion in stocks represents a good investment opportunity. I find that difficult to believe.

Fewer Fishermen

Although they are quite accessible, many overseas stocks remain less visible. If U.S. investors, for example, are confined to North American markets, right off the bat, they limit themselves to about half the world's opportunities. Researching only the U.S. and Canadian markets, for example, may net 10,000 possible stocks for consideration. In contrast, if you look globally, you can be toe-to-toe with as many as 35,000 stocks, a much greater universe to explore. Again, it really just comes down to the numbers.

Whether you are investing in a developed country like the United States, developed non-U.S. markets, or emerging markets, it's easier to find bargains when there are fewer bargain hunters around. Perhaps because they're underanalyzed overseas, value stocks are also under *chased*. That is, the majority of U.S. investors who look overseas still favor doing so using growth investing strategies.

A Tale of Two Companies

Sometimes a great company comes in a package that you don't recognize. Yet, it can be just as attractive as one that you do know. Everyone knows wireless services provider AT&T, Inc. In 2014, AT&T had about 116 million wireless subscribers in regions all over the world, with about a 30 percent share of the U.S. market. I think anyone would consider this to be substantial market penetration.

There is another wireless company whose subscriber base is just a few million shy of AT&T's, and it also has about a 30 percent market share that is steadily climbing. But it's not Verizon Wireless. The company is Telefonica Brasil SA, a São Paulo–based firm that is the largest wireless operator in that country. Telefonica Brasil is also the incumbent (dominant) fixed-line and broadband operator serving São Paulo, Brazil's most populous city.

With AT&T having more than three times the market capitalization of Telefonica Brasil, the Brazilian company may appear smaller, but the prospects for growth for a company serving the fifth most populous country in the world make it much bigger in scope—especially for the long term. This is just a glimpse of the tremendous and often overlooked investment opportunities that are available when you cast your net overseas—and not only in developed markets, but also in emerging countries. The world's emerging markets—countries such as South Korea, Brazil, Argentina, Turkey, China, Russia, and India—offer many compelling opportunities.

Lower Risk

Putting all your money into the stocks of one country is a limiting strategy. Sensible investors diversify, and cross-border investing is an important part of that approach. Ironically, some investors equate the phrase "foreign stock" with risk. The exact opposite is true. Often, the inverse, or noncorrelating, relationship between stock markets can *reduce* risk (again, as defined by volatility) in a diversified portfolio. I go further into risk in the value investing world in Chapter 17.

You should always expect that there typically will be regions where stocks outperform those in your home market over any specified time period. Even if your home market has been at the top of the rankings for a while, you're still likely to find opportunities elsewhere, too. In fact, an extended period at the top is usually followed by a significant decline. When you see one market rise, it can soon retreat and another rise, and so on. I talk more about correlation in the next chapter—and it's actually not always considered good.

Then there is the value card. Risk (the potential for losing money when investing) can be reduced through long-term investments in companies whose stock is undervalued in relation to the real value of the business. The world's various stock markets offer tremendous opportunities to find just such businesses. Remember, value investing believes that no single factor tends to lower one's risk more than buying a company at a favorable price.

Wider Opportunity Set

When you go global, you can also look beyond larger-cap companies. Attractive bargains and compelling opportunities can be found within the small- and mid-cap segments of international markets. Smaller caps may offer enhanced return and diversification benefits, particularly for U.S. investors.

Smaller-cap stocks, because they tend to attract scant analyst coverage, can be ideal targets for diligent value investors. Additionally, the dearth of attention devoted to smaller companies around the world can create opportunities for value investors to identify and capitalize on pricing inefficiencies (see Figure 7-1).

Keep in mind that investing in smaller caps often includes certain risks that may not be as prevalent among larger caps. Unique risk factors can influence stock prices in the short term, but I think they're largely irrelevant for long-term investors. Over time, I believe investors in markets worldwide eventually come to recognize an undervalued business—regardless of the firm's size or where its headquarters are.

From a historical perspective, value investors who broadened their investment horizons to include stocks in various countries may have been able to take advantage of (or avoid) a number of irrational price anomalies in markets around the world. For example, valuations in Japan in the early 1990s—P/E ratios of 40 to 50 and earnings yields of barely 1 percent—made no sense. For that matter, Japanese stocks trading at 3 times earnings in 1963 made no sense either. Similarly, the U.S. market in 1981 offered a number of attractively priced stocks, while a great number of stocks were extremely overvalued

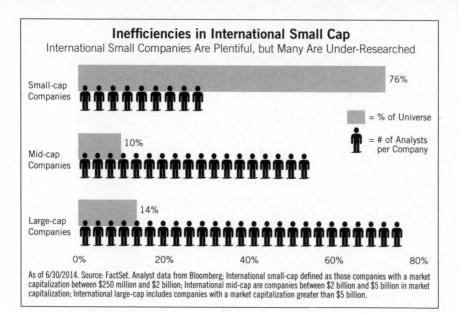

Inefficiencies in International Small Cap

International Small Companies Are Plentiful, but Many Are Under-Researched

Small-cap Companies — 76%

= % of Universe

= # of Analysts per Company

Mid-cap Companies — 10%

Large-cap Companies — 14%

0%   20%   40%   60%   80%

As of 6/30/2014. Source: FactSet. Analyst data from Bloomberg; International small-cap defined as those companies with a market capitalization between $250 million and $2 billion; International mid-cap are companies between $2 billion and $5 billion in market capitalization; International large-cap includes companies with a market capitalization greater than $5 billion.

Figure 7-1 The smaller the number of analysts watching a stock, the more opportunity there is for those who do. Small-cap stocks are the least followed stocks, yet they represent the largest percentage of companies in the investable universe. This creates a wider opportunity set for patient value investors.

by early 2000. Following the financial crisis of 2008–2009, U.S. stocks offered some bargains, but there were fewer pickings beginning in 2012, and this remained the case as this book went to press.

Why do markets swing to such extremes? Jeremy Grantham, a renowned investor, shared his thoughts: "The market[s are] gloriously inefficient. . . . The manifestations of the inefficiency are that they horribly emphasize comfort and discomfort. . . . They extrapolate today's conditions forever so if inflation is low, they assume inflation will be low forever. . . . The real world is mean reverting."[3] Value investors who recognize market swings as opportunities often can uncover attractive investments in markets around the world.

Target Companies, Not Countries

As a proponent of a bottom-up investment style, my firm has no use for the strategy that determines stock purchases based on country targets. Bottom-up investors choose the stock first. Where the company happens to be domiciled plays a role in the decision-making process only to the extent that prudent managers should be cautious about becoming overly concentrated in the securities of any single country and the extent to which uncertainties demand a higher margin of safety.

Rather than using top-down strategies, we are more interested in *hunting* down individual companies—those with promising fundamentals and attractive prices. Our assumption is that individual companies can be welcome additions to the portfolio—regardless of where the business is based.

The Emerging Markets "Bump"

The advantages of applying a global value approach where information is scarce or seldom analyzed couldn't be more prevalent than in emerging markets. To be honest, I felt this way long before it became popular.

Before reviewing the opportunities there, let's look at what makes up this important segment of the world's markets.

Not all emerging markets offer securities that are worth researching, and many don't even have a stock market at all. I also take issue with labeling a market *emerging* just because it's less developed. Many of these emerging markets can be better described as *submerging*, at least from time to time. The emerging markets that I consider are those with sufficient infrastructure (both for the economy and for the stock market), reasonably substantial companies, and potential for economic growth in the longer term.

According to the World Bank, markets considered to be "emerging" are those in nations with per capita gross national income (GNI) of no more than $9,205. Some countries with larger economies may still be considered emerging if their capital markets are small. Of nearly 200 sovereign nations around the globe, the average per capita GNI of all those classified as emerging is a little over $1,000. By comparison, per capita GNI in the United States is more than $51,000.

From a benchmarking perspective, the Morgan Stanley Capital International (MSCI) Emerging Markets Index stands out among the leaders. It comprises more than 800 securities in 23 emerging countries' indexes as of 2014. Overall, MSCI is a leading provider of global indexes. The following countries are included in the EM Index: Brazil, Chile, China, Colombia, the Czech Republic, Egypt, Greece, Hungary, India, Indonesia, South Korea, Malaysia, Mexico, Peru, the Philippines, Poland, Qatar, Russia, South Africa, Taiwan, Thailand, Turkey, and the United Arab Emirates. Although it doesn't happen often, the list can change. Greece, for example, was for many years considered developed, but the heavy toll from its sovereign debt crisis in recent years challenged its economic health relative to that of other developed nations. Consequently, MSCI reclassified it as an emerging market in 2013.

Among the arguments in favor of investing in emerging market stocks are:

1. *Strength.* Emerging markets are not necessarily third world countries; they include some very substantial economies, in terms of either population (Brazil) or GNI (South Korea). The nearly 10 billion people living in emerging nations account for more than 85 percent of the world's population.[4] One of the largest and best-performing economies is China, which is predicted to migrate into the developed market category before long.

2. *Undercapitalized.* Output from emerging economies represents roughly 30 percent of global GDP, yet emerging markets are capitalized at just 11 percent of the aggregate value of the world's equity markets.[5] These data suggest that there is considerable room for share-price appreciation and broadening of the equity markets, even without above-average economic growth.

3. *Economic growth.* Economic growth in emerging markets has exceeded that in developed countries by more than 3 percent and is projected to continue that pace through 2018.[6]

4. *Flexibility.* Emerging markets can quickly adjust to periods of expansion and contraction. This is a direct result of their minimal wage and employment restrictions. If the economy of an emerging country is experiencing a slowdown, companies are better able to adapt by adjusting production capacity than are companies in large industrialized countries, which often have strict minimum wage legislation and employment protection laws.

5. *Inherent inefficiencies.* Since emerging markets are generally the least researched segment of the equity universe, they can be a great source for undiscovered value.

These conventional arguments, combined with the lack of competition from other well-informed, disciplined value investors, make a compelling case for investing in emerging markets. But there's one more aspect of it that to me is very appealing, but to others may be somewhat controversial: volatility.

Emerging markets can swing from euphoria to despondency in relatively short periods of time. As a result, their collective performance (as measured by the MSCI EM Index) has been as spectacular as 78.5 percent (2009) or as awful as −53.3 percent (2008). Over longer periods, their gains have been substantial: the average net annual increase for the 12-year period ending in 2013 was 11.5 percent, which to me just reinforces the potential opportunity.

The end result is that there are periods when most investors either will not go near emerging markets or will drop them at the first sign of trouble. Meanwhile, value investors who pursue bargains during the perceived bad times may be ridiculed by their peers (or, in my case, by their clients). But this is exactly when the patience and discipline of the true value investor may pay off spectacularly.

This actually just happened in early 2014. After an astounding run-up that began in 2008, the once-darling emerging markets arena was hit hard by a triad of concurrent setbacks that sent investors running for cover practically overnight. China showed signs of economic sputtering and revealed several banking missteps. Meanwhile, Argentina faced its steepest currency devaluation in more than a decade. Making matters worse, Russia's annexation of Crimea fanned political tensions and concerns over natural gas and oil supplies throughout eastern Europe. My heart goes out to the citizens who are directly affected by their country's woes. At the same time, emerging markets are not a homogeneous group. As one struggles, so do all, goes the paradigm. This is not the case. And when the group is on its back, that's when we go to work to find the gems in the crowd. As I write this, emerging markets on the whole have yet to recover, and I think it may take time to regain investors' trust in them. But from a value investing point of view, we took the flight in stride. They will return. They always do.

Access Improvements

Investing overseas has never been easier to do. Not too long ago, however, a U.S. investor couldn't just pick up the phone, purchase stock that trades exclusively on the Tokyo exchange, and call it a day. There were currency hurdles to contend with and settlement time to factor into the trade, among other things. Technically, there still are.

But as more investors turned to international sources for growth potential, the industry has stepped up to make international investing more accessible and relatively hassle free. It's more convenient than ever for individual and institutional investors alike. Among the big contributors to improvements are:

- *Depository Receipts.* These securities are designed to make investing beyond your home country a lot easier. There are two types:

  - *Global Depository Receipts (GDRs).* GDRs are typically designed for investors outside the United States who seek to purchase shares outside their home country.

  - *American Depository Receipts (ADRs).* ADRs are designed for U.S.-based investors who want to purchase shares of non-U.S. companies.

- *Prepackaged investments.* These are mostly open- and closed-end mutual funds focused on global, international, and emerging markets strategies, among others. They're designed as a one-stop alternative for investors who would rather leave the work to someone else.

- *Improved liquidity.* With more market participants come more buyers and sellers to execute trades more handily.

- *Settlement efficiencies.* ADRs and the advent of electronic trading have especially shortened the time it takes to settle a trade. In some cases, same-day processing is possible, compared to months in the not too distant past.

- *Access to information.* In addition to its trade processing benefits, the Internet age has also offered effective channels of communication for an ever-wider swath of company types and locales. Information is good for investors, but again, only when they know how to use it.

- *Accounting standards.* International Financial Reporting Standards were strengthened in 2001 to help create a common global financial language for businesses across Europe and other stretches of the globe outside the United States, which still relies on generally accepted accounting principles (GAAP), although changes to this are underway.[7]

- *Trade agreements.* The Office of the U.S. Trade Representative, part of the federal executive branch, is responsible for investment treaties and frameworks that provide the principles for agreements between the United States and foreign parties. The department's bilateral investment treaties establish helpful procedures for fair treatment, payment, transparency, and access relative to the non-U.S. controlling parties of investor holdings. The World Trade Organization (WTO), formed in 1995, is also an important cog in the international commerce wheel. Agriculture, intellectual property, tariffs, labor standards, and other global matters of interest are areas that it oversees in the interests of promoting free trade—a vital component of an efficient global investing landscape.

Why Corner Yourself?

Walls tumble, nations are born, and economies and private enterprises blossom. The world has gotten a lot smaller in the last 40 years, while investment opportunities have grown. Today, there is a tremendous universe of companies that may fly undetected under the radar of investors and the market.

Rationality will never fully determine market values—in *any* market. The gamut of human emotions—from greed and optimism to fear and pessimism—can alter perceived or short-term values and send prices spinning up or down, always creating opportunities for the perceptive investor with a global scope.

As you have gathered by now, my conviction concerning the need and the benefits of standing your investing ground around the world, especially in emerging markets, can't be overstated. In Chapter 8, I'll expand on a few topics I just highlighted and discuss additional considerations for value investors in overseas (non-U.S.) markets.

CHAPTER 8

SEARCHING FOR VALUE IN A VOLATILE AND DYNAMIC GLOBAL ARENA

Information inefficiencies are one way for global value investors to find opportunities. But the bigger pool is fed by the pricing inefficiencies created from investors' short-term orientation and over-reaction to widely disseminated, very publicly available information.

—Charles Brandes, in an interview with *Outlook Business India,* June 2014

In the fall of 1990, I spoke to a national gathering of high-net-worth financial advisors on my usual topic, the merits of long-term value investing. A nagging bear market was in full swing, so I had more than enough real-world value company examples to share with the crowd. My firm had just opened our international strategy as well, so I was particularly excited to show how we could bring utility to their clients' portfolios. Things were humming along until we wound down to the Q&A segment, which quickly turned the moment into what my grandchildren would call, "a total buzz kill."

The first question fired at me was no softball, and almost hostile: "Are you telling us, as armies of the world converge on the oil fields of the Middle East—the most volatile region of the planet—for what could turn into World War III, that *now* is a good time to be buying stocks?"

"Absolutely, if they're the right stocks," I replied, emphasizing that my view is rooted in fundamental valuations, not in what the market's reaction to a Persian Gulf conflict might be. I empathized with their concern over the global situation, which was getting tenser by the day. Iraq had invaded neighboring Kuwait just a few weeks earlier, and, in response, a U.S.-led coalition of forces was rushing everything it had to the region to take it back, an action known as Operation Desert Shield. It was the most politically charged five months that the world had experienced in a very long time. It was the precursor to the 1991 Iraq conflict, a relatively quick endeavor compared to the subsequent U.S. military involvement, yet one that captured our constant attention as war suddenly, and irreversibly, went "real time" via the ceaseless coverage by the likes of CNN and other 24/7 cable news outlets.

Nevertheless, hostilities wouldn't begin for several months, and the advisor's question still hung there in the ballroom. At the risk of appearing tone deaf, I continued. "This is a good time to buy if you look at how cheap the stock market is today compared to historical prices. For many reasons, valuations of good companies are very attractive practically everywhere in the world right now. I'm thinking long term for these companies based on what I *can* see in front of me, not on what I *can't* see, and certainly not on speculation concerning what *could* happen because of imminent war with Iraq and its allies."

I don't think I convinced them totally, but such is the life of a value investor. We often take an unpopular or contrarian view. We don't ignore the macroeconomic environment, but neither do we let it help us pick stocks. At the very least, the attendees and I agreed to disagree, and the room's temperature grew a lot more comfortable for me.

Value First, Global Second

The fact that company fundamentals can still reveal opportunities amidst uncertain economic, political, and social change is one reason that I've always been drawn to markets outside the United States. International investing can be intellectually challenging on many levels. My first non-U.S. investment came early in my career: in 1974, right after I started my firm. There was no grand calling or sudden awareness that pushed me toward non-U.S. stocks. From the start, global investing just seemed like a natural extension of a purpose-built value discipline. In fact, I didn't even consider it global investing—it was *value* investing. After all, when you're looking at a business from the ground up, the soil it sits on really doesn't matter most of the time.

By 1977, my firm held positions in Bayer, the German chemical maker; Royal Nedlloyd, a shipping firm based in Holland; Jardine Matheson, one of Hong Kong's successful international trading houses; and Nestlé, the Swiss food company, which at the time was just a fraction of the giant it is today. These were solid companies then, and some of them still are, but few U.S. investors held them, or even knew that they could.

In 1982, however, my team turned up the dial on our overseas exposure to one of the outlier categories of international equities, emerging markets, starting with Mexico's Telmex, which I mentioned in Chapter 1. This time, I am bringing up Telmex to make a different point about information inefficiency.

Information Underload

One of the challenges of being an early adopter is that you're also the first to beat the path. It was the same with global investing back then. As Mexico struggled with its debt crisis that year, we pursued a hunch that state-owned companies there might be feeling some undeserved downward price pressure.

Unlike the plethora of information that is available on U.S. stocks, the research infrastructure for non-U.S. equities was really just being built at that time. In many cases, one of which was Telmex, there was little to go on other than the annual S&P Stock Guide and about two years' worth of then-named Telefono de Mexico's balance sheets and income statements. You could consider the lack of information a challenge that we didn't even know we had. By today's standards, our data was pretty near to piloting a plane while wearing an eye patch.

Today, we could gather terabytes of information from Telmex and other sources by clicking a mouse to download annual reports and other public documents, not to mention a personal visit by our global research team. But the full weight of our decision to invest still rests in the metrics behind the fundamentals of *precio, ingresos, y flujo de caja.*[1]

Some 40 years later, my team leaves its footprints overseas every week. It's not just that we get around. Rather, we get inside. We open the books, we kick the tires, and we meet with management—whatever it takes to understand the companies in which we invest beyond our borders.

Macro Appeal

The bigger picture has its place in value investing, but it's not a dominant factor. It's not realistic or prudent to dismiss the conditions that create the climates in which we invest. If you do, you simply can't function as an effective investor of any kind in the real world.

Global insights are part of our research process, and they provide context and awareness of the environments within which companies function and produce wealth. Why? Because the economic forces of inflation and growth, high-impact regulations, international banking agreements, government intervention, corruption, and the dynamics of the markets can all affect the value of the companies that you own or hope to buy. Notice that I said they can affect the *companies*, not the *stocks*—a big difference in the mindset of the value investor. Both are part of the equation, but the company takes priority if you're taking a long-term stance.

How we view the world, countries, industries, and sectors around the globe is usually a by-product of where we find companies. Even when we interpret global or macro activity, we do so from a bottom-up perspective. So, rather than trying to make economic forecasts, we ask questions like: How would rapid inflation and the weakness of the currency in this country affect the salability of that company's product, and hence the company? What would a slowdown in GDP do to this company's earnings? Might it affect its operations or impair its ability to compete? All these questions relate to how the macro factor affects the company, and all of them are geared to help us better understand whether its stock price is becoming unmoored from its intrinsic value.

Going Our Own Way

Graham-and-Dodd value investing can often be a lonely discipline, especially on the global level, where investors tend to herd to the "hot dot" countries or regions. Independence is part of the value investor's DNA. In fact, the *only* way that long-term active value investing can outperform is by separating from the pack. Value investors operate differently; the truly focused ones are distinct from their peers, and their portfolios are often clearly miles away from their benchmark or index. Indexes are effective standardized gauges for performance comparisons, but other than that, value investors have little use for them.

I've never built a portfolio or a strategy to mirror an index. I wouldn't turn to the MSCI All Country World Index (ACWI) and decide to allocate 12 percent of a global portfolio to emerging markets companies just because the benchmark does. We may, however, find an assortment of attractively valued emerging markets value companies that could, when you add them up, represent 12 percent of a portfolio. Even then, they probably would not be the same exact companies across the board. Here, too, the thought process and approach of the value investor and the overall market are completely different, for the most part.

We go where the value is, and this usually takes us to places where most investors won't venture, at least for the moment. If everything works the way it should, the party eventually catches up with us because capital will always flow to where the opportunities exist.

United States Versus Europe

One example of the nonsynchronous nature of global markets was felt well into 2014, as U.S. equities soared to new highs and we found fewer value opportunities in that market. At one point, our global strategies managers generally held half the weighting in U.S. stocks of the MSCI World Index, their primary benchmark. At the same time, just the opposite was happening in Europe, which made up some 41 percent of our global strategies portfolios, versus 28 percent for the benchmark. In this case, a diverse range of select bargains revealed themselves there, while investors were generally training their sights on the United States for the upward ride.

As we've seen in past hot market cycles, it's hard for the crowd to leave when the party really gets going. Plus, Europe's prolonged, tepid economic climate beginning in late 2010 looked much too dire on the surface to be much of an alternative. But underneath the doom and gloom there lay solid companies such as Norwegian commercial bank DNB ASA, that country's largest financial institution. In 2011, DNB offered a compelling valuation when in 2011 its shares sold off during a flare-up of the euro zone and the pervasive sovereign financial crisis. At the time, DNB was one of the few global banks that value investors believed had possessed all of the following high-quality characteristics: a dominant domestic franchise in a financially strong sovereign nation, solid asset quality, strong capitalization, and a high dividend yield. Given its low cross-border exposure, some investors believed that DNB would be relatively well positioned if there happened to be a euro breakup. Meanwhile, the market seemed to be more concerned about regulatory uncertainty in Norway and DNB's shipping-loan book (the bank is highly exposed to shipping and oil interests). Gradually, these fears receded.

Distinguishing Among Emerging Markets

A value investor's willingness to go against the grain is always being tested. This was certainly the case when emerging markets got a little uncertain starting in late 2013. After an incredible run that began in 2008, emerging markets swiftly felt the brunt of sudden investor concerns about a slowdown in China, currency struggles in Argentina and Brazil, and political turmoil throughout Turkey, among other developments.

Investors dropped out, and the MSCI Emerging Markets Index sank dramatically, but we took a different tack. From our vantage point, emerging markets are not a homogeneous group. Yes, there is a tendency for crises to spread from one emerging markets country to another relatively easily. But when the contagion spreads, it just demonstrates to us the importance of discriminating among emerging markets countries and, more important, emerging markets companies.

Most investors believed that the emerging markets crisis began in China, whose astounding 30-year economic expansion was indeed a unique success story. In reality, however, despite its size and influence, China in and of itself does not represent emerging markets as a whole. Much of the fear over China was an overblown reaction to such events as a default on a large trust product and concerns about a potential hard landing if economic growth were to slow meaningfully. Although it was an important check mark in the macro column, this was not the country's first default. Also, its so-called slowdown equated to about a 4 percent annual gross domestic product—still twice the growth rate of most *developed* countries at that time.[2]

Yet, especially in China, you have to be selective. There are value opportunities and some traps, so it really depends on where you look. For years, opportunities have been created from the country's growing urbanization, expanding middle class, productivity improvements, and, most important, attractive valuations in select industries—particularly those that reach an ever-growing number of domestic consumers. Since 1980, China's economic engine has managed to lift almost half its population of 1.3 billion above the poverty line, creating generations of demand for houses, cars, clothes, higher-quality food and beverages, natural resources, and so forth.

People's Food Holdings Limited, a national distributor of meat and meat products founded in 1994, is one example. Value investors saw its competitive position as a low-cost producer with solid growth opportunities for pork in a country that consumes more of it than any other country. It also showed a consistently strong balance sheet and had historically generated robust returns on capital and free cash flow.

The market seemed to be attributing very little value to all the positive aspects of the company, and was instead pricing People's as an undifferentiated, cyclical, and commodity-like hog processor. Moreover, investors were generally skeptical of small-cap Chinese companies following a spate of negative press.

The company went on to generate meaningful free cash flow, and expanded its differentiated consumer packaged goods segment into chicken and beef sausages. It also initiated a major retooling to emphasize food safety, which was beneficial given a number of food safety scandals in China.

Here, There, or Everywhere?

By now you may have noticed a pattern: when some global markets are up, others are challenged, and still others are somewhere in between. Given that there are so many unique markets in today's global mix of investing opportunities, it's rare when they go in the same direction at the same time. The few times this happens, the temporary direction is usually acutely downward, such as during the Great Depression of 1929–1933 and the financial crisis of 2008–2009.

Even the most basic comparison of U.S. to non-U.S. developed markets shows a clear cyclical pattern over more than 40 years (see Figure 8-1).

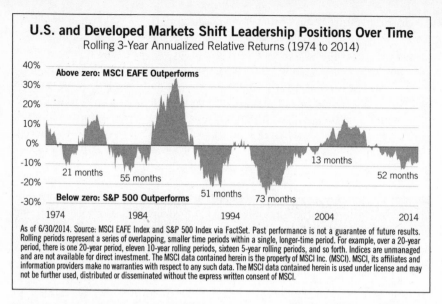

U.S. and Developed Markets Shift Leadership Positions Over Time
Rolling 3-Year Annualized Relative Returns (1974 to 2014)

Above zero: MSCI EAFE Outperforms

Below zero: S&P 500 Outperforms

21 months 55 months 51 months 73 months 13 months 52 months

1974   1984   1994   2004   2014

As of 6/30/2014. Source: MSCI EAFE Index and S&P 500 Index via FactSet. Past performance is not a guarantee of future results. Rolling periods represent a series of overlapping, smaller time periods within a single, longer-time period. For example, over a 20-year period, there is one 20-year period, eleven 10-year rolling periods, sixteen 5-year rolling periods, and so forth. Indices are unmanaged and are not available for direct investment. The MSCI data contained herein is the property of MSCI Inc. (MSCI). MSCI, its affiliates and information providers make no warranties with respect to any such data. The MSCI data contained herein is used under license and may not be further used, distributed or disseminated without the express written consent of MSCI.

Figure 8-1 This chart shows when and for how long U.S. and other developed markets have changed leadership positions over time. The history of the two markets' unsynchronized performance is a telltale sign of the importance of pursuing a little of both, especially for value investors.

Low to No Correlation

A more granular, country-by-country look reveals that the world's stock markets usually take turns at the top, such as during the 20-year period shown in Figure 8-2.

Is Correlation Important?

Some global investors focus on these *zigs* and *zags*—that is, they are obsessed with short-term price volatility and the notion of "correlation," which basically is an indicator of how closely returns in one market parallel returns in another.

Most investors track correlation to maximize the risk-reduction benefits of diversification. So, correlation is important only if you're worried about short-term price fluctuations. But I'm not convinced it always helps. In fact, I've seen studies that conclude that investors who constantly move to minimize risk or chase the next big thing at all costs can actually be the primary catalyst for *higher* correlation; the more they herd, the more extreme the correlation and the short-term price fluctuations can be—exactly the opposite of what they're hoping to avoid. I get further into this self-defeating pattern as part of a discussion on risk in Chapter 17.

Trying to gauge the level of your global diversification based on trending correlation is speculative and similar to market timing. For long-term value investors, correlation should not be an area of emphasis. Instead, I hold fast to a meaningful exposure to international equities in order to fully participate in the long-term appreciation potential that markets—and companies—throughout the world can provide.

Market Leaders Change

Year	Top Performing Market	Return	U.S. Market (S&P 500)
1993	MSCI Hong Kong	117%	10%
1994	MSCI Finland	52%	1%
1995	MSCI Switzerland	44%	38%
1996	MSCI Spain	40%	23%
1997	MSCI Portugal	47%	33%
1998	MSCI Finland	122%	29%
1999	MSCI Switzerland	153%	21%
2000	MSCI New Zealand	6%	-9%
2001	MSCI New Zealand	8%	-12%
2002	MSCI New Zealand	24%	-22%
2003	MSCI Sweden	65%	29%
2004	MSCI Norway	53%	11%
2005	MSCI Austria	35%	5%
2006	MSCI Spain	49%	16%
2007	MSCI Finland	49%	5%
2008	MSCI Japan	-29%	-37%
2009	MSCI Norway	87%	26%
2010	MSCI Sweden	34%	15%
2011	MSCI Ireland	14%	2%
2012	MSCI Belgium	40%	16%
2013	MSCI Finland	46%	32%

As of 12/31/2013. Source: MSCI via FactSet. Sampling includes only developed market countries as defined by MSCI. Past performance is not a guarantee of future results. The MSCI data contained herein is the property of MSCI Inc. (MSCI). MSCI, its affiliates and information providers make no warranties with respect to any such data. The MSCI data contained herein is used under license and may not be further used, distributed or disseminated without the express written consent of MSCI.

Figure 8-2

Correlation Catalysts

Low correlations among global markets can result from any of a number of factors. The most common reason is nonsynchronous economic cycles. For example, one country's economy could be falling into recession while another nation's economy may just be gathering steam. Currency, politics, fiscal policy, popular sentiment, and other factors also may come into play to create different economic landscapes from one market to another. Let's take a look at some of these.

Currency Fluctuations

Like correlations of returns among markets, changes in global currencies are cyclical and have some effect on global investors at different times. All currencies, from U.S. dollars and euros to Japanese yen and Mexican pesos, can fluctuate in relative value just like stocks (see Figure 8-3). They affect us all when we travel, but currency moves can influence returns for the global investor as well.

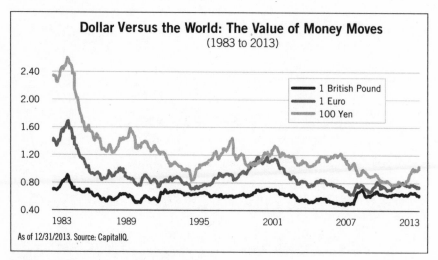

Dollar Versus the World: The Value of Money Moves
(1983 to 2013)

Legend: 1 British Pound, 1 Euro, 100 Yen

As of 12/31/2013. Source: CapitalIQ.

Figure 8-3 Currencies around the world are in constant flux. Here we show the pattern of movements of currencies compared to the U.S. dollar over a 30-year period (pre-euro data use the former German deutsche mark).

Many factors influence the value of a country's currency. A currency doesn't necessarily move in simultaneous lockstep—or even in the same direction—relative to the monetary units of every other nation. Although there were short-lived attempts in the 1980s to bring nations together to artificially manipulate exchange rates and please everyone (see Chapter 11 for more detail on the Plaza and Louvre Accords), the price of a nation's currency relative to another country's is essentially set by supply and demand. Speculators and central banks can distort these trends over short periods, but economic factors tend to prevail in the long run.

For example, in the 40 years from the 1950s to the mid-1990s, the yen and the deutsche mark had periods of appreciation in price against the dollar, as the Japanese and German economies saw rapid growth, low inflation, and trade surpluses. Later, rising deficits and the fiscal crisis in the United States throughout the 2000s led to a weaker dollar versus the euro for much of that time. Still later, changes in the emerging markets ushered in a Mexican peso that was stronger against the U.S. dollar as that country passed major reforms to improve its state-run telecommunications and energy sectors. Meanwhile, political unrest in Turkey and inflation concerns in Chile led to slow but steady double-digit weakening of the lira and the peso, respectively, versus the dollar.

One large exception is China, where the government has openly circumvented market forces to artificially keep the value of the yuan relatively weak versus other currencies, thus making the country's exports competitive overseas. In part because of peer pressure from global trading partners, the country began loosening up this policy around 2005. Even so, any appreciation is usually well choreographed at the whims of the central bankers.

Investing in Money

The currency "market," also called the foreign exchange market, is the largest and most heavily traded market in the world. It runs 24 hours a day, 5 days a week and electronically prices and moves more than $5.7 trillion in currencies each day.[3] Currency trading is complicated, fast moving, and crucial to a smooth-running international investing infrastructure. As an investment, currency strategy funds are now popular "alternatives" to equities. Even bellwether bond portfolios have increasingly leveraged an array of financially engineered currency derivatives to help augment their core holdings and attract new investors.

As a rule, I don't recommend direct investment in currencies or their distant cousins: derivatives, swaps, futures, and forward contracts. They're not stocks. They offer no ownership interest in a single business enterprise. Currencies may help measure wealth, but they don't create wealth or value the way a business can. As one currency goes up, another goes down, creating a continuous zero-sum game. Where is the value in that?

Even if you believe that it is important to control the currency exposure in your portfolio, managing it is virtually impossible. For example, you can certainly increase or decrease your euro *positions*, but it's difficult to assess your underlying *exposure* to the currency security by security.

(continued)

The same goes for currency hedging, which seeks to eliminate or reduce the impact of underlying currency movements while retaining exposure to the related investment.

Currency hedging programs have grown in the past 30 years, fueled by lengthy periods of volatile performance by most of the world's major currencies and a more accommodative trading and pricing infrastructure. Tools such as forward contracts, futures contracts, and currency options are available for those who wish to manage currency exposure, but there are trading costs associated with using each of them. Ultimately, the question investors should ask before hedging currencies is, "What is the *real* cost if I do it wrong?"

Value investors don't need to hedge currency. Based on what I have seen, the impact of currency hedging has not been consistent over time. The reasoning behind why an international investor would want to hedge currency is sound—protection from loss—but this goal is typically best pursued by the same golden rule applied to any other aspect of a portfolio: don't allow it to get overconcentrated in any one company, industry, asset class, or, in most cases, a single country. Spread your exposure among undervalued companies, not currencies.

In my view, there's a strong and rational argument for doing nothing with currencies. There can be exceptions, such as for investments in Canada where the Canadian dollar moved from 0.62 to 1.02 against the U.S. dollar over the 20-year period ending in 2002. In a globally focused value portfolio, however, exposure to a range of currencies comes with the territory and can help add another layer of diversification. Not only are you diversified by stock, by industry, and by geography, but you are also diversified by currency—it's part of the process.

Political Risk

In the post–World War II era, political fallout has had a unique way of seeking its level. Sometimes it can affect a wide swath of countries around the globe, such as during both Gulf Wars, the aftermath of 9/11, and the eurozone crisis. It can also be limited to single nations. In either case, we all have seen how quickly an ideal political scenario can sour, and vice versa.

In some extreme situations, political upheaval can wipe out an entire portfolio. Anyone who happened to be fully invested in Chile when Salvador Allende began nationalizing major industries in 1971 could have lost everything. On a more contemporary note, the U.S. government's takeover of Fannie Mae and Freddie Mac at the height of the 2008 fiscal crisis was very much like nationalization, and shareholders now allege that it "destroyed their value and trampled their private ownership rights," according to a pending lawsuit against the federal government. The point is, these events can happen anywhere, but they are usually very rare. I'll offer more about these government-sponsored agencies and the takeaways from the financial crisis of 2008–2009 in Chapter 10.

Up until now, I have stressed the benefits of individual security selection: a bottom-up, company-by-company approach to investing worldwide. So why even address political risks? Do political considerations, including a country's fiscal policies, even matter for an investor who focuses on individual business fundamentals and builds a well-diversified portfolio? The answer is yes—to a degree.

Consider how concerns about an economic crisis surfaced in Brazil in 2002 when the country's unemployment rate spiked and the inflation rate in neighboring Argentina passed 20 percent. Brazil's debt crisis also raised fears of a contagion that would spread across Latin American economies. But it was in the *political* arena that many investors raised the most serious doubts about the countries.

By July 2002, investors were voicing concerns over the presidential election polls, which showed a lead for left-wing candidate Luiz Inacio Lula da Silva. While outgoing President Fernando Henrique Cardoso's government had paid careful attention to the markets, da Silva's social issue agenda left many worrying about the country's debt obligations and economic health. As da Silva's lead in the polls widened prior to the October election, Brazil's stock market tumbled. In the third quarter alone, the market lost 39.4 percent, as measured by the MSCI Brazil Index.

Investors fled in hopes of avoiding a political and economic crisis. And how did Brazil fare? The crisis never seemed to materialize. Just months after his election, da Silva was being lauded by investors around the globe for his commitment to controlling inflation and luring investors—and rationality—back to Brazil's markets. The situation illustrates how markets can suffer even in the absence of an overt political crisis.

Not all crises are imagined, however, and some can be acute and be destructive to an otherwise prosperous region. Consider Thailand, where in May 2014, the military ousted acting prime minister Niwattumrong Boonsongpaisan in an overnight coup—the country's twelfth since gaining independence in 1932. Thailand was one of the world's fastest-growing economies for more than a decade, but political disruption since late 2011 has reduced its growth to less than 3 percent (barely half that of neighboring Vietnam, the Philippines, and Indonesia). Major industries, especially tourism, were soon struggling, while a handful of influential companies—automakers among them—began to rescind plans for expansion into key urban centers. Popular protests, although quashed at first, grew rapidly via social media. At the same time, undocumented migrant workers, who are a key component of its prosperous business model, fled the country by the thousands, fearing a crackdown by the provisional government. By late summer 2014, however, coup leader General Prayuth Chan-ocha was appointed by the country's legislature as prime minister. Meanwhile, Thai consumer confidence had actually strengthened, with a larger number of residents indicating that they felt a better sense of stability.[4]

Cutting Through Crisis

It's not as easy as it looks, but seeing through political uncertainty can often be rewarding for the value investor. In addition to the examples that I've offered earlier in the book, here are a few more outlier situations that I've run into over the years:

Italy, 1994. A major election surprise routed the Christian Democrats after their 50-year hold on the country's political reins. The untested center right coalition's assumption of power sparked a major banking crisis. I viewed this as a misplaced overreaction and increased our holdings in several of the country's leading banks.

Spain, 1995. The majority Socialist government suffered a number of financial scandals that put the country's currency, the peseta, in a downward spiral. We took value positions in a major bank and telecom company, competitive firms offering services that were essential to the nation's consumers. These companies prospered as the government proved resilient and made big strides toward Spain's gaining a solid foothold in the evolving European Union.

Saudi Arabia, 2011. Widespread government and social upheaval in the Middle East, collectively known as the Arab Spring, created short-term challenges for some otherwise well-run companies in the region. Among these were Air Arabia, the first and leading low-cost airline in the Middle East, whose stock price retreated as a result of temporary disruptions in commercial air traffic and a spike in jet fuel prices.

Greece, 2012. The height of the country's sovereign debt crises and austerity measures had a severe impact on this country's place in the world, but it didn't affect a Greece-based small-cap manufacturer of jewelry, watches, and fashion accessories that had steady overseas demand for its products.

Brazil, 2014. For a country hosting the World Cup and the Summer Olympics within two years of each other, Brazil is an interesting case of dual identity. Its currency, the real, has been getting crushed for years, and inflation has hovered at a miserable 7 percent. You already know where I'm going with this: we had more Brazil stocks than you could shake a stick at, representing some 18 percent of our emerging markets portfolios, compared to just 11 percent for the strategy's key benchmark. We found great margins of safety in a major aircraft manufacturer and the country's largest financial institution, among others, and as South America's single largest economy found its way back, these and other significantly undervalued companies certainly benefited from the rising tide of investor interest.

An evaluation of the political terrain can affect the assessment of a company's underlying business value and help investors decide at what price shares should be purchased. When evaluating political risks, my firm also considers the attitudes of opposition political groups, the level of stability in the labor market, the country's economic sensitivity to energy costs, and the government's policies regarding foreign investment and private enterprise. I also think political factors can influence how large a position a security should occupy in a well-diversified portfolio.

An assessment or forecast of a country's political environment is not a starting point for individual stock selection. That's why most of the time, one of the best defenses against political risk is diversification. I tend to limit investments in a single country to the greater of 20 percent of portfolio assets or 150 percent of that country's weighting in a comparable index. I believe this provides both diversification benefits and flexibility to my strategies. By limiting exposure to any one country, only a portion of the total portfolio is being exposed to particular political risks, depending, of course, on the region.

Value investors are long-term holders of a stock and are willing to endure temporary drops in a country's stock market. My firm introduced this guideline around the time of the Tiananmen Square massacre in 1989, when Hong Kong stocks fell substantially. But the ever-patient value investors eventually saw stock prices gradually surpass their original values.

Some value investors even view political risk in a positive light, since the resulting uncertainty can create good buying opportunities. As was the case with Tiananmen Square, political developments can have tragic consequences. I'm not suggesting that investors ignore such tragedies or develop a callous nature. But in the wake of such occurrences, speculators may be motivated by emotional impulses. However, the value investor remains focused on the objective evaluation of businesses and the prices being paid for their shares. Sometimes the best time to buy is after stocks have plunged and a market is selling at an absolutely cheap price. Long-term investing is likely to span periods that include events that could be described as shocking, bewildering, or horrifying. Investors—as opposed to speculators—need to retain their discipline in *all* market environments.

Accounting Systems on a Global Scale

The challenge for global stock pickers is to compare companies' earnings on a worldwide basis, despite national accounting discrepancies. It's a challenge that we as value investors welcome because it gives us a leg up on the competition in the hunt for bargain stocks. If uncovering the bottom-line truth about a company's financial status were a quick and easy task, less diligent investors would do it too.

What's more, any lingering challenges created by the incongruencies between U.S. and non-U.S. standards are just part of the day in a life of the value investor. I discuss these differences in more detail in the next chapter.

All Things Not Being Equal

What lessons should we learn from the past performance of global markets? Did the benefits of international investing disappear after the first or the second Gulf War; after the 1990s crises in Sweden, Mexico, and Thailand; or after practically everything went south in the financial crisis of 2008–2009? Absolutely not. In fact, as this book is being prepared, the *majority* of opportunities for undervalued companies are still *outside* the U.S. market.

If there's one takeaway from my more than 40 years of value investing abroad, it's that not all companies in any country are equal. More often than not, I have seen companies react differently—for better or worse—to the same stimulants. On the other hand, global value investing is no different from investing in the United States in one important way: the paramount importance of focusing on individual companies.

I urge you not to allow fear or uncertainty about global investing to keep you from participating in these potentially rewarding markets on the company level. As a society, we have learned to embrace brand names—Airbus, BP, 7-Eleven, Nestlé, Budweiser, Firestone, Church's Chicken, Holiday Inn, Trader Joe's, and Sony—that we regularly come in contact with, yet that are owned by international companies. Products and services from businesses around the world are an integral part of our lives in the United States. As we have long lived in a global age for our gas, food, clothes, and cars, we also should think globally when it comes to investment opportunities. More often than not, they are just as compelling, if not more so.

CHAPTER 9

ANALYSIS AND ACTION

GLOBAL VALUE INVESTING IN THE MODERN AGE OF GOVERNANCE, ACTIVISM, AND ACCOUNTING

You guys need to get a handle on the numbers. The real numbers. Figure out the size of the real hole. Not the made-up hole. Go contract by contract, like bottom-up work. This isn't like you're (just) going to be late on your credit card bill!

—JPMorgan Chase chairman James Dimon, reprimanding AIG's Brian Schreiber, head of strategy, August 2008[1]

Th is telltale quote from *Too Big to Fail* attests to the fact that no matter how thorough you are in looking inside a company's books, not all businesses—even the giants—will be 100 percent transparent to you. The book provides a tight chronology of the painstaking patchwork and negotiations hammered out by the upper echelons of government and finance in the days leading up to the global financial crisis in the fall of 2008.

Years later, I still wonder whether the leaders of American International Group or any of the other financial giants that were affected much cared that no one had any idea what was coming. I doubt it, now having the benefit of knowing that their books contained a maze of half-truths and had the opacity of a cataract. Warren Buffett, whom AIG desperately approached to solicit a last-minute buyout, couldn't see through the ledgers to find any value in the insurer. "I've looked over the 10-K," Buffett said. "The company is too complicated, and I don't have enough confidence to do that. Nothing is going to work with us, so don't waste your time."

In the interests of remaining fair and balanced, let me say that my firm owned a good amount of AIG shares. So did a lot of money managers, and we collectively got burned in the aftermath of its colossal takedown by insurmountable forces. As a firm, we had several takeaways from the AIG mess, foremost among them the belief that there is always a possibility that situations like this could happen again. All the regulations, principles, guidelines, and general practices that oversee and mechanize the way companies do business are not helpful when they're not used. Deciding to follow the rules is a choice. As value investors, we prefer to own companies that make the right choices. This keeps things fair, aboveboard, transparent, and, most important to us, more predictable. I get into much more detail on AIG and the financial crisis of 2008–2009 in Chapter 10.

So far, we've examined the fundamentals and environment of a company's performance that help our search for value opportunities. Now, I'll offer some insights into the areas of company research that, on the surface, should appear cut and dried, but that are often subject to additional scrutiny, interpretation, and judgment. In other words, as we look at financial reporting, leadership, and social responsibility, we turn from examining *what* businesses provide to *how* they provide it effectively, profitably, and consistently.

Opening the Books

When my firm researches companies, we delve deeply into their accounting statements and scour the footnotes. We seek to answer such deceptively simple questions as, "What does this company do?" and "How does this company make money?" In cases where, after a thorough investigation, we cannot answer these questions with a high degree of confidence, we will generally avoid the company—as we did with Enron and WorldCom. We have had, and continue to have, a bias in favor of companies with proven business models and relatively strong balance sheets.

Despite our focus on business specifics, there is no immunity to the risk that a company may engage in deceptive accounting or go bankrupt. While my firm did not purchase shares of Enron, for example, there is no guarantee that we won't purchase shares of a company like Enron in the future—especially given the "against the grain" approach that is the hallmark of value investors.

Global Accounting Challenges

In sports, all teams play by the same set of rules. Scoring a goal in soccer is the same whether the game is played in Africa, Asia, Europe, or North or South

America. There can be disputes over what constitutes a goal and penalties applied to those in the game, but everyone pretty much buys into 95 percent of the process. Keeping score is a lot more confusing in the international investment arena, where many countries have their own set of accounting rules and corporate disclosure practices. And even when the terms are the same, they don't necessarily mean the same thing. Confusing? You bet. But that same confusion creates opportunity for those who understand the differences in global accounting methods.

In the United States, the Financial Accounting Standards Board (FASB) oversees U.S.-based companies' adherence to generally accepted accounting principles (GAAP). Any non-U.S. company that is listed on a U.S. exchange must also satisfy reporting standards that conform to GAAP. Some multinationals fulfill this requirement by issuing two sets of accounting statements, one to meet local standards and a second for purposes of U.S. GAAP. Other companies use a single report and publish results in accordance with their own national accounting requirements. Within the framework of that same report, numbers are converted into U.S. GAAP terms. To say the least, there are a lot of numbers thrown about, but according to FASB, these standards "govern the preparation of financial reports and are officially recognized as authoritative by the Securities and Exchange Commission (SEC) and the American Institute of Certified Public Accountants."[2]

Outside the United States, the International Accounting Standards Board (IASB) oversees the adoption of International Financial Reporting Standards (IFRS) by many nations. These standards are now widely accepted, with some 100 countries—most of the European Union, Australia, Canada, New Zealand, Brazil, Mexico, and Russia among them—mandating or permitting some or all of their application. About 450 non-U.S. companies listed on American exchanges use IFRS as well.

The Push for Global Uniformity

In October 2002, the IASB and the FASB announced an agreement to work together to combine international and U.S. accounting standards. More than a decade later, adaptation of IFRS in the United States is projected to begin in 2015, with total convergence by 2017. In the meantime, IFRS standards have been a big help in developing accounting consistency overseas.

I often cite China as being home to a wonderful opportunity set of value companies in emerging markets. But this is not true for all industries, primarily because of unreliable accounting. I'm referring to China-based financial companies, especially banks, an industry that was unattractive to my firm for many years. On the surface, it looked in 2013 as if a sharp pullback in the prices of Chinese bank stocks was simply reflecting the market's reaction to a measurable slowdown in the country's GDP growth. The banks seemed adequately capitalized, and they had the total support of the state if something tragic were to happen. Return on equity was reported at a respectable 20 percent, too. From a purely fundamental perspective, many banks appeared to be great value plays.

But you never know what you're going to get with Chinese bank reporting. "We don't have any idea what's in there," was the often-repeated assessment of Jim Brown, one of my esteemed, very expressive, and veteran firm partners who led my financials research team at the time. "Their lending operations are black boxes, and when their loan book is growing by 30 or 40 percent a year, there is no way we can be confident in the quality of their portfolio."

Especially troublesome was our concern about their expanding use of trust and wealth management products to provide financing in the shadow of the legitimate banking system, which flew in the face of the government's valiant effort to tighten domestic credit. By 2013, China owed some $1.2 trillion to Asia-Pacific banks alone, much of it short-term loans backed by copper, aluminum, and other market-sensitive commodities.[3] In spite of the relatively large pullback in prices, we had too many concerns about what we didn't know and couldn't find out, so we kept them at arm's length.

Other reporting rules around the world are not necessarily better or worse than U.S. GAAP; they are just different and, in some cases, more widely used. Financial accounting is a somewhat judgmental process. In addition, accountants often make assumptions about the future that understandably differ from country to country. Although many countries are adopting components of IFRS, there are slowpokes among the crowd; foremost among them is Japan, but the tide is turning.

Dealing with Differences

Although IFRS has made significant strides abroad, not all countries have adopted it completely as their own universal standard. And, considering the slow-moving convergence with U.S. GAAP, there are some pockets of accounting variations that value investors regularly identify, interpret, and weigh into the equation.

Revenue

Some overseas companies, particularly when reporting extraordinary earnings from sales of subsidiaries or real estate, may report these earnings less conservatively than they would under U.S. GAAP standards.

Sales

There are nearly 100 rules for documenting sales under GAAP, which can vary by industry. IFRS uses just two.

Earnings

Some countries, such as Switzerland, Germany, and Japan, are more conservative than others when it comes to reporting earnings. To help cut through this, my global research team usually compares cash flows rather than reported earnings (see Figure 9-1). Although cash flow per share requires adjustment for differing accounting methods, the statistic is generally more comparable than earnings.

Cash Flow Is a Better Gauge of Value in Some Countries (U.S. vs. Japan)				
	MSCI Japan Index		MSCI U.S. Index	
Date	P/E	P/CF	P/E	P/CF
12/31/1992	38.9	8.1	22.7	10.2
12/31/1993	67.8	9.8	22.1	10.4
12/31/1994	98.2	11.6	16.9	9.1
12/31/1995	105.2	12.9	17.2	10.0
12/31/1996	108.7	12.1	19.3	11.2
12/31/1997	41.9	9.5	22.9	13.7
12/31/1998	185.2	9.7	30.2	18.1
12/31/1999	-295.4	16.2	30.7	19.5
12/31/2000	57.5	11.4	26.1	15.7
12/31/2001	39.8	8.5	33.3	16.0
12/31/2002	-126.2	8.8	22.6	12.1
12/31/2003	66.0	8.4	21.6	13.6
12/31/2004	22.5	7.8	19.4	12.7
12/31/2005	23.7	10.2	18.6	12.3
12/31/2006	21.1	10.2	17.8	12.1
12/31/2007	17.5	8.4	17.2	11.8
12/31/2008	12.0	4.7	13.8	7.1
12/31/2009	-35.1	11.7	28.6	11.7
12/31/2010	16.6	6.1	16.5	10.2
12/31/2011	18.6	5.7	13.9	8.9
12/31/2012	24.8	7.2	14.6	9.5
12/31/2013	17.6	8.5	18.6	11.7

As of 12/31/2013. Source: MSCI. Past performance is not a guarantee of future results. The MSCI data contained herein is the property of MSCI Inc. (MSCI). MSCI, its affiliates and information providers make no warranties with respect to any such data. The MSCI data contained herein is used under license and may not be further used, distributed or disseminated without the express written consent of MSCI.

Figure 9-1 Differences in earnings reporting (conservative versus liberal) can result in P/E ratios varying from country to country. But if you compare price-to-cash flow multiples, the variation is often reduced and you get a better reading on value opportunities. Japan is a case in point. In this table, P/E ratios for Japan look very expensive. But on a cash flow basis, the valuations look more reasonable during the same 20-year period.

Depreciation

U.S. companies generally rely on the straight-line method, while the Japanese, for example, use the double-declining-balance method of depreciation, thus often understating fixed assets and earnings. If Japanese companies employed the straight-line method, their earnings would increase on average between 10 to 15 percent.

Regardless of the method used, the amount of depreciation will be the same over the life of the asset, but value investors have to spot how straight-line depreciation can present a more favorable earnings picture.

Goodwill

This represents the values of a company's intangible assets, such as product or service brands, customer relations, experience of employees, and management. U.S. firms tend to show higher book values because of their method of accounting for goodwill, especially relative to their non-U.S. cousins.

Japanese companies normally amortize goodwill arising from consolidation over a five-year period. Since in the United States, goodwill is revalued at least annually and written down to market if necessary, asset values for U.S. firms could be over or understated, depending on the situation, compared to those in Japan.

Revaluations

Revaluation of fixed assets can significantly increase a company's reported net assets, particularly during periods of inflation. In the United States, only historical cost amounts may be used for depreciation purposes. In the Netherlands, however, fixed assets may be revalued and stated at amounts in excess of historical cost. This upward revaluation of assets could conceivably allow a Dutch company to borrow more than a company in the United States. Given this, we would expect net income to be lower under Dutch Civil Code standards than under U.S. GAAP.

Taxation

Tax considerations affect the way in which non-U.S. companies report their earnings. Under U.S. GAAP, net income before taxes as reported to shareholders often differs from net income as computed on the company's tax return. For instance, a U.S. company could use one depreciation schedule for reporting to its stockholders and a different one for reporting to the Internal Revenue Service.

In Germany and Switzerland, tax authorities do not permit businesses to maintain two sets of books. The shareholders and the tax authorities receive identical earnings reports. Therefore, reports to shareholders minimize earnings to avoid a heavier tax bite.

Inventory

Differences exist between U.K. and U.S. inventory accounting, primarily in the use of the LIFO (last-in, first-out) method, which is not permissible for tax purposes in the United Kingdom and is seldom used. LIFO is used by a large percentage of major U.S. firms.

During periods of rising prices, a U.K. firm's reported cost of sales would be lower than that for a U.S. company using LIFO, and the U.K. firm's net income would be higher.

Restatement of Accounts

In Brazil and Argentina, where high inflation has often rendered financial statements meaningless, restatement of accounts is used to reflect changes in price levels.

In such cases, we typically mark up most balance sheet accounts, including fixed assets and equity, by the level of inflation seen over the course of the year and run gains and losses either through the income statement or directly through the equity account. Fortunately, U.S. GAAP has never required inflation adjustments to the financial statements, although certain inflation disclosures were required in the footnotes during the 1970s.

Options Accounting

Options have come under fire because of the different ways companies issue them to employees and account for them on their books. They can be significant drains on the bottom line, but many companies don't even book them as an expense, contending that because no money is actually paid out (unlike a salary, for example), they aren't really a cost. Even if they were, these firms would argue, there is no accurate or commonly accepted way to value them.

This is nonsense. There are always costs associated with the issuance of options that need to be recognized, and you *can* assign a value to them. It's just simple math; something that is *given* to employees reflects something that is taken away from equity holders.

Taiwan Semiconductor is a large semiconductor manufacturer that does a great deal of outsourcing business. Software engineers at Taiwan Semiconductor may receive a total compensation package of $150,000 to $170,000. However, their base salary may be only $30,000, with the rest paid in stock bonuses. Stock bonuses are similar to options in that stock is essentially "given" to employees. If these bonuses are treated as expenses, it significantly raises the costs associated with salaries and decreases the firm's earnings. In some cases, expensing options and stock bonuses may reduce a company's earnings by up to 50 percent. Thus, a business that at first appears to be attractively valued may turn out to be quite expensive after a closer investigation.

For the value investor who is seeking a sound business at an attractive price, financial statements are a vital element in the decision-making process. As we have indicated, however, financial accounting is an inexact discipline at best. Attaching hard numbers to dynamic and perpetually changing business conditions is a difficult task.

The reams of estimates and assumptions that are part of an accountant's stock in trade are invariably subject to uncertainty and interpretation. Some accountants obviously display a great sense of humor when they attempt to report asset values and earnings down to the last dollar. In addition to being humorists, however, some accountants seem to be in the beauty makeover business. As investors, we must be wary of accounting techniques that dress up corporate results to make them look better. These practices, while strictly legal, can confound readers of financial statements.

Now, let's pull our heads out of the books and instead go face-to-face with the individuals whose sole purpose should be to create value for the company and ensure its long-term success for the benefit of its shareholders.

Accounting for Accounting

Following Enron and other high-profile scandals of the early 2000s, a wave of accounting improprieties surfaced at a large number of otherwise perfectly legitimate companies. These irregularities ranged from overstating earnings and insider trading to siphoning cash out of the company for personal use.

Such highly publicized examples of fraud also prompted new laws designed to bolster investor confidence in the validity of corporate accounting and corporate governance. Foremost among these was the Sarbanes-Oxley Act of 2002, known as SOX. Opponents argue that implementing it is a major corporate expense. But the core elements of the measure are aimed at helping to ensure better oversight, auditor independence, enhanced disclosures, transparency, and accountability for fraud, among other things. As someone who focuses on the long term, I think these pluses outweigh the costs.

Corporate governance essentially focuses on whether the company's managers are looking after the interests of shareholders and following the appropriate rules, processes, and safeguards in doing so. In practice, it doesn't always work out like that, as several examples have illustrated over the years. The high-profile scandals involving Enron and WorldCom are the ones that everyone remembers best in that era of malfeasance circa 2002. But missteps can show up anywhere, and they did, and my firm's holdings were not immune. Here's a list of just a few names associated with some form of scandal, most of which were spotted and pursued by authorities under the then brand-new SOX:

- Royal Ahold (2002): inflated vendor rebates, which represented far more revenues than the company actually received.

- Bristol-Myers (2002): exaggerated revenues.

- Duke Energy (2002): round-trip trades, an activity that pumps up the volume of buys and sells on the same company asset to create the illusion of higher revenues and volume.

- El Paso Corporation (2002): round-trip trades.

- Merck & Co. (2002): recorded co-payments were not collected.

- Parmalat (2002): false documentation.

- Tyco International (2002): CEO Dennis Kozlowski was later convicted of unauthorized bonuses, payouts, and purchases of rare art with company funds.

- Health South Corporation (2003): accounting fraud; its CEO, Richard Scrushy, took the brunt of the blame.

I believe that there will always be the potential for fraud. Yet we have come some distance over the last two decades to help curb it. Whether this is the result of SOX, other post-Enron regulations, or just heightened investor awareness of what proper accounting should look like, accounting statements for the vast majority of businesses today reflect greater integrity and accuracy.

Corporate Governance and the Value Investor

Throughout my four decades as a company leader, I have instilled in my research and investment teams the discipline to search for companies that are managed in the same way that we manage our own business—with a long-term vision. For example, I seek companies that are run by executives who are committed to building shareholder value, not personal empires. However, there are situations in which companies do not have these favorable attributes, but can still be good investments at the right price.

When my firm buys a company's shares at a discount, we're expecting that its intrinsic value will eventually be reflected in its market price. If management of the company we own is acting in a way that keeps this from happening, then they are interfering with the rationale we used when we made the investment. Put simply, they stop us from obtaining a good return on our investment. Sometimes this interference reflects a difference of opinion—or conflicts of interest—between management and shareholders. In rare instances, we see cases of outright dishonesty.

Running a public company is not easy. Management must constantly balance the often competing interests of a variety of constituencies beyond just shareholders, such as partners, customers/clients, creditors, regulators/politicians, distributors/suppliers, employees, and the community.

Nevertheless, sound corporate governance can make the job of managing a corporation easier for executives by creating a framework for the execution and review of important management decisions, and by providing a way for shareholders to make their views known when this is appropriate.

Ensuring Sound Governance

Is there a relationship between good corporate governance and shareholder value? My experience says yes. If corporate governance is designed to provide a blueprint for success, then *good* governance should result in a *good* business and enhanced shareholder value.

Close on the heels of the high-profile accounting scandals of the early 2000s, the Securities and Exchange Commission in 2003 approved new listing standards concerning the composition of boards and board committees.[4] Generally, publicly traded companies listed on the New York Stock Exchange and Nasdaq were required to maintain the following:

1. The board of directors should have a majority of independent, non-executive directors. In other words, most of the board members should have "nonmaterial interest" in the company itself.

2. The board must have a nomination committee that is responsible for proposing director appointments.

3. The board must have a compensation committee to establish fair and transparent compensation of management and directors.

4. The board must have an audit committee that is responsible for interacting with outside accountants and ensuring the integrity of the company's financial information.

5. A company should have effective, transparent, and fair procedures for conducting shareholders' meetings and for allowing shareholders to exercise their votes.

When the new guidelines were put in place that year, I considered them a good start, but they have limitations. They apply only to companies that are not owned by a majority shareholder. That is, if a person or holding company owns at least 51 percent of the stock, the company is exempt. And, other than delisting the company, there is no penalty imposed by the exchanges or the SEC on listed companies that do not meet the minimum independent director levels.

Nevertheless, the United States leads other developed nations in the appointment of independent directors. And it's getting better abroad, too. The International Finance Corporation (IFC), part of the World Bank, works with firms in 180 countries to promote the adoption of good corporate governance standards. The IFC's Corporate Governance Development Framework was established in 2011 and has been adopted by some 30 financial institutions in developed and emerging markets to help assess companies in which they invest.[5]

From a longtime global investor's perspective, all this is also an excellent beginning. But there is still a long way to go. That is, there are a few additional criteria that help companies go above and beyond the minimum required guidelines to ensure a truly independent mindset among boards:

1. Remove the board member selection process from corporate management.

2. Mandate that there be more candidates than vacancies to give shareholders a real choice.

3. Provide a reasonably simple way for any significant group of shareholders to make a nomination to the board.

Although they were never formally approved, these criteria were floated following Enron. Advocates believe that such additional safeguards would have gone a long way toward preventing or recognizing the accounting frauds that eventually brought that company to an acute and ugly end. We can never be certain, and sometimes it takes more than just rules to makes things run well—such as active involvement by shareholders.

Shareholder Activism

Assuming that the board is following the rules, sometimes it's not enough for shareholders to sit idly by and watch things happen. What if goals aren't being met, shareholders' interests aren't being considered, or the management team does not have all the skills and/or vision necessary to maximize the value of the shares?

In these types of situations, shareholders have three choices:

1. *"Hold and hope."* Keep their shares and believe that better times are ahead.

2. *"Sell and shrug."* This is also referred to as the "Wall Street walk" or "voting with your feet."

3. *"Push and prod."* Attempt to change the situation.

The first two options are docile approaches, while the third—attempting to bring about a change—is referred to as *shareholder activism.*

Activism has many catalysts, objectives, and participants. The media and Hollywood often showcase its extremes—from the frail elderly widow who bravely argues against the majority at the annual shareholders' meeting to the high-profile majority owner using his influence to bring about mergers, spin-offs, increased share buybacks, and special dividends.

When shareholders, whether individual or institutional, believe that something needs to be done to realign management with the interests of the shareholders, there is a broad array of tactics available to them within an active investment strategy. These range from thoughtful proxy voting at one end of the spectrum to aggressive legal challenges, such as a proxy battle or a lawsuit, at the other end. I have rarely found the most extreme measures necessary or effective, as it is often possible to effect some change through private discussions with management.

Activism's Roots in Value

In *The Memoirs of the Dean of Wall Street*, Benjamin Graham gives an account of his first experience as a shareholder activist. In 1925, he believed that the shares of Northern Pipeline were trading at a significant discount to the company's underlying value. Northern Pipeline was one of 31 companies created following the U.S. Supreme Court's decision in 1911 to break up the Standard Oil monopoly. Graham discovered that Northern Pipeline owned large amounts of high-quality bonds, was operating with a large profit margin, carried no inventory, and "therefore had no need whatever for these bond investments."[6] Enthusiastic at the results of his research, Graham wrote: "Here was Northern Pipeline, selling at only $65 a share, paying a $6 dividend—while holding some $95 in cash assets for each share, nearly all of which it could distribute to its stockholders without the slightest inconvenience to its operations. Talk about a bargain security!"

When Graham had acquired about a 5 percent stake in the company, he attempted to "persuade Northern Pipeline management to do the right and obvious thing: to return a good part of the unneeded capital to the owners, the stockholders. Naively, I thought this should be rather easy to accomplish."[7]

Later Graham would write:

> *When, in all innocence, I made my first effort as a stockholder in 1926 to persuade a management to do something other than what it was doing, old Wall Street hands regarded me as a crackbrained Don Quixote tilting at a giant windmill. "If you don't like the management or what it's doing, sell your stock"—that had long been the beginning and end of Wall Street's wisdom in this domain, and it is still the predominant doctrine.*[8]

Through research and persistence, Graham described how he eventually became one of the first people not directly affiliated with the Standard Oil system to be elected to the board of directors of one of its affiliated companies. Eventually, Northern Pipeline followed Graham's advice and distributed unneeded capital and newly created shares to existing shareholders. Graham wrote that the value "of the new Northern Pipeline stock plus the cash returned ultimately reached an aggregate of more than $110 per old share." Keep in mind that when Graham began his research, the shares were selling at $65 per share.

Graham's effort reflects the value of pursuing an activist strategy in *certain* cases. In light of the premium that investors are willing to pay for sound corporate governance and what I believe to be the potential for unlocking additional shareholder value at certain firms, shareholder activism remains an option for institutional money managers and pension plans to consider on a case-by-case basis in seeking to foster long-term wealth creation.

Although it's been around in different forms for decades, shareholder activism rose sharply (62 percent) after the financial crisis of 2008–2009, according to a *Financial Times* study. In Europe alone, activism campaigns tripled between 2010 and 2013. On the surface, it sounds as if more shareholders are taking an interest in the quality of their stocks. But I'm not totally convinced that activism translates that easily to a "town hall" meeting. For example, much of the increased activity cited in that study is attributed less to a rising concern for good governance and more to the activist hedge funds or whale investors who are in it only for the short-term benefits to themselves or their firms. So it seems that those who are taking more interest are actually just those with the most skin in the game.

Here are just a few motivations behind some of the more vehement activist initiatives:

- Hedge fund Starboard Value LP, with a 6 percent share in Darden Restaurants, Inc., pushed hard through a bitter proxy fight to replace Darden's *entire* 12-member board of directors in 2014. Battles for complete control are increasing, but coups are rare and can be destructive to shareholder value.[9]

- In 2013, Dow Chemical faced pressure from Daniel Loeb's Third Point LLC to split the giant into two companies, one focused on petrochemicals and the other on specialty chemicals, a massive undertaking that went well beyond Dow's original intention to simply restructure toward the same general goal.[10]

- The iconic billionaire activist Carl Icahn demanded that Apple offer more share buybacks to the tune of $150 billion, arguing that the cash-rich company might be a Wall Street darling, but it was not a bank. Apple budged a little, making an $18 billion repurchase in early 2014 that actually helped set the tone for other companies to follow suit that year.

- Pershing Square Capital Management chief William Ackman, after quietly gathering about 10 percent of the shares of successful Botox maker Allergan, Inc., pushed for the takeover of that company by Valeant Pharmaceuticals International at a price in the neighborhood of $53 billion. In an unusual twist, Credit Suisse Group became an advisor to Ackman on the initiative. Banks have usually steered clear of activists, so this sends a clear message of activism's growing influence among Wall Street's major institutions.[11]

Almost in lockstep, companies have raised more barriers to defend themselves against these and other potential (and usually undesired) instances of shareholder influence. Stricter poison pill guidelines are being adopted by more companies—Hertz Global Holdings, Aeropostale, Inc., and J.C. Penney come to mind—to help prevent unwanted takeovers. Poison pills, which trigger the issuance of a flood of new shares as a dilution mechanism, traditionally would kick in when a shareholder garnered about 20 percent of a company. Stricter triggers between 2010 and 2014 brought that number down to 10 percent.[12] And poison pills are being used more frequently. From 2006 through 2013, poison pill deals jumped threefold (from 9.6 percent to 30 percent).[13] In terms of board infiltration, companies like Pfizer, Inc., and Agrium, Inc., have revised company rules to help restrict outside board appointments.

Why Be Active, Sometimes?

Based on what I've seen and done, the vast volume of successful activism is focused more on high-level corporate governance values, such as accountability, transparency, and the establishment of proper shareholder democracy, than on detailed operating issues.

Shareholders should still have the platform to offer opinions on "micro" issues. However, activism is more likely to garner support among the board, officers, and other shareholders if it is directed at key governance values, rather than social issues or matters that clearly involve business judgment.

Activists' efforts also tend to have a greater chance of success when they are carried out by institutional investors rather than individuals. Since they are managing money on behalf of thousands of individuals, institutional investors simply have larger collective ownership stakes, more extensive resources, and greater leverage than individuals.

For example, the California Public Employees' Retirement System (CalPERS), the largest public pension fund in the United States, is one of Apple's largest shareholders. In 2012, Apple finally caved to a longstanding but ignored shareholder demand to require a majority (not just a plurality) of votes for someone to be elected to its board. For a company that pretty much received a rubber stamp on board approvals, it was quite a shift of heart after spending years rebuffing the issue.[14] What made the difference in 2012? CalPERS had formally taken up the cause.

Being Passive on Activism

"Perception is reality," goes the timeless and ubiquitous quote coined by political strategist Lee Atwater. Those three simple words basically affirm that no matter what you do, you're going to make an impression, and it may or may not be the one that you intended to make. Along these lines, even well-intended shareholder activism can send the wrong message to influential recipients. So it is sometimes best to take a pass on being publicly active.

Some of the bigger reasons include the costs, legal issues, and the possibility of adverse publicity. Engaging in activism is often expensive. It may demand outside legal and accounting advice, proxy solicitation assistance, and public and media relations consulting. Furthermore, the expense of hiring these external experts must be added to the costs associated with the diversion of the time and talent of the firm's *internal* resources.

Managers must also evaluate the possibility that existing clients could be sensitive to the diversion of time and talent that activism entails, or may even view activism as an expensive rationalization for poor stock selection. Furthermore, if managers engage in activism, there is the potential for negative media coverage, even if the managers are successful in bringing about the changes they seek. Finally, the tone and content of media messages are often difficult to manage, and publicity may have adverse effects on how the managers are perceived.

Here is one example of how a less openly engaged and more "behind the scenes" type of activism can work well. In a 2014 politically charged shareholder vote, Warren Buffett abstained from a measure on executive pay at Coca-Cola, of which Berkshire Hathaway is the largest shareholder. For months leading up to the vote, Buffett had repeatedly stated that the package was "excessive," so it surprised many followers when he opted to look the other way. At the 2014 shareholders' meeting, he stated that forcing board-level changes can sometimes be rude behavior. "You keep belching at the dinner table, you'll be eating in the kitchen," he said.[15] It later came out that he had held private talks with Coke about the pay plan, which eventually underwent a major cleanup that made it more to his liking.

The Social Responsibility "Era"

As members of a global community, we all tend to react the same way to tragic events, suffering, and nefarious wrongdoing. As much as I trumpet the benefits of removing emotion from investing, I am like everyone else: human. I can't help but want to try to remedy or fix whatever is broken or threatened. I tend to do this, however, beyond the scope of my value investment strategies.

The popular belief is that socially responsible investing is a relatively new trend. In fact, there are many new *names* for it, but a general framework concerning the merits of social investing is documented as far back as the 1700s, with the religious and moral underpinnings typical of the times.

In 1843, the ever-prolific Charles Dickens reversed Ebenezer Scrooge's all-profit motives with one billowing howl from the ghost of his dead partner, Jacob Marley: "Mankind was my business. The common welfare was my business; charity, mercy, forbearance, benevolence, were all my business. The dealings of my trade were but a drop of water in the comprehensive ocean of my business!"[16]

Today, we are under a lot of consumer pressure to be more socially aware in our investing disciplines. Sensitivities toward enterprises such as gaming, firearms, tobacco, nonrenewable energy, conflict diamonds, and many others have long been increasing—and understandably so. Among the leading considerations are a company's impact on, or commitment to, the environment, human rights, consumer protection, public health, social justice, and corporate governance. Socially responsible investment managers believe that companies that leave no destructive footprints in these areas have a competitive and profitability edge. Their advantage is often measured in terms of potentially lower liability costs and access to growing markets outside the United States, where consumers are believed to be more socially engaged and loyal to like-minded businesses.

(continued)

This is a worthy endeavor, and there are more than 300 retail mutual funds alone that specialize in ESG (environmental, social, and governance) strategies. However, can one be completely socially responsible in one's investing? It's one thing to identify companies that engage in obvious deception, malfeasance, misconduct, or subterfuge. When my investment teams see them, we avoid them. But it's another thing altogether when companies are simply following the rules of the road in their respective arenas. It can be hard to tell what's right if you're also trying to stay objective. Here are a few examples, with a question to ponder for each:

- In 1970, six years after an eye-opening surgeon general's report linked tobacco use to increased health risks, President Richard Nixon signed into law the Public Health Cigarette Smoking Act. Among other things, the measure banned cigarette advertising on U.S. television and radio stations and mandated warning labels on all packages. Proponents argued that advertisers had a "responsibility" to warn users of any dangers in their products.

  Q: Since big tobacco has been complying ever since, aren't these companies being socially responsible?

- Throughout the 1980s, U.S. laws and United Nations resolutions pushed for divestiture of (or no further investing in) companies and public infrastructure in South Africa as part of a global admonishment of that country for its discriminatory apartheid system.

  Q: Were the South African businesses—employers of thousands of people of all races and economic backgrounds—socially irresponsible for being based there, even if they didn't adopt apartheid practices?

- In 2010, a tragic disaster on a drilling rig in the Gulf of Mexico spewed more than 200 million gallons of crude oil into the region over 87 days—the industry's worst spill in history.[17]

  Q: If this convinced you to never invest in BP plc stock, does the same avoidance apply to your car's gas tank? If you instead buy a competitor's fuel to get to work, do you see that company as more socially responsible?

I offer these questions not to be glib or insensitive, but to point out that there are no easy answers. We are blessed to live in a country where we can express our opinions and stand up for what we believe. This is exactly the point with socially responsible investing. It comes down to a personal choice.

If you do pursue a socially responsible investing path, I would suggest that the filters used to profile companies within a socially responsible framework are somewhat of a work in progress. Many managers who have been leaders in socially conscious investing have told us that there is no standard best practice for overlaying the "social factor" with basic company fundamentals and valuations. That said, protecting the environment and standing up for equal rights are valid and noble considerations. It's also important for you to be sensitive to all the variables in our shared world that influence each company's unique situation.

My firm engages in activism very selectively. We have held discussions with senior management, traveled to shareholders' meetings to present ideas, and challenged mergers and acquisitions—all with the intention of better unlocking shareholder value for existing clients. A more detailed example concerning our holdings in Ono Pharmaceutical is described in Chapter 11. Our success in these pursuits has varied. Regardless of whether we achieve our objectives, however, if we believe that we can make a positive contribution to shareholder value through activism, we will consider it.

Our approach to global value investing has carried my firm to many crossroads. Since our founding, we have searched the world for mispriced companies, wading through often disruptive backdrops of cyclical prosperity and recession, peace and conflict, crises and confidence. And I don't expect that we'll ever see a perfect agreement on rules and regulations any time soon.

In any event, the macro environment provides only color in terms of our singular focus on individual businesses—wherever they may be. With more than 40 years, thousands of companies, and millions of travel miles in our wake, we can't help but have a few good stories to share. There have been many lessons from our journeys that shape our views, validate our convictions, and keep us humble. Value investing works over the long run, of that I'm certain. There are also milestones along the path to mark when it doesn't, no matter how closely you stuck to the map. And that's OK, as long as you learn from your experiences and apply that learning going forward. In the next two chapters, I share a few of these lessons from our wins and losses with you.

PART III

LESSONS LEARNED AND PRINCIPLES APPLIED

E very day, the market brings investors a voice. It whispers in our ears and tells us that things are good or not so good. We are then left to decide whether what it says is correct or whether it even matters where the market goes.

For the most part, value investing looks beyond this annoyance. But there are times when the person on the other end of that voice, Mr. Market, can challenge us and put our value principles to the test.

Whatever challenge he brings, the important thing to remember is that we need to apply anything we learn from it to what we do going forward. Then we're always a little wiser and ever more effective as we go into the next round.

If such wisdom comes from being responsive, it's just as important to be proactive about it. Staying committed, on target, focused, and active all boils down to surveying the terrain at all times. Thought-provoking research and useful analysis of market structure, investor psychology, and the product arena is vital to the mission. So is sharing this with the world for all who also wish to benefit.

Now, I invite you to Part III, an inside look at some of my firm's experiences with Mr. Market and our constant commitment to thought leadership through the Brandes Institute.

CHAPTER 10

STAYING COMMITTED:
MR. MARKET TAKES VALUE TO TASK–PART 1

We don't fear market volatility; we try to take selective advantage of it.

—Charles Brandes, in an interview with the *Washington Post,* 1997

This chapter and the next each offer a comprehensive example of my firm's experiences with value investing in the real world. I feel that the best way to show how value investing is in constant motion is through a vivid chronicling of two very distinct scenarios, one revolving around a country and the other around a cataclysm. Keep in mind that these exposés are individual inside views of just two of the many value investing propositions that my firm has handled.

Japan is at the center of the next chapter's narrative, but you shouldn't take this to mean that my firm sees value investing is anything other than a global strategy. Likewise, this chapter's discussion of financial organizations, real estate, and auto companies by no means suggests that our approach to value investing sets its priorities through top-down sector or industry analysis.

We focus on companies, and this was exactly what we were doing as the first scenario unfolded during the financial crisis of 2008–2009.

September 9, 2008

Another last-minute meeting invitation had popped open on my computer screen, and just like the previous three that morning, it was a convening of one of my firm's seven investment committees. This was the fifth so far for the workweek, and it was only Tuesday afternoon. Typically, a weekly meeting to discuss new buy ideas and portfolio construction is considered sufficient, given that we hold concentrated portfolios, and that *minute-to-minute* adjustments are not part of a value investing approach. However, the financial crisis evaporated trillions of dollars in quoted net worth throughout the global capital markets in the fall of 2008. So we needed up-to-date information to be sure that we were on top of what might be happening to our holdings on a fundamental basis.

Crisis Mode

Market cycles repeat, and only their stripes change to fool you into thinking that this time it's something new. But this crisis really *was* different in both its depth and its intensity. So we did whatever it took to stay on top of it, even if it meant four investment strategy sessions or more a day. I was sure that this scenario was being repeated at hundreds of companies across the country that were facing the same type of hurdles.

I was early for this particular meeting, but the conference room was already standing room only. "Uh-oh," I thought. "With everything changing so fast, *everyone* being in the same room can't be good." As I crossed the threshold, I caught the end of an analyst's colorful parable: "Wells Fargo taking over Wachovia is like getting a Rolls-Royce for the price of a Toyota Corolla," followed by nervous laughter. It was a microburst of conviviality, but the situation was no laughing matter. "And JPMorgan Chase taking over Washington Mutual is like getting a Toyota Corolla for the price of a Schwinn bicycle," came another barb. I shared a grin, but I remember thinking that the setting resembled a situation room. The financial crisis of 2008–2009 was enveloping our holdings, and we were soon swept up in trying to decipher and come to grips with an event that was similar to—but perhaps worse than—what happened in 1973–1974.

Credit Crunch

Most of the industry's struggle had developed over several years and come to a head over several months. Yet, there was one frenetic weekend in Washington in which, by Monday, the U.S. corporate financial world was unraveled by policy makers and then patched together into an unprecedented tapestry. When it was over, Wells Fargo had taken over Wachovia, JPMorgan Chase had enveloped Washington Mutual, Bank of America had purchased Merrill Lynch, and Lehman Brothers—also an iconic financial institution with a 164-year track record of success—had disappeared. In the surrounding weeks, the fates of Fannie Mae and Freddie Mac were also sealed, as was that of the insurance giant AIG—all targets of a government buyout on the pretext of saving them from going under. Soon afterward, two of the big three U.S. auto companies became the subjects of government takeovers: GM and Chrysler, both straining under the weight of peaking oil prices and a demand shift to more fuel-efficient cars that they just didn't have.

Back in 2007, we knew that there was a huge bubble waiting to pop, but few people anywhere knew or even suspected that it would get this bad. We had purchased a lot of these stocks after things began to deteriorate and prices had already fallen materially, based on what we saw as textbook discounts of about 35 to 50 percent in intrinsic value and other carefully considered filters for long-term potential contribution to our strategies. Like most money managers who shared the pain with clients, we soon found ourselves navigating a disastrous "70-year flood" that forced to the surface very unusual events for these companies that very few people believed were possible.

Rewind a Few Years

For more perspective on my view of the financial crisis of 2008–2009 and what my firm experienced during the crisis, we should backtrack to what led up to it.

Around 2002, the markets and leading industrials were starting to gain some traction. Housing was on the upswing around the country, thanks to several years of the Federal Reserve pumping liquidity into the economy—a trend that started right after the 9/11 attacks. At my firm, many of the seeds that we sowed during the tech bubble and its aftermath were now beginning to show their true value. Again, these were the "boring" and "tired" stocks in manufacturing, telecom, materials, consumer staples, and food products that I discussed earlier. Value investing in general began a strong and steady four-year climb, and our portfolios certainly benefited from the market's rediscovered affinity for Graham-and-Dodd strategies.

Large inflows eventually pushed most of our investment strategies toward their respective maximum capacity. Some of this burgeoning came in fits and spurts, as large institutional clients would grab the entire mandate of specific strategies without batting an eye. By the end of 2005, we were obliged to close the majority of our strategies to protect the interests of current clients. International and Global had been closed a few years earlier.

Performance Insights

Closures are a frustrating irony of the asset management business. In most businesses, the better your results, the wider your reach for new clients should be, but this is not always the case with investment portfolios. Value investing, which often results in a fairly concentrated portfolio, can end up with a limited number of high-quality companies that have the requisite discount to intrinsic value. In fairness to those clients who have been with you all along and are paying for active results, you have to close your doors to new clients or, in extreme cases, *any* inflows.

On the important point of performance reporting, I believe that it is sometimes overemphasized and too narrow. When I started in this business in 1968, I learned very quickly that showcasing Go-Go or Nifty Fifty stocks drew attention to the wrong things, with dire consequences. More than four decades later, I still try never to hang my hat on short-term outperformance, because value is eventually around the bend from an out-of-favor cycle. In fact, although my firm produces it in order to be in line with industry standards, quarterly portfolio reporting is not something that I advocate. I think it is too short term to give a clear picture of how value investing is supposed to work. Nonetheless, it's hard *not* to appreciate the moment when things are going your way.

Moreover, when they are chasing performance, too many investors often don't care about your process. They may not appreciate that returns—especially for value strategies—are not always going to be this "hot" or this consistent. So, you often attract investors or institutions that have unrealistic expectations that are not necessarily congruent with long-term superior growth. This was the situation for us. Our emerging markets, global, and international small- and large-cap strategies were all the outperforming poster children for our biannual institutional conference in 2006. Yet, attendees didn't seem to care much about how we got there—they were just anxious to hear how long it would be before they could get in on it again.

U.S. Bank-Free Zone

Throughout the good times and up until 2007, my firm had limited itself to a handful of U.S. financials. For example, we had moved into and out of American International Group (AIG) over the years. Our U.S. focus at this point, however, was on the value opportunities in telecom, where we outweighed the index fourfold. Consumer staples had a big role, too. We also held a large number of overseas financials—many of which were key contributors to our performance for several years.

Meanwhile, however, U.S. banks were also now generally doing quite well. Still, we could never justify their valuations. Their 18 percent return on equity dwarfed their 12 percent historical levels. But the same was true of their price-to-earnings ratios, which were around 14 times versus their traditional average of around 11 times. We knew that this couldn't last, but we were hard-pressed to convince clients why we held a de minimis weighting in financials when the major indexes were showing around 30 percent in them. Against some strong client pressure to jump in, we stayed out of U.S. financials, which was precisely the best move we could have made at the time. After all, these were not value companies, yet. But given the general signs that we were starting to see in late 2006 into 2007, we believed that they would be value plays relatively soon. What we and most of the industry didn't know at the time was that these companies weren't showing all their cards. And, new regulations such as mark-to-market accounting would create almost historic difficulties for these financial companies.

Bubble Trouble Emerges

In the summer of 2007, the signals of what we had believed all along became more apparent—the overheated real estate market was starting to correct. It was also now more obvious that a great deal of questionable lending was going on at the large banks. As I mentioned earlier in the book, not being able to totally see through to the "black box" of a bank's loan book standards can be the norm. In this unique environment, however, we deduced that too many mortgages were getting into the hands of risky borrowers, and the cagey veil of bank secrecy made it hard to confirm just how bad this was. What we *could* see was a record-high ratio of home prices to median income (see Figure 10-1). There was no way this could be sustainable, was our conviction. The gray area for us, however, was knowing just how far the eventual fall would be.

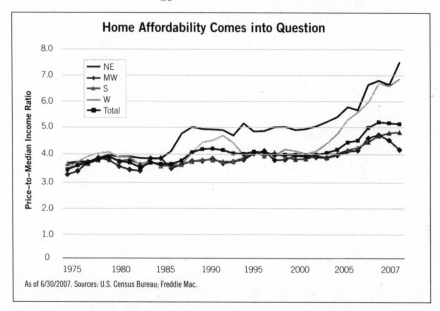

Figure 10-1 A Brandes analyst report in the summer of 2007 revealed a record high ratio of average home prices to median income in most major U.S. markets. This was a key harbinger of the inevitable real estate correction, and our signpost to start looking for value opportunities. Determining the intensity of the correction would be another matter altogether.

As trouble began, we did what we do best—search for undervalued companies in a challenged environment. We set our sights on a key area of the housing market that was experiencing potential hiccups in light of the nascent correction: the dozen or so leading providers of housing development and construction, which we refer to collectively as "the homebuilders."

These primarily small- and mid-cap companies were all experiencing some measurable setbacks after having a solid showing for decades. Few of those in their management teams held the same opinion as to when their operations would return to normal. Some predicted 12 to 18 months, others by the next earnings period. None of the 12 firms' estimations came close to the extended downturn that occurred.

Modeling the Past

Housing market indicators told a sad but not surprising tale. They also appeared to be in line with what had happened in previous recessions, such as 1973–1974 and the early 1990s. Foreclosures were at 1.3 percent when the downward cycle began, but the homebuilders blamed this on the subprime segment, which supposedly accounted for just 5 percent of their total sales.[1] Overall, our assessment put the homebuilders in retrenchment mode, as they were making virtually no land purchases and were using their large amounts of emerging free cash flows predominantly to decrease their debt or increase their cash balances.

Other factors that we considered in our valuations included:

- These companies had $4 billion in land owned and option deposits that were seen as impaired, and none of them had plans to purchase new land.

- Their balance sheets were improving, and the companies were using cash flow to pay down debt that they had incurred to purchase larger inventories during the boom.

- Net debt-to-equity ratios were at reasonable levels, with minimal dependence on lines of credit in the rapidly declining market.

- Home deliveries were down 30 percent compared with 20 percent for normal recessions.

- Staff layoffs were in the 10 to 20 percent range, historically typical for tough times.

- Shares were trading at below tangible book value, very close to the trough multiples seen in the prior real estate–led recession.

We believed at the time that the market was factoring in substantial amounts of bad news, and that most of the homebuilders would do much better than just break even in the coming years. Therefore, by the second half of 2007, our indicators revealed that a comfortable margin of safety existed for this group, and we slowly began taking positions in them in basket form. "This is not for the faint at heart," wrote Brandes senior analyst Ralph Birchmeier. "We expect significant nails-scratching-on-a-chalkboard volatility in both stock prices and underlying earnings for the foreseeable future." Although we got into the homebuilders a tad early, we then averaged down, and many of them would be accretive to our U.S. mid-cap strategies over time.

Banks Appear Attractive

By the summer of 2007, the real estate market appeared to be severely challenged. However, we saw the federal initiatives and other measures to prop up the mortgage industry as well timed, constructive, and necessary to help stave off, or at least mitigate, the inevitable collapse. In this context, financial stocks were caught up in the market's dragnet of negativity and were down at least 50 percent, and in some cases as much as 70 percent, by the third quarter of 2007. Naturally, we rolled up our sleeves and got to work, not only scrutinizing commercial and investment banks, but also looking into the interconnected sectors of consumer finance, thrifts, insurers, and even U.S. auto companies, all of which were losing steam for pretty much the same apparent reasons.

Our analysis of the banks' financials overlaid our experiences during past recessions and the tendency for banks to overreact during tough times. These overreactions (1974, 1980, 1991, and 1995) turned out to be highly profitable for investors on the back end, my firm included. Seeing relatively similar opportunities now, we pressed ahead and steadily took or added to positions in the United States, including in AIG. Meanwhile, overseas, we brought on a handful of banks and insurance companies there too.

Our valuations of these holdings included a "mental model" of a worst-case 10 percent nationwide housing correction, which hadn't occurred on a national level in modern history. This model also factored in potential sharper declines in the northeastern and western markets, which had run up the most during the boom. Few people knew that we were facing much more than a worst-case scenario. Based on the information that we had at the time, I still believe that this was a smart value disposition, and it would have worked well for many of the holdings we applied it to, had it not been for forces and developments that we, like many others, unfortunately did not foresee.

Coal Mine Canaries

The first warning signs of looming trouble appeared in the summer of 2007, when two Bear Stearns hedge funds specializing in securitized subprime mortgages suddenly failed. Despite a month of intense yet fruitless restructuring and bailouts by the parent company, the hedge funds eventually filed for bankruptcy at a loss of more than $1.5 billion in shareholder assets.[2]

Hedge funds are the most misnamed securities in the industry. The simple concept of hedging is supposed to help protect the fund against certain risks, such as exposure to currency fluctuations. But many hedge funds are far from simple, and some of them can be convoluted, intricate, and misunderstood by investors. For the Bear Stearns funds, the added layer of rapidly failing mortgage-backed securities catapulted them to dangerous levels of leverage, more commonly known as debt.

Leverage Concerns Emerge

The sequence of events in the long chain of failures, mergers, takeovers, and bankruptcies is well documented. I highlight Bear Stearns, however, because it hit me hard. We didn't hold the parent company's stock, but the failure of its two funds still shocked me, as it showed how dangerous excess leverage had become to the entire global financial arena. Financial technicians at Bear Stearns and other companies had been engineering creative, complicated products for years, some of which were designed to mitigate risk to the bottom lines. But at the end of the day, you need to have capital at the ready when the time comes. Bear Stearns had none. It didn't take the world very long after these failures to discover that few of the other financial giants had it either.

In the wake of the Bear Stearns fund failures, the market absolutely punished banks for their dicey loan books. Meanwhile, the Federal Reserve scrambled to do its part by freeing up as much liquidity as possible, including a ramp-up to its extended series of "quantitative easing" programs. The central bank sequentially pushed target rates lower and launched an armada of "lending facilities" lifeboats to help support federal agency debt and mortgage-backed securities. The system needed money, and fast. Although there were a lot of sick patients, triage pointed to one priority: housing. "Fix housing, and you'll fix the crisis," was the general consensus from Washington.

Soon enough, there were two more canaries: the mortgage companies IndyMac and Countrywide Financial; we held a sizable position in the latter. We knew that there were problems at Countrywide long before we invested in it. Value opportunities often involve investments in companies with problems—often problems that may take time and patience to work through. It was well known that the secondary market for nonconforming mortgage securities, of which Countrywide was among the largest underwriters, had all but dried up. Such droughts had happened before, and Countrywide had made it through them, coming out ahead at the other end. Other positives were that it was drawing on an $11 billion credit line at major supporting banks and had laid out initiatives to restrict nonconforming loans to 10 percent of its book.[3] These didn't help. The extent of the credit crunch and the growing leverage problem were just too much to withstand. By July 2008, the takeover of Countrywide by Bank of America was finalized at a bargain-basement price of $4 billion.[4] Four months earlier, Bear Stearns—which we did not own—had finally failed, after valiantly struggling to keep up since the hedge fund debacle of the prior year. It too was sold to a larger suitor, JPMorgan Chase, at just $2 a share.[5]

With the sure and steady flow of liquidity into the system, we had little reason to suspect that all the other financial institutions would face the same dire credit challenges as Countrywide and Bear Stearns. Based on what anyone could see, most of the surviving banks appeared to be well capitalized, and our team had full confidence that in a worst-case scenario, they would have the strength to see things through. We were not alone in our convictions. Even the new CEO of Wachovia, Robert Steel, was buying his company's stock for his own account to help send signals of the company's stability.[6] Everyone who was looking for opportunities, including us, suspected that there was trickery going on under the banking shroud, but most of us were coming to the same conclusion: this too shall pass, and these essential businesses will normalize in due time.

Three Conspiring Forces

Normal was not to be. First, short sellers working the angles were becoming a major obstacle to long-term investors. Whether they were "naked" (selling without first borrowing) or operating within portfolio strategies, all of them were betting against the struggling financials. A temporary SEC ban on the short selling of a select group of "systematically important" financial institutions did little to help the situation. A small handful of targeted firms tried to ease their plight through new issues, but this just made their situations worse. The further below book value they were, the more destructive any new issues were to their share price. For some institutions, this became self-fulfilling very quickly, as short sellers continued to bang away wherever they could through 2007 and much of 2008.

Second, the unstable structure of creative mortgage-backed products began to buckle under its own weight. Problems began when auditors began to write down the values of the mortgage-backed securities dealers' holdings significantly. Credit ratings on mortgage obligations also became increasingly foolhardy and unsound. As the rush played out, raters had created entirely new classifications of subprime mortgages that made them appear less risky than they were. Tranches of junk were subdivided into multiple layers of junk, with the best junk among the group being labeled AAA. This was a dangerously misleading classification on any level, let alone when it was multiplied by the billions by all the major banks. Knowing this, how could anyone be sure of the quality of an institution's book of business?

Third, if the junk got too risky, the banks weren't overly concerned. They had taken out insurance to hedge against the possibility of a subprime mortgage failure. They just used credit default swaps (CDSs), and there were plenty to go around. CDSs were designed as a hedge instrument for this very purpose, but things went from bad to worse when they came to be seen as profit generators as well. The emerging irony was that CDSs not only were helping banks hedge against their own subprime loans, but were also enabling them to bet against their own customers. We'd never seen anything like it. As they were rapidly commoditized and bought and sold like securities, they fueled the speculative rush that eventually led to the systemic failure in credit. "With this complicated intertwining of bets of great magnitude, no one could be sure of the financial position of anyone else, or one's own position," wrote economist Joseph Stiglitz. "Not surprisingly the credits markets froze."[7]

Back to Crisis Mode

Return to that day in the fall of 2008, our fifth investment committee meeting in two days, with an unprecedented credit crisis in our laps. This time the discussion pivoted to another incalculable factor working against us: government intervention. Even when you set out to do everything by the book, sometimes the rules are changed on you, and things get beyond your control very quickly. Earlier in the book, I touched on how the challenges and uncertainties of global investing turned tragic when Chilean president Salvador Allende nationalized most of the private companies upon his assumption of power. If you think that couldn't happen in the United States, it did.

At the height of the crisis, the U.S. government decided that it had to stop the bleeding in the financial industry immediately. As a result, companies that we owned, and that we saw as solid, well-run businesses with significant margins of safety, practically evaporated before our eyes as the U.S. government stepped in. The playbook had just changed on many of our key holdings, and while we could discuss the implications, there was little we could do to change their course.

The first to be acquired were Fannie Mae and Freddie Mac, the two primary government-sponsored enterprises (GSEs), which were placed into conservatorship on September 6, 2008. "They can't survive," argued then Treasury secretary Henry Paulson. "We have to fix this if we're going to fix the mortgage market." Although they were burdened by the weight of their subprime holdings, both GSEs had disclosed 18 months earlier that they were through with new purchases of these troubled securities. They saw the handwriting on the wall before almost anyone else did, which to us showed prescient leadership and integrity—another reason that we had taken positions in them. We believed that it was just a matter of time before their ship was righted as they worked the existing junk off their books. The only focus of the conservatorship that was forced upon them was to protect their senior and subordinated debt and mortgage-backed securities. "Common stock and existing preferred shareholders will bear any losses ahead of the government," was the official line from the Federal Housing Finance Agency. From where we stood, they certainly called that one right. We believed that these entities still offered a fantastic opportunity over the next several years, but instead they were caught up with the industry in something much larger and irreversible that would trump even our most conservative fundamental value models.

Fannie and Freddie's situation paled in comparison to the September 16 Treasury takeover of American International Group. AIG was ready to implode under the weight of the credit default swaps it had sold to insure nearly $450 billion in collateralized debt obligations. When the markets collapsed, investors came for their money in accordance with the contract, with Goldman Sachs being the biggest and more successful player that was now expecting to get paid. AIG's ratings downgrades and the subsequent pressure to post additional collateral to back up the swaps became a complicated tale, of which you probably know the outcome. AIG received the largest government bailout in U.S. history. Things suddenly may have looked brighter for AIG after that move. But for its investors, like my firm and the rest of the world, things quickly got a lot dimmer. We were beside ourselves, feeling frustrated and helpless to do much about it. The one thing that we in the value investing world were most concerned about had just happened: a permanent impairment of capital. Volatility? Bad headlines? Bring them on. But when we have an average cost of $30 a share—with a view that the long-run fair value should be much higher—and then are forced by the Feds to sell at $7 a share, this brings to life our worst nightmare.

U.S. Autos

Financials weren't the government's only targets. The big three automakers also received assistance, except that they were more proactive in obtaining it. Leaders from struggling GM and Chrysler approached Congress for a large piece of the initial $700 billion earmarked for the Troubled Asset Relief Program (TARP).[8] After some wrangling, they got a series of generous U.S. tax-payer–funded measures of life support in one form or another that would add up to about $80 billion. Ford, which was doing comparatively well, soon spoke up too and took government loans to pay for "retooling" and other expenses. In hindsight, not taking free money would probably have been an unwise move for Ford, as it could have put the company at a competitive disadvantage at the time. Generally, these loans weren't a government takeover as much as life-giving injections into a struggling private industry.

For GM, the government's actions created about a 60 percent U.S. Treasury ownership stake. The upside is that the money helped. It saved jobs, kept U.S. automakers competitive overseas, protected pensions and other liabilities, and possibly prevented an even larger disaster. We'll never know for sure on that last point, especially when you consider that both companies made out OK when the dust eventually settled.

Although they began in the financial crisis, the challenges facing the auto companies extended to 2009. Year-over-year sales volume was cut in half, as consumers were hard-pressed to secure loans and those who could secure them were looking for the gas-saving qualities that imports offered. For nearly 20 years, U.S. car companies had really bet the farm on the SUV, which was highly profitable but was falling from grace after six years of rising gas prices.

Examining all angles, we built positions in both GM and Ford and continued to average down as their prices dropped. Fewer people were buying cars. We factored this in going in. Who would want to buy a car on the brink of a recession? Or who could, when lenders were tightening up? Among our information resources, however, was a 70-year history of car buyer trends, which consistently showed a boom following cycles of delayed purchases like the one that was underway. Moreover, we believed that the infusion of government funds was helping to prop up the companies' short-term cash flow until the new buyer cycle kicked in. But this just didn't happen.

Our auto positions during this tumultuous 18 months generated many opinions, not only among our investment teams, but between the firm and its clients. While prices were dropping, we all agreed that GM and Ford would eventually return to the mean, but we differed on when. Clients were furious. Some of them saw GM singlehandedly accounting for an 8 to 10 percent drop in their portfolios, even though it had just a 1 percent weighting—an unavoidable symptom of an averaging-down strategy when the stock price is falling rapidly. By the end of 2008, some six months before GM's bankruptcy filing and subsequent removal from the S&P 500 Index, we had liquidated all of our shares. (In an odd twist, it was readded to the benchmark four years later to replace Heinz, which went private when value investor Warren Buffett bought it.) Our ill-fated holding in Ford was also dropped by late spring of 2009 at a gut-wrenching $2 per share.

Everything we had found, scrutinized, and modeled pointed us in the direction of value for these car companies. But what on the surface looked like a 30 percent discount turned out in reality to be a 90 percent chasm when other influential factors suddenly sprung up—these being the unprecedented credit crisis, a tectonic shift in the industry, and a game-changing government intervention (at a loss to taxpayers of $10 billion by the time it was over).[9] Sometimes you have little choice in the matter; you have to just walk away. These unprecedented times were one such moment.

Was a Takeover Necessary?

Regardless of which way you lean politically, you'd be hard-pressed to prove that these government intrusions were truly necessary. Those with more extreme opinions argue that the government's actions represented an outright theft of shareholder value. I partly agree, but I strongly believe that the government acted too soon and, in the case of GM and Chrysler, failed to follow the correct protocol with respect to the companies' debtholders. At GM, for instance, bond owners were offered a swap deal for a small percentage of the stock, but it was evident very quickly that whatever stock they would have received would disappear in an eventual bankruptcy. It took years to unwind the mess.

The auto companies may have been struggling, but they were far from dead. Our hand was forced, and we sold the companies that had been "nationalized" at significant losses. Even with the best intentions, government intervention offers little consolation for current shareholders. It does the government little good, either, when it takes so much debt onto its books by buying them. While GM and Ford later had admirable turnarounds, you'll never convince me that the ends justify the means when the shareholders get hurt in the short term.

Throughout the crisis, we stuck to the playbook, making some adjustments along the way. It wasn't pretty for us, or for anyone else who was managing money that year. Our setbacks in these holdings were not the result of getting them wrong. Actually, we were quashed before we could prove we were right. My investment teams were absolutely convinced then (and still are) that had the government stayed out of it, many of these companies would have done our clients proud. The circumstances were no laughing matter, but I could relate to Kentucky Senator Jim Bunning's lament at a hearing about what he considered a sudden left turn in American enterprise: "When I picked up my newspaper yesterday, I thought I woke up in France. But no, it turns out socialism is alive and well in America."

After the Crisis

Industry fallout from the crisis lingered for years. As the receiver of Bear Stearns and Washington Mutual, JPMorgan Chase bore a costly weight of subsequent lawsuits over fraudulent mortgage-backed securities practices by those firms, and eventually settled for $13 billion in 2013.[10] Bank of America settled related civil charges, many of which were levied directly on some of its top-rank executives, while Citigroup paid $7 billion for its part in CDO improprieties leading up to 2008, releasing it from any further liabilities.[11]

The collapse also forced changes on the U.S. regulatory front that resulted in certain insights into companies going forward. These included tighter stress test rules for banks, such as limits on leverage levels, and consumer protection guidelines under the new Dodd-Frank Wall Street Reform Act. Morgan Stanley and Goldman Sachs, the two major investment banks left standing, agreed to convert to commercial bank status and be subject to tighter oversight. I remain skeptical, however, as banks have a history of making themselves look good, even when they're not, for a very long time.

Looking at our examples, GM and Ford weathered the storm and went on to do relatively well for themselves. But it was years before my firm would consider them again. When GM reemerged as a public company in September of 2010, its relisted stock closed its first day of trading at about $34 per share.[12] Ford, which never filed for bankruptcy, quadrupled its share price by year-end 2009 and hovered at around $15 to $18 for many years.

AIG emerged a leaner, more profitable business and shook off the government yoke by year-end 2012. Fannie Mae and Freddie Mac became relatively profitable and efficient, albeit needing some long-term unwinding that analysts expected would keep them somewhat distracted for decades. Finally, most of the surviving banks, as you know, began a prolonged turnaround in March of 2009.

Financial Crisis Takeaways

A Chinese proverb reminds us that the most important lesson to learn is *not* to learn the wrong lesson. The financial crisis of 2008–2009 was a watershed—a once-in-a-career event for anyone who had a role in managing money or serving clients. Therefore, it's a daunting task and probably ill conceived to over-analyze any textbook-changing impact the crisis may have had on what we do as value managers.

Could we have delayed the purchases of stocks that were falling in price until a little later in the cycle? Are we now more sensitive to a company's leverage situation? Is there more awareness of the interconnectedness and codependence among companies in the same portfolio? To these and similar questions, I respond, perhaps. But you could ask the same questions in 2009, 1974, or 2014, or at any time in the future, and get the same answer. And it will always come back to one theme: it depends on the company.

The financial crisis was an investment climate that I hope we will never see again, for everyone's sake. But it wasn't all bad, either. While the United States bore the brunt of the storm (Europe's major woes came two years later), we found opportunities overseas, particularly in Japan. By selling certain Japanese financials, which hadn't suffered nearly as much as U.S. banks, we were able to pick up a substantial number of undervalued small- and mid-cap telecom and manufacturing companies in that region. These worked out quite well, but they were underappreciated within the larger context.

On another bright note, I couldn't have asked for a better team to work through it. Partners and analysts alike stayed sharp and focused, seemingly tireless through the endless meetings and debates. And there were plenty of debates. But that's what teamwork involves sometimes. Passionate ideas and constructive feedback are the nexus of effective, meaningful client service. Teamwork was exactly what we needed to face this crisis—not to mention a lot of conferences. We didn't make drastic changes in our positions, but the information deluge was so drastic that we made sure to stay in constant touch in case anyone had anything new to share.

The adage that something can be greater than the sum of its parts is spot on when it comes to describing our team-based value investing approach. My firm makes investment decisions by having select committees dedicated to certain strategies. To me, the team-driven approach has always worked well for value investing, and it still does. It's the most effective method for continuously vetting a cross-pollination of original ideas, not to mention continuous checks and balances among a wide range of talented and persistent professionals. It also encourages camaraderie and mentoring of future investment leaders. It can, of course, create tension. But discourse is always kept constructive and respectful by remembering that it's all about the clients, not about us.

Whether we're in crisis mode or on an average day, the disciplines of value investing are solid and apply to any date on the calendar. With informed and persistent process, people, and patience, value gets it right most of the time. When it doesn't, there is something abnormal or unprecedented that foils it. This time, it was both of these: an extended backdrop of hopped-up real estate, excessive leverage, a systemic credit collapse, misleading financial reporting, and an acute market panic. "What we thought was a crack was actually a crevice about 5000 feet deep," reflected Brandes senior partner Jim Brown several years later. "We weren't alone, and our first reaction was to stick to our guns. But it was almost impossible in those conditions to see how serious this was going to be."

What Would Ben Think?

When value does go wrong on the outlier, how do you adjust? How do you factor a government takeover of an otherwise solid company into a price-to-earnings multiple? Will an acute and lasting global dissipation of capital affect a company's book value when its sole purpose is lending money? Would you always factor a catastrophic 30 percent collapse in real estate prices into a builder's cash flow? These are anomalies that even Ben Graham, who lived through the Great Depression, probably wouldn't have imagined possible as single events, let alone occurring as they did—all at once. However, I can't help but wonder what he would have thought if he had seen it all for himself.

Ever humble, especially around his students, Graham often opined that value isn't always perfect even under the best conditions. One insight in particular is forever captured in a transcript of a 1946 lecture at Columbia University:

> *I don't believe any of us have the pretension of believing that by being very good analysts, or by going through very elaborate computations, we can be pretty sure of the correctness of our results. The only thing that we can be pretty sure of, perhaps, is that we are acting reasonably and intelligently. And if we are wrong, as we are likely to be, at least we have been intelligently wrong and not unintelligently wrong. (Laughter.)*[13]

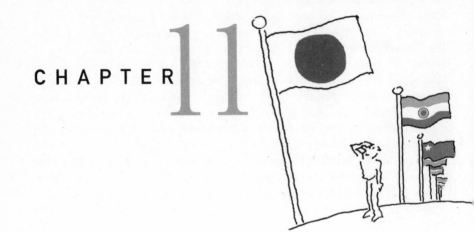

CHAPTER 11

STAYING COMMITTED:

MR. MARKET TAKES VALUE TO TASK—PART 2

井の中の蛙大海を知らず

—Ancient proverb (Translation: "A frog in a well does not know the great ocean.")

The Asian proverb that opens this chapter is about accepting only what you see around you as reality. One version of the folktale has the frog being happy to live at the bottom of a very dark well because that was all he knew. Life was satisfying and unthreatening there. When another frog invited him to see beyond these confines, he accepted. However, he quickly returned to the well, where he was most comfortable, and failed to ever see what the bigger world could have offered him if he had just given it a chance.

This chapter is a reminder that many investors sometimes end up like that frog in the well—they are satisfied to judge things by taking a narrow view while missing out on greater things beyond it. This time we are focusing on Japan, another important example of the contrarian drum that value investors often beat—sometimes for an extended period of time.

Like the situation we examine in Chapter 10, this account is intended to serve as a case study in value investing, for which many scenarios can continuously play out all over the world.

The Lost Decades

After Japan's nearly 45 years of growth following World War II, a powerful real estate and banking collapse in 1989 ushered in a period of economic malaise known as "the lost decades." A subsequent series of banking system and public policy failures and other missteps didn't help to reverse the situation, and the prolonged downturn made the country persona non grata in almost all investment circles. Chronically low inflation, even deflation, productivity woes, and a number of economic growth fetters kept most investors at arm's length for a very long time. *Time* magazine and other periodicals' cover stories during this period helped perpetuate a sense of total hopelessness: "Can Anyone Save Japan?," "Japan's Meltdown," "Deflation Nation," and "Japan's Amazing Ability to Disappoint." From its peak at nearly 40,000, the country's bellwether Nikkei 225 Index sank to 7,400 by mid-2009.

A 45-Year Miracle

Japan had long been considered the miracle of the twentieth century. It began in a very desperate situation in 1945, but over time and through the 1970s, all indicators pointed to a nation that was doing everything right. It was averaging 10 percent annual GDP growth rates, with modernized industries and productivity gains pushing it toward a game-changing shift to exporting dominance.[1] This was a big deal for a partially nonarable island sovereignty that was forced to import much of its food.

Asset Bubble

Enter the 1980s, which for Japan were off the charts. It seemed as if Japanese businesses couldn't do anything wrong. Autos, entertainment, engineering, medicine, and manufacturing all simultaneously whistled while they worked, and the world embraced them. Output credibility made major strides, and the label "Made in Japan" was no longer associated with something cheap or shoddy. Better-quality cars, innovative video games, and high-demand personal electronics and computer peripherals reached new acceptance levels abroad. Decades of inbred quality improvement disciplines started to kick in. If you've ever had the opportunity to compare a ride in one of the early Honda Civic hatchbacks (circa 1975), to one in a later-year Civic, you know exactly what I mean about dramatic improvements.

Kaizen, which means "good change," had been ingrained in Japanese business for decades, but it was now being heard and seen everywhere. The word was heralded as a philosophy in enterprise and a way of life that permeated

Japanese industry and its loyal workers. Soon enough, it became a major export in its own right. U.S. cultural, motivational, and business speakers alike jumped on the *kaizen* quality-control bandwagon—with an immutable forewarning that we needed to start thinking like the Japanese soon, or else.

Against the backdrop of Japan's many wins, we saw all the classic signs of a bubble. In addition to the overheated Nikkei 225, a big problem for us was the rapid expansion in consumerism after a decades-long pattern of frugality as the accepted norm. While higher consumer spending is usually a sign of a strong economy, the Japanese are traditionally the most aggressive savers among developed nations. We felt that if the Japanese were spending, they probably weren't saving as much. And if they weren't saving, what were the Japanese banks using to make all those loans to stock market and real estate speculators? To us, a potential drought in credit and the growing popularity of real estate (on an archipelago only the size of California) could only mean trouble, as the supply could never keep up with the demand.

Japan's Monetary Might

In the early 1980s, Japan's success sparked some concerns about whether it was doing a little *too* well for everyone's comfort. Its longstanding restrictive import policies combined with a consistently weak yen made it a trading powerhouse at an especially vulnerable economic time for the United States and its European allies. Stopping short of potentially destructive protectionism, the Reagan administration summoned finance ministers from Britain, West Germany, France, and Japan to the posh Plaza Hotel in New York City. They were expected to hammer out a deal that everyone could live with before things spun out of control.

The resulting Plaza Accord of 1985 was basically a planned and methodical devaluation of the U.S. dollar against several major currencies: the pre-euro deutsche mark and French franc and, most important to the world at the time, the weaker yen. In theory, everyone—including Europe—wanted to help make American exports more competitive overseas. At first, this worked. By 1987, the dollar and other currencies had fallen about 50 percent versus the yen. Perhaps not coincidentally, the U.S. economy also got a much-needed lift. But it took yet another international pact to put the brakes on the dollar's continuing slide. This one was a comprehensive trade agreement signed in Paris by the G6. The Louvre Accord was a historic step toward adapting the individual fiscal and monetary policies of nations to a global platform, with fair trade hanging in the balance. Even with the best intentions, however, the measure eventually fizzled, leaving the path clear for the current system of floating exchange rates mostly governed by the basic laws of supply and demand.

For Japan, participating in these well-intentioned accords was a huge victory in one sense and a huge defeat in another. On the upside, the accords offered long-needed recognition of the country's growing importance to the international monetary system. However, many observers considered them too restrictive on Japan's central bank, which had to force monetary policies into place that did more harm than good to the country's economy.

We were OK with a little potential slowdown in Japan. We thought the relatively minor recession that hit there in 1986 would help cool the jets and open the doors to value. But things came roaring back by 1987, and more loosening of the money supply meant that nothing was standing in the way of those who wanted to join the speculation party. Taking advantage of cheap money, Japanese leaders of industry and real estate soon joined the ranks of the world's wealthiest landowners. Real estate moguls extended their reach, purchasing iconic properties in New York, Chicago, and Los Angeles. Hawaii was an especially desirable hotbed of investment in resorts and private homes, with an estimated 40 percent of Waikiki condominiums sold in 1987 going to Japanese nationals.[2] An expensive market even in a down year, Aloha State home prices were driven to record levels, to the chagrin of many locals, for whom housing suddenly became practically unobtainable.

At their peak, Japanese real estate prices reached ridiculous levels, averaging ¥6.4 million ($45,000) and ¥890,000 ($6,000) *per square meter* for residential and commercial property, respectively.[3] We saw skyrocketing rents in Tokyo, forcing millions of workers to pull up stakes and move to surrounding prefectures (jurisdictions), doubling the average commute time to as much as two hours each way.

Domo, No

While most of the market lauded the success story, my firm watched from afar and had no interest in investing in Japan. The mere fact that the relatively small Nikkei 225 had become the most highly capitalized stock market in the world was all we needed to tell us to keep our hands off the merchandise.

Our aversion to Japanese stocks was met with some unpleasantness. "You may want to consider finding another line of work," began one financial advisor's written account-closure notification. "You're not just overlooking opportunities here; you're missing out on the biggest stock story in decades." The acrimony prevailed for years. But we knew in our minds that this was *not* going to end well for investors in Japan.

Besides, we were landing plenty of fish in other waters—with all the attention being focused on Japan, we found quiet victories in other corners of the world. We found opportunities in places like Germany, Holland, and even Japan's backyard—Hong Kong. At the end of the day, our bruises from dissatisfied clients were more than soothed by our steady international and global portfolio outperformance for most of those years—largely because of our near-zero weighting in Japan.

Then, Collapse

Although 1980s Japan and the financial crisis of 2008–2009 discussed in Chapter 10 were two very different sets of circumstances, they share a common thread. Both had their roots in a systemic failure in credit, but with differing outcomes.

"Once you're so far out there on the tree limb, it doesn't take much for the wind blowing in either direction to cause things to fall," recalls Matt Johnson, a tenured associate of the firm who often presents our Japan investment strategies. "As in a lot of bubbles, there was more than a kernel of truth to what was being done very well in Japan throughout that time, but it was all overhyped."

Besides the fact that excess and speculation will always come home to roost, much of the blame for the inevitable Japanese asset price collapse fell on the ill-timed and weak monetary policies of the Bank of Japan (BOJ). We agreed with the eventual consensus that the BOJ had placed too little emphasis on stabilizing inflationary asset prices at home, in favor of strengthening the currency situation.

By 1989, property values had fallen to one-third of peak prices and the air was being sucked right out of the banking system. Banks had no liquidity to support them during the failing loan debacle that quickly unfolded. Even the country's *keiretsu*, an interlocking system of businesses, stock cross-ownership, and shared financial risk, couldn't work right. *Keiretsu* was designed to help stabilize and grow postwar Japan, and it usually helped businesses weather difficult times. But it just couldn't operate effectively in these dire conditions. The bubble burst, the market crashed, the loans went bad, and the money needed to turn it all around just wasn't there.

This is not to suggest that we knew the crash would be as sudden and extended as it was. Providing specific predictions of the future is not our business. Our emphasis is on using the past, combined with a disciplined focus on company fundamentals, to help *position* ourselves for the future. That said, this omnipotent downturn that was now on the history books adroitly flipped our view of Japan. The country now began to show opportunities among the good companies that this still very industrious nation could offer to value investors like us.

Same Coin, Other Side

There's a popular assumption that when the dam breaks, value floats to the top. The truth is that it's not that simple. Stock prices may become unlinked from real company values during an economic malaise, but it can take a while to sift through the mud when something as big as Japan occurs. "Japan is still too hot, even after the bubble burst," I told *Barron's* as late as 1990. "Value opportunities are out there in the world, but you're still more likely to find value in a cement company in Monterrey, Mexico than in Oita, Japan right now."

I wasn't joking, either. Cheaper doesn't always mean cheap. Even when things started to go south in Japan, it was still a very expensive market across the board by historical standards. But patience is the *sine qua non* for value investing. Eventually, opportunities started to show themselves by 1993.

What Brought Us Back

Figures 11-1 to 11-3 offer a glimpse of why Japan soon became a viable opportunity set for value investing and remained so for quite some time. For example, our research revealed valuation dispersions that were the widest among the developed markets. In fact, Japan began an extended period of offering non-U.S. value opportunity sets that were well above those of the United Kingdom, Europe, and Canada.

Throughout this time, key considerations for our valuations of individual Japanese companies included:

- *Deleveraging progress.* It took the better part of two decades to complete, but an emphasis on deleveraging followed the bursting of the asset bubble almost immediately, leaving many Japanese corporate balance sheets relatively strong.

- *Substantial cash flows.* Soon enough, the number of Japanese companies with more than 25 percent of their market capitalization in cash far exceeded that of any other nation.

- *More profitable than they appear.* Japanese companies typically have lower returns on equity than U.S. companies, but in many cases this is a function of conservative accounting and a rather complicated tax structure (discussed in Chapter 7). When valuations of Japanese companies are adjusted for the excess cash on their balance sheets, their price-to-earnings ratios tend to be significantly lower, and their returns on equity are often higher. This is especially true of pharmaceutical companies.

- *More focus on shareholders.* An increased focus on managing costs and a ramp-up in dividend payments and share buybacks showed us that Japanese companies were focusing more on returns to shareholders rather than life support.

- *Unwinding keiretsu.* Japan's extensive and cozy cross-shareholding system, *keiretsu*, which has historically protected underperformers and insulated many companies from change, has been rapidly unwound (cross-shareholdings between Japanese companies fell to 21.3 percent of total outstanding shares by 2013).[4]

- *Improved Sino-Japanese relations.* Agreements between China and Japan allowing companies to convert their respective currencies directly into each other without first converting them into U.S. dollars were a boon to large Japanese companies that had to rely on a more costly currency regime.

Many of these considerations are among the primary reasons that Japanese companies, particularly in the small-cap range, offered many "net-net" value opportunities. Recall from Chapter 6 that net-net involves calculating a company's value by subtracting all of its liabilities from its current assets. A company with positive net-net current assets theoretically could pay off all its liabilities with cash and securities and still have some left over. As long as the company was also generating profits, net-net was an effective way to identify the more appealing value companies in Japan for many years.

Discovering Japan

Three Primary Focal Areas for Finding Value Opportunities in "the Lost Decades:"

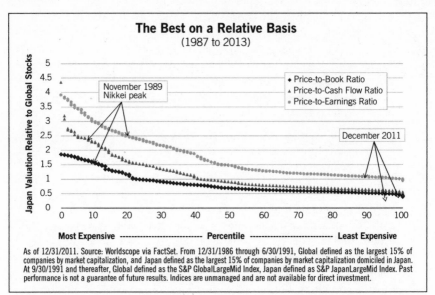

Figure 11-1 After the asset price bubble burst in 1991, Japanese companies in the Nikkei 225 began a steady slide to record low valuations in the three key metrics of price-to-earnings, price-to-book, and price-to-cash flow.

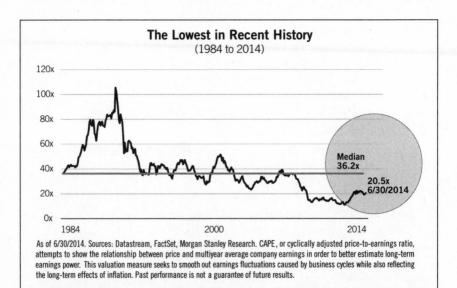

Figure 11-2 Price-to-earnings ratios for the Tokyo Stock Exchange remained at historic lows for a very long time following the bursting of the bubble, especially in the post-financial crisis years of 2009–2014.

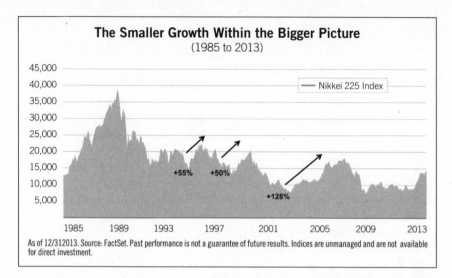

The Smaller Growth Within the Bigger Picture
(1985 to 2013)

Nikkei 225 Index

+55%   +50%

+128%

As of 12/312013. Source: FactSet. Past performance is not a guarantee of future results. Indices are unmanaged and are not available for direct investment.

Figure 11-3 Most investors focus on the bigger story—a 25,000-point decline in the Nikkei Index from peak to trough over more than two decades. However, within this time period, there have been some opportunities to participate in positive market returns.

Oh Yes to Ono

An example of some of these important attributes in full bloom is Osaka-based Ono Pharmaceutical Co., Ltd., a mid-tier drug manufacturer with about a 2 percent share of the Japanese market. We initially purchased Ono in 2001, around the time that clinical trials of a potentially important new drug were halted in the United States. Other potential dents in the company's armor were a high patent expiration risk and a relatively weaker product pipeline than its peer companies. But we also couldn't overlook its strong balance sheet, cash flows, and year-over-year return on equity.

In addition to what we felt were hospitable valuations, Ono had significant cash and investments, which at various points on the timeline represented more than 50 percent of the company's market capitalization. Investors seemed overly punitive in valuing Ono's research and development drag, mainly because of the company's noticeable dearth of late-stage drug candidates; however, we knew from experience that pipelines can and do turn around.

We also saw most of the market as overreacting to Ono's revenues and earnings being derived from one market, Japan, where the government mandates potentially painful biennial price cuts. We also thought that there was too much focus on the *perceived* inefficient capital structures of the day. That is, no allowance was

(continued)

made for the *potential* for cash deployment—for example, acquisitions, dividend payouts, or share buybacks.

These were just signs of the times to us. Like many Japanese companies, Ono was stockpiling as much cash and investments as possible on its balance sheets. This was normal practice during the 2000s. The long shadow of uncertainty, a fragile financial system, a deflationary environment, and a vigilant desire to *save for a rainy day* normally fueled a constant conservative mindset. We were OK with that, too.

Ono reflects our long-term, patient investment philosophy on several levels. In an industry where the R&D pipeline often requires 10 to 15 years to bear fruit, the ability, willingness, and patience to see beyond short-term market concerns are the keys to success. But patience sometimes requires a little nudge, and Ono is one of the companies in which my firm engaged in shareholder activism.

Throughout our long holding period, we initiated many constructive meetings with Ono's leaders, some of which led management to improve the company's balance sheet. As a 7 percent stakeholder in the company at one point, we felt obligated to step up in the interests of all shareholders and get Ono to up the ante on its return to shareholders. After some back-and-forth, Ono eventually increased its dividend, bought back shares, and deployed its capital to license products in its pipeline.

Is Japan a Value Trap?

Despite the evidence, there was a popular countercontention that Japan was just a value trap. In concept, a value trap suggests that stocks may be selling cheap, but they will never recover from the weight of the larger issues that they face. Before we knew it, we heard that all-too-familiar drumbeat kick up again. The flack was coming at us, only this time from the reverse angle. Now, instead of wanting us to run *into* Japan with cash in hand, clients and brokers wanted us *out* of there. "Don't you know that their population is just getting older?" was the most common jab. "Where is the value in that?" My personal favorite was, "Your team must work in a basement, because your line of sight just can't see that the Nikkei has sunk to somewhere around the floor joists."

We knew that Japan had an aging demographic, which could put a strain on the cash-hungry national retirement system. But there was much more to that story. Although the official retirement age in Japan remains low compared to most western countries, the de facto retirement age—when individuals actually retire—is very high. This propensity for older Japanese to continue to work means that the demographic situation in Japan as it relates to pension strain is far less acute than we are led to believe.

As for the market itself, the Nikkei had lost its thunder, to be sure. But there were short yet sustained periods of market gains during those infamous decades, such as 55 percent here, 50 percent there, and a 128 percent uptick from 2002 to 2006 (see Figure 11-3) that offered periods of growth for undervalued companies. Among them were three Japanese auto giants—Nissan, Honda, and Toyota—that were beginning to reflect their intrinsic values again. We have owned all three at one point in time or another.

Over the years, the market has taken a constant negative view of Japan for many macro reasons, including sovereign fiscal deficits, high taxes, and a general lack of confidence about whether the country would be able to overcome the economic challenges that have plagued it since 1991. But we never let these factors overshadow the unique opportunities that many Japanese companies presented to the rational, long-term value investor. We may have been among only a few believers, but our diligence in Japan had established a noticeable, consistent pattern of benefiting our global and international strategies as we approached the twentieth anniversary of the bubble bursting.

The 2011 Tsunami

Just when it was showing some consistent progress on a macro level, Japan suffered a tragedy in March 2011 that piled on new misery: the Tohoku earthquake and subsequent tsunami that started the Fukushima nuclear plant disaster.

Our hearts were torn by the massive loss of life and catastrophic damage to the Japanese countryside and psyche. It also hit very close to home for Brandes, as one of our senior analysts, Shingo Omura, was near the end of a 10-day research trip to the country. Fortunately, he was in Tokyo, so he was not in the damaged area and was able to return to our headquarters the following day.

Our scramble to evaluate the situation was well underway by the time Shingo landed in San Diego. We developed a plan to reach out to everyone that we knew or served who may have been affected by the tragedy. Our analysts reexamined every Japanese holding for potential impact, checking everything we could on the deepening nuclear crisis against the possible implications for the companies we held, their people, and whatever else we could think of at the time. The firm's client-facing professionals, as well as the communications team led by Ray Lewis, worked over the weekend to put together a client outreach initiative. A webinar for clients and brokers alike was held early that week, led by senior international investment team members and a freshly rested Shingo. We also wrote personal letters to the management of every Japanese company that we held, just to remind them that they were in our thoughts and that we were here if they needed us.

Not surprisingly, our Japanese holdings were hit hard in the immediate aftermath, starting with a 20 percent drop along with the market within just a few days.[5] However, it wasn't that long before they began to recover, and the overall Japanese economic picture brightened again in the following months.

Fast-forward just a few years, and Prime Minister Shinzo Abe was taking dramatic steps, known as *Abenomics*, toward long-term improvements. Abe's "three-arrow" approach targeted monetary easing, fiscal stimulus, and structural reform. Other macro tailwinds, such as a weakening yen (making exports competitive overseas) and a stabilizing euro (a big market for Japanese products), continued to provide a backdrop for opportunities, albeit not as many as before. And that's OK, too. If we're finding fewer value companies in any country, we'd much prefer that it be because that country is prospering than for any other reason.

Finding Value in Japan

Generally, my firm navigated the touch-and-go decades with allocations to Japan that were roughly one-third in defensive industries and sectors (such as pharmaceuticals, telecom, and consumer staples), one-third in exporters (such as technology companies and autos), and one-third in financials (including banks and property and casualty insurance companies). We believed that this three-legged stool offered holdings that—in normal circumstances—were in well positioned, globally competitive companies with an attractive market presence and clean balance sheets.

Japan's Improving Path

Today's picture of Japan is one of a country with a very high quality of life that continues to improve. Advancements and better access to healthcare are further increasing life expectancies, which typically surpass those in the United States by some 10 years for men and women. The country's unemployment rate is consistently lower than that in other developed nations, usually at about 4 percent, and has typically been half that of the United States at practically every turn.

Housing prices have yet to return to where they were before the boom, but deflation seems to be much less of a threat after years of central bank booster shots to the country's money supply. From a business development perspective, Japan has led the world in commercial building, even during its darkest years, constructing nearly 100 high-rises (buildings of more than 50 stories) during those lost decades, compared to about 50 in Chicago, 60 in New York City, and less than 10 in Los Angeles for the same period. As a general observation, I find Japan's major cities vibrant and the efficiencies of its airports, trains, and other transportation infrastructure excellent.

"Japan's achievement is all the more impressive for the fact that its major competitors—Germany, South Korea, Taiwan and, of course, China—have hardly been standing still," was one 2012 *New York Times* guest opinion from economist Earmon Fingleton, who had also predicted the 1990 bust. I agree.

With the wounds from the lost decades still so fresh, everyone quickly gets worried about growth in Japan any time its market flinches. But in a slow-growth environment, the Japanese market usually offers companies that are extremely cheap on the basis of their net asset value, profits, and cash on their balance sheets.

Time and again, despite occasional, even powerful macroeconomic forces, the best indicator of a company's long-term stock price movement is derived from that company's underlying fundamentals and the price one pays to acquire its shares. This was true during the asset price bubble in Japan, when bullish investors ignored well-above-average prices and valuations in favor of positive macroeconomic forecasting, only to get burned in the end.

Whether it is in or out of favor, Japan will always be held up as a miracle just for what it accomplished in the decades following World War II. Its diverse economic machine continues to offer value investors opportunities in a wide range of industries, from technology to tobacco and from pharmaceuticals to farming equipment. I'm convinced that great things are still ahead for Japan, and that value opportunities will be revealed to those who are willing to venture beyond the restrictions of "the well" and take the time to look around for them.

CHAPTER 12

STAYING ON TARGET:
INVESTIGATING
INVESTOR BEHAVIOR

Market knowledge and experience are essential: But having insight into investor behavior and how it is influencing the value of companies is empowering.

—Charles Brandes, in an interview with *Australian Financial Digest*, 2011

Investors have long demonstrated a strong penchant for using their hearts rather than their heads. In *Security Analysis*, Ben Graham and David Dodd introduced the term "the investment fraternity" to refer to people who are motivated "as much by eagerness for quick profits as they are by ignorance and by lack of interest in the fundamentals of security values."[1] In his follow-up book 15 years later, Graham admitted that he did not choose *Intelligent Investor* for the title to suggest a higher IQ. Instead, he meant patient, focused, and with a desire to constantly learn—"a trait more of the character than of the brain," he wrote.[2]

When done correctly, value investing gets you up close and personal with companies in ways that no other investment strategies can. You get to see how companies work, and to interpret the context in which they make money. You also need to understand how most investors value companies and the ways in which their actions and reactions can separate a company's stock or bond price from the underlying value of the business. That's why you always have to be on top of trends and understand the influences of human behavior.

"If It Isn't Behavioral . . ."

In Chapter 4, I touched on behavioral biases that influence the way people see and respond to information. While these psychological understandings have been around for a long time, applying them to the investment world is a more recent development. Seeing *how* investors react and the impact of their decisions was easy. Understanding *why* they made these decisions remained a mystery until behavioral economics became the framework for interpreting investor behavior.

Berkshire Hathaway vice chairman Charles Munger identified the need to study the impact of human psychology on economics and markets in 1995. At a guest lecture at Harvard University, Munger was ahead of his time in sharing his modern view on "the psychology of human misjudgment." He worked through a list of well-known behavior catalysts such as incentives, reinforcement, association, reciprocation, and social proof and concluded that economic theories must embrace them all if they are to account for inconsistencies. "If there is anything valid in psychology, economics has to recognize it, and vice versa," said Munger. "People that are working on this fringe between economics and psychology are absolutely right to be there. . . . How could economics *not* be behavioral? If it isn't behavioral, what the hell is it?"[3]

Munger, and others who shared his logic, argued that convergence was more than just an assortment of general observations, and he challenged those in the room "to array facts around the terribly important question of *why*." The floodgates were thereby opened. Many books were subsequently written, and a growing recognition of and appreciation for the inseparable bond between investment decisions and basic human emotional responses emerged.

Soon enough, behavioral finance blossomed in academia. Nobel Prize–winning economist Dr. Robert Shiller was among the leaders with his best-selling 2000 book *Irrational Exuberance,* a term that had been coined four years earlier by former Fed chairman Alan Greenspan to refer to the tech bubble. In his book, Shiller laid the groundwork for the investor psychology that had led to the bubble's bursting, which coincidentally began almost on the day the book was released. "News events that are more likely to be transmitted in informal conversations are in turn more likely to contribute to the contagion of ideas," wrote Shiller.[4] "Envy of others who may have made more in the stock market than one earned at work in the past year is related to painful feeling, especially so in that it diminishes one's ego."[5]

Irrational Exuberance inspired a wide range of scholastic interest in the topic of behavioral finance. The winners of the 2002 Nobel Prize in Economics, for example, were Daniel Kahneman and Vernon L. Smith, who integrated psychology into their studies of economies and financial markets. The Royal Swedish Academy of Sciences lauded Kahneman for applying psychological factors to "human judgment and decision making under uncertainty." His experiments showed that investors tend to exhibit "short-sightedness in interpreting data that could explain large fluctuations on financial markets."[6]

In 2007, Richard Peterson went even further in investigating the workings of investors' thought processes with *Inside the Investor's Brain*. A former trader, Dr. Peterson argued that investors' self-defeating tendencies were as much physical as mental, and that most humans just weren't hard-wired to be effective at making money in the financial markets. "Such biased behavior is rooted in the brain's hard-wired cognitive and emotional systems," he wrote. "As a result of their deep subconscious origins, such biases are challenging to identify in oneself, much less correct."[7]

Behavioral finance insights were soon everywhere, with additional ideas emerging regularly. Today, there are many differing opinions about investor behavior, but one thing everyone agrees on is that it will always be a driving force in the markets, and vice versa.

Vetting Market Sentiment

Misdirected investor behavior usually leaves some interesting footprints. Beyond the predictable tendency to separate a company's price from its value, market sentiment can offer some interesting and useful hard data as well. Numbers don't lie, and when you're looking for answers to hard questions that affect what you do, you need them practically in real time. For example, my firm constantly wants to know the current answers to standing questions like:

- Is investor sentiment aligned with what is actually happening in the market?

- Are there metrics to support a frequent investor aversion to specific investment styles?

- What disconnections might there be between where investors are looking for opportunities and which products are actually more beneficial to them?

- To what extent is the changing product landscape affecting the effectiveness of individual and institutional investors?

- How do today's attitudes compare to traditional views on risk, retirement income, and asset allocation, and are any differences helping or hurting investor effectiveness?

We need to ask these and other important questions at every turn, not just for my firm's sake, but for clients, brokers, plan sponsors, high school and college educators, and students of finance—anyone who is interested in bettering his or her own investment knowledge. We quickly discovered that inquisitiveness was one thing, but finding the answer was another matter. So, around 2001, we decided to take matters into our own hands and laid plans for a new division of the company that could devote time and resources not only to asking honest questions like these, but to sharing the answers beyond our walls.

The Brandes Institute

In 2002, we launched the Brandes Institute. At first, the goal was to create an in-house barometer to gauge weather conditions for the market, with an obvious tilt toward value topics. This soon expanded into a think tank with a broader mandate. Today, the Institute comprises an 11-member advisory board of majority non-Brandes academics, public trustees, plan sponsors, and industry observers who contribute and share information to help *anyone* make better-informed decisions.

The Institute is now a vital component of Brandes's commitment to thought leadership. Its larger mission is to serve as an objective research and reporting arm to challenge perceptions, raise awareness, and educate colleagues, clients, consultants, and the broader investment community on various topics of interest.

"Value Versus Glamour"

One of the first subjects the Institute tackled was updating the academic "Value Versus Glamour" study that had been released years earlier. The concept's origins were in the Graham-and-Dodd sentiment that unpopular value stocks are often those of companies that are experiencing hard times, operating in mature industries, or facing similarly adverse circumstances. The general consensus is that they're boring, unloved, and slow. Meanwhile, fast-growing firms tend to function in dynamic industries that many people associate with faster-paced activity. They're cutting-edge, exciting, and *glamorous*. This stark contrast between the firms' "softer" attributes naturally leads to the question: Are there hard quantitative data on these two types of stocks that can show which performs better?

The original idea to compare the two camps, as I introduced in Chapter 3, came from three university professors who referred to them as "Value Versus Glamour." In 1994, the respected academic periodical *Journal of Finance* published the work of Professors Josef Lakonishok, Andrei Shleifer, and Robert Vishny (collectively, LSV). At the time, "Contrarian Investment, Extrapolation, and Risk" was one of the most detailed performance comparisons between the two stock types that had ever been made.[8] Without a deep dive into the study's mechanics, suffice it to say that LSV's meticulous trials drew a resounding, well-documented conclusion: value stocks consistently outperformed glamour stocks by wide margins. The original trend line of their results is captured in Figure 12-1. An important aspect of the original LSV study that we left intact was its methodology of sorting the entire universe of stocks into deciles, based on valuations. The 10 percent with the highest price-to-book ratios were grouped in the first decile, those with the second-highest 10 percent were placed in the second decile, and so forth through 10 deciles. Thus, deciles 1–3 represented glamour stocks, while the higher valuation measures of deciles 8–10 represented those with metrics reflecting value stocks (lower price-to-earnings, price-to-book value, and price-to-cash flow metrics).

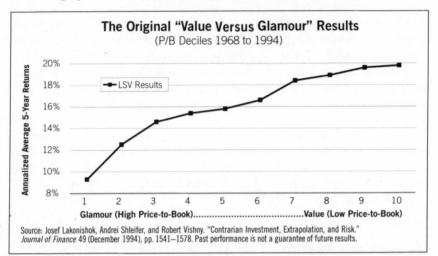

Figure 12-1 The original LSV study results showed how stocks with a "value" tilt outperformed those with a growth or "glamour" label, based on the price/book valuations of the sampled stocks. Each plot point represents annualized performance for the groups over five years. Stocks with glamour (growth) characteristics tended to perform worse than value stocks over the period. The complete methodology is available at www.brandes.com/institute.

Bringing the Data Closer to Home

The LSV study was an excellent foundation, but nearly a decade later, the Institute "retested" it with a thorough revisit and expansion of the original but dated output. We had to know whether value was still working as well as it had been, because so much had changed for the strategy and for the markets during those years. Bringing the study up to date included widening its scope to include stocks beyond the U.S. markets and overlaying some volatility implications and investor expectations, the latter of which I reviewed in Chapter 4.

Following in the footsteps of LSV, the Institute started with all the firms traded on the New York and American Stock Exchanges in 1968. It then added stocks so that it included the universe of Nasdaq issues, trimmed the smallest 50 percent of the sample (to make the expanded universe more representative of an institutional investor's investable universe), and also split the revised sample into large- and small-cap companies.

Our results from later years helped reinforce our convictions: value still works, and this is equally apparent among large and small companies (see Figure 12-2). In 2012, the Brandes approach told the same story overseas, echoing another ongoing sentiment that value knows no borders. A wide array of global value stocks outperformed glamour stocks not only in the United States, but in non-U.S. developed and emerging markets as well. We have continued to extend the data as years go by, with one such report in 2012 being summarized in Figure 12-3.

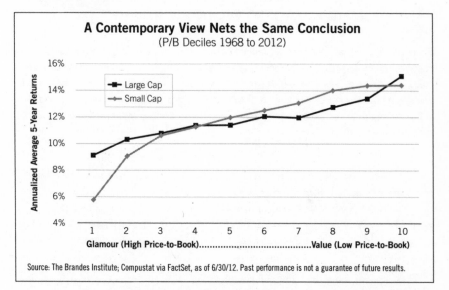

A Contemporary View Nets the Same Conclusion
(P/B Deciles 1968 to 2012)

Glamour (High Price-to-Book)..Value (Low Price-to-Book)

Source: The Brandes Institute; Compustat via FactSet, as of 6/30/12. Past performance is not a guarantee of future results.

Figure 12-2 With the LSV methodology having been refined and widened by the Brandes Institute, later studies showed that average returns for glamour stocks were significantly lower than average returns for value stocks for both small- and large-cap stocks. If the markets were actually efficient, as most investors think they are, these lines would not slope upward from left to right. Over time, we see a very clear value premium, a reward that accrues to value investors who have had the patience to stick with it.

Value versus glamour remains a key focal point of the Institute, whose wide mandate also includes investigating areas beyond behavioral finance, such as portfolio construction, risk, and market trends. The most recent body of work is available to the general public at www.brandes.com/institute and includes some important work on behavioral topics and risk, such as:

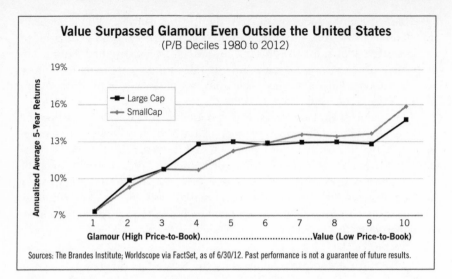

Value Surpassed Glamour Even Outside the United States
(P/B Deciles 1980 to 2012)

Annualized Average 5-Year Returns

- Large Cap
- SmallCap

Glamour (High Price-to-Book)..Value (Low Price-to-Book)

Sources: The Brandes Institute; Worldscope via FactSet, as of 6/30/12. Past performance is not a guarantee of future results.

Figure 12-3 Periodically, the Brandes Institute extends the value versus glamour comparison methodology first used by LSV to include later years. Through 2012, results continue to show that stocks that lean toward a value style (lower valuations) have offered better returns than those that lean toward glamour, or a growth style (higher valuations), over the long run. In this example, the outperformance extends overseas among both small- and large-cap companies.

Boomers behaving badly. Fear and misinformation may be prompting the world's baby boomers to adopt a far-too-conservative approach to their retirement assets. With interest rates uncertain and people living longer than ever, increasing the portion of their investments allocated to stocks—even during retirement—may prevent investors from outliving their assets.

Behavioral finance and investment management. This includes firsthand accounts of the effects of biases on investment selection, asset allocation, and risk management, and tips for countering those biases.

The role of expectations. Expectations about company earnings have played a key role in investors' assessment of value and glamour stocks, a pattern of events that has allowed value stocks to outperform over the long term. Chapter 4 highlights some points from this study.

Broad is the new narrow. Passive investing, particularly in emerging markets, has become an increasingly popular means of quick, "diversified" exposure to a particular segment of the markets. But the presumption of diversification can lead investors astray. Many passive investments are, in fact, extremely concentrated because of the disproportionate size of their largest holdings and blindly weighting by market capitalization.

Death, taxes, and short-term underperformance. Just about every active manager has taken its turn at the bottom of the performance rankings. These studies—on various classes—show that short-term underperformance, especially for long-term leaders, can be as inevitable as death and taxes.

Risks of risk parity. While risk parity offers potential advantages, its success hinges on key assumptions and a favorable environment for bonds. It can also use a narrow definition of risk and fail to take into consideration a critical element in long-term investing: valuations.

Floating-rate bonds. Floating-rate bonds (FRB) and FRB funds are attracting investors who are searching for more income and capital protection. Strong performance has compounded the attraction. The primary benefits of FRBs seem compelling, but there are risks: credit risk, liquidity risk, concentration risk, and valuation risk.

Private equity versus public equity. While private equity (PE) may offer exceptional return potential, investors should be extremely cautious when contemplating this asset class. The current, widely used method for calculating the internal rate of return (IRR) for PE funds can be misleading. Because of various factors, including costs and lack of liquidity, investors may be better served by investing in public equities, particularly small-cap stocks.

Applying What We Have Learned

Decades before the term *behavioral finance* was coined, Graham knew very well that investing in sound businesses was an important component of long-term success—but not the *only* component. He was also aware of the market's occasional irrationality, and he urged investors to exploit its short-term swings in temperament by purchasing out-of-favor stocks when they were offered at bargain prices, and selling them when *emotion* drove them toward or beyond their true underlying value.

Little changed in the years that followed. "Nothing sedates rationality like large doses of effortless money," went the Buffett quote in 2001,[9] followed by his iconic, "Try to be fearful when others are greedy and greedy only when others are fearful," from 2005.[10]

Behavioral finance helps to explain the tendency for investors to emotionally and consistently separate market prices from company valuations, enabling value investors to purchase high-quality securities "on sale." The Graham-and-Dodd principles may be timeless, but on the superhighway that is the modern market, it helps to keep them roadworthy. You have to revisit them, double-check them, and, above all, validate your course. Munger's 1995 challenge at Harvard to keep asking why was soon followed by LSV and the Brandes Institute asking the very same thing as they blazed ahead with value versus glamour.

With discovery comes a sense of obligation to share what you learn and encourage open discussion. Value strategies often benefit from human folly. So, I think that investors, clients, and anyone else who follows the value beacon can benefit from thought leadership on the topic, whether it comes from the Institute or from any other curriculum honed by the school of rational thought. "To leave the world a better place . . . this is to have succeeded," wrote Ralph Waldo Emerson. I agree that we should all give something back, and I earnestly believe that it's also in every value investor's best interest to put in the time for oneself, observe human tendencies, and interpret any findings.

CHAPTER 13

STAYING FOCUSED:
EVERYTHING OLD IS NEW AGAIN

Isn't life a series of images that change as they repeat themselves?

—Andy Warhol

In the late 1970s, the wildly popular Van Halen hit *You Really Got Me* introduced a classic to a new generation. It ushered in a unique and exciting sound for rock music, but to my ears, it was just a remake of the Kinks' original song from 14 years before.[1] If you're around long enough, you start to see these repetitive patterns in all walks of life.

In the music business, cover versions and samplings are usually a form of flattery. In financial services, trying to repurpose an old investment as the next big thing is a little more complicated, but it's done all the time. Investors are constantly hit with newfangled approaches to long-tried tactics and financial products. To me, these inventions are just old and sometimes fishy approaches repackaged in new wrappings.

Then and Now

Let's take a look at some of the more obvious repackagings that I have seen over the years (Figure 13-1).

Then & Now	
What Once Was...	**Later Became...**
Top-Down Forecasting (1960s on)	Macro Hedge Funds, Risk-On Risk-Off
Portfolio Insurance (1987)	Derivative Protection
Commodities, Swaps, Commercial Real Estate (1970s on)	Alternatives, Currencies, Private Equity
Flight from Equities (1979 to 1983)	Portfolio Derisking

Figure 13-1 What may have been tried before, *and often not been effective*, is often repackaged as something new and different as time goes by.

Macro hedge funds, also known as *global macro strategies*, invest broadly in instruments like currencies, interest-rate swaps, and indexes based on economic policies and capital movements around the world. The same is true for *risk-on risk-off* approaches, which typically entail moving asset-class risk selection up or down based on perceptions of market volatility. Except in name, these approaches barely differ from the "big picture" *top-down forecasting* strategies that many mutual funds have used for decades.

Derivative protection refers to strategies designed to hedge your bets, typically with a complicated basket of options "derived from" price changes in the underlying investment (but not the actual investment). *Portfolio insurance*, which was a computer-based version of the same principle, was a short-lived approach in 1987. It was among the leading causes of Black Monday on October 19, 1987, the devastating crisis with which I opened this book.[2]

Since the 1970s, *commodities*, *swaps*, and *commercial real estate* have helped investors step out beyond the traditional asset classes of stocks, bonds, and cash. Somewhere along the line, however, commodities were rebranded as *alternatives*, such as precious metals, hard assets, and natural resources. Similarly, the basic concepts of *swaps* and *commercial real estate* are part of the frameworks of modern, but not necessarily better, *currencies strategies* and *private equity*.

The *flight from equities* was heralded in the 1979 *BusinessWeek* cover story "The Death of Equities," which I discussed in Chapter 1. Willing investors in the stock market dropped to historic levels as the perfect storm of rising interest rates, inflation, and a recession pushed them away, but only temporarily. Fast-forward to a similar hangover from the financial crisis of 2008–2009, and a fear of the "risks" of stocks created a market that was hungry for the "safety" of fixed-income and cash instruments. In turn, *derisking* became the new vernacular.

Complicating Matters

Especially disconcerting to me is the ever-expanding number of complicated products that are not well thought out and can come back to haunt investors. Many of these products have so many layers of mechanical processes and structure that there is a lingering question as to whether investors really understand what they own. What's more, I'm convinced that so much choice is not necessary.

Robert Maynard, the chief investment officer for the Public Employee Retirement System of Idaho, summed up the situation even better in his 2013 study "Conventional Investing in a Complex World": "The capital markets are a complex, interactive, tightly coupled, and adaptive world. But the best response is *not* automatically a complex, tightly organized, and highly opportunistic investment structure."[3]

An accomplished pension steward, Maynard concluded that even in a complex and turbulent market, the best response was a simple, transparent, and focused portfolio—both for long-term returns and for purposes of real risk control.

But Wait, There Is More

The proliferation of sophisticated product offerings became especially prevalent following the financial crisis of 2008–2009. Here's my perspective on a handful of the more highly touted offerings that have captured investors' attention over the years—not to mention their assets.

Shorting

Shorting represents everything that I do *not* do as a value investor. As I see it, shorting is little more than a zero-sum game in which there can be a winner only if there is a loser. Shorting takes value from one entity and gives it to another. It adds no *real* economic value.

In terms of returns, the long-term track record of shorting is poor. When shorting does generate outperformance, it is typically short-term only and rarely sustainable. Shorting can also be challenging in the near term. For example, when the markets hit new highs in 2013, short-selling hedge funds trailed the S&P 500 Index by an average of 23 percent for the year, according to the Bloomberg Hedge Funds Aggregate Index. In addition, shorting has limited upside and unlimited downside risk.

Long-Short and 130/30

I don't consider long-short strategies as being as much of a zero-sum game as pure shorting. However, investors may be well served by knowing that the long-term returns of long-short funds tend to fall behind the market.

For many years, I had the honor of chairing the investment committee for a nonprofit medical research group. After just 10 years, I observed that the long-short funds that we had hired (which I never recommend as a rule) had underperformed the market by at least 4 percent on average during periods of normal markets and economic conditions. The managers of these funds typically claimed that these lackluster results also came with less downside *risk* during the 10-year period. However, if we eliminate just one key year from results—the significant decline of 2008—any evidence of those managers' ability to keep up with the market completely disappeared. Therefore, for investors who believe that a 2008-like event will happen again soon, I suspect that a long-short strategy may give them some protection from short-term quotational loss. But I am skeptical that such approaches will offer long-term outperformance.

The notorious long-short fund fee structure of "2 and 20" must also be factored in as a contributor to performance drag. A quick glimpse at decades of public equities performance clearly reminds us that a 2 percent annual management fee on assets *plus* a 20 percent performance fee on profits will, on average, almost guarantee underperformance for the investor. On the other hand, it could generate great returns for the manager.

Through all these years and for all these reasons, there are no clear-cut leaders in the long-short strategy arena. There are no *famous* long-term short traders who can demonstrate that they have added real value to their investors' portfolios. This is one reason why picking an effective long-short manager is much more difficult than choosing a long-only manager. Adding to the challenge is that long-short managers tend to have much smaller amounts under management, usually rely on just one stock picker, and tend to close their funds much more often, typically to start up another hedge fund or return to managing their own money.

While some investors show a preference for shorting strategies and alternative investments, it is important to note that long-only strategies have withstood the test of time, with equities producing the highest returns compared to all other asset classes over extended periods.

Target Risk and Target Date

These strategies draw from modern portfolio theory and efficient market theory and attempt to match an investor's asset allocation to a specified risk tolerance. The difference is that *target date* funds will adjust allocations as the investor approaches an established date, which is ideally a retirement year. My problem with these strategies is the fact that markets are not always efficient, as we learned in the black swan event of the financial crisis of 2008–2009. When everything went south, these funds were especially challenged. Also, the upside capture that they offer in good markets can be constrained by their tilt. That is, if you're in a conservative portfolio, that's usually the level of growth you can expect on its best day. Another typical drawback is high fees. These portfolios are often constructed as "funds of funds," which adds additional expenses from the underlying managers who are selected to run a portion of the asset-class mandates within them.

Strategic and Tactical

These are supposed to be classic opposites, but the lines have blurred as more convoluted product types and investment parameters have entered the mix. Those who favor *strategic* methods advocate developing a blueprint of asset classes and sticking to that knitting. Those who favor *tactical* methods give you some leeway to take advantage of shifting market conditions, perhaps by changing allocations. Portfolios in both camps suffered during the crisis, and this created client confusion as to what the strategies actually did and when they could do it.

Many brokers shared stories with me about how challenging it was to explain the difference. Among the top questions was, "If it's strategic, why are they moving things around? Doesn't that make it tactical?" To me, investing is *both* strategic *and* tactical, based on the preliminary and ongoing decisions that you need to make along the way. Even the academics agree that you need a little of both, no matter where you begin. The original guidance for modern portfolio theory, the most strategic approach imaginable, argues for a combination of "statistical technics and *judgment*."

Active Versus Passive (Indexing)

The chasm between these two camps keeps getting wider. *Active* proponents (and I'm certainly one of them) agree that the only true path to long-term outperformance is best guided by a professional. *Passive* enthusiasts lean the other way. They are convinced that, with rare exceptions, there is no way to beat the market over the long run. So, why pay the extra money for a manager? One reason is that an index can't look inside itself and exploit the inefficiencies that occur constantly over time. I go further into the arguments for active versus passive investments in Chapter 14.

Active and Passive ETFs

Passive exchange-traded funds (ETFs) were introduced in the early 1990s and haven't looked back since. ETFs are baskets of securities that track an index, but are traded like individual stocks. The most visible passive ETFs include SPDRs, or "Spiders" (which attempt to track the S&P 500 Index), Diamonds (which are designed to track the Dow Jones Industrial Average), and QQQs, or "Qubes" (which are designed to track the largest 100 Nasdaq firms based on market capitalization).

In the early 2000s, *active ETFs* were introduced as the next generation. Almost everything else about them is generally the same as their earlier cousins, but active ETFs involve a manager or management team that is maneuvering the product around its benchmark. That is, the managers will reallocate and trade within the ETF, and sometimes among investments that are not held by its mirror index, to try to outperform. Does this sound complicated? It is, and it's far from transparent. It's tough to know what you own. To me, ETFs are just another way to index, only with a little more opportunity for liquidity when you change your mind about them.

Quantitative and Absolute

The *quantitative* method applies sophisticated mathematical models, usually of the manager's own design, to increase the fund's ability to outperform the benchmark index. It was pioneered in the 1970s, but the number of adopters grew dramatically in the early 2000s leading up to the financial crisis as tracking software became more effective. This approach is more likely to leverage the skill set of someone with a doctorate in statistics, mathematics, or computer engineering than of a credentialed investment professional. Their long-term success remains a hotly debated topic in the industry. In contrast to relative returns, which seek to beat an index or competitors, *absolute* return strategies apply alternative techniques like short selling, futures, and options in the quest to outperform. Absolute and quantitative methods share a penchant for unconventional measures, particularly in the hedge fund arena.

Smart Beta

Considered to be the intersection of passive and active management, *smart beta* tries to improve upon index investing. The approach follows an index, but it uses one that is built with an alternative weighting composition based on company fundamentals, as opposed to the traditional capitalization- or market size–weighted structure of most indexes. It attempts to deliver a better risk/return trade-off than conventional indexing by focusing on a "rules-based" index. It is a relatively new approach, with less than 20 years of proven track record to validate its long-term effectiveness. However, I would typically prefer a passive product with a "tilt" toward factors that make sense to me, such as valuations, rather than simply owning the entire market.

Municipals and Tax-Efficient Portfolios

Municipal bonds, nicknamed "munis," are bonds issued by local governments or other government agencies to raise revenues. The interest that they pay is usually exempt from federal income tax, and possibly from state tax as well, depending on where the investor lives. The extent to which the tax savings is of any real benefit depends on how much interest the bonds pay, your tax bracket, and sundry other factors. The same is true of *tax-efficient investing*, which involves a complicated menu of taxable, tax-deferred, and tax-exempt offerings that is best left to a financial advisor to help sort out. Generally, all investing should focus on long-term growth objectives before taking the tax ramifications into account.

Fixed Income

By the late 2000s, the combination of a general aversion to equities and a desire to limit exposure to short-term volatility lit the fire under investors' demand for bonds and fixed-income mutual funds. I believe that bonds have a place in an effective allocation mix, but not to the extent that they were being consumed for many years. The land grab simply fueled a gradual mass movement to low-quality credit in a desperate search for competitive rates. All this eventually opened the doors to a world that was suddenly perplexing to the average investor. In Chapter 16, I offer more perspective on how fixed income applies in the value investing arena. Here, I touch on some of the complex fixed-income products that contributed to the inundation.

- *Floating rate bonds.* Just another name for adjustable, these debt instruments are primarily tied to the London Interbank Offered Rate (LIBOR). Issuers tend to be non-investment-grade, which means that investors are trading down in credit quality in return for better rates. Also, they offer few diversification benefits, as their returns have moved more in line with equities than those of other bond types.

- *High-yield bonds.* In the fixed-income space, if you want higher yields, you have to give something up in terms of credit quality. As an asset class, high-yield bonds certainly have offered long-term returns in line with the broader equities market, and sometimes with less volatility. But like any security, outperforming over the long run comes down to selection of undervalued issues based on individual merits.

- *Duration-managed bonds.* This is a simple label that suggests nimbleness and responsiveness to changing interest rates, but duration is a complicated by-product of an investment mandate. Is the goal high income? Short duration? It's best to know the objective before developing the strategy.

- *Treasury Inflation-Protected Securities (TIPS).* These are U.S. Treasury securities that are adjusted in accordance with the Consumer Price Index, ideally to hedge against inflation. Just know that if inflation is in check, so is TIPS' growth potential.

- *Foreign bonds.* These are credits that one country issues in another country, using the latter's local currency. In my opinion, they require a strong stomach for risk, because not only do you take on the usual credit and interest-rate concerns, but currency and possibly political uncertainty risks are also present.

Keep in mind that there is a thoughtful, value-based approach to investing in fixed income, which I share in Chapter 16.

Other Hard Assets

The historical evidence regarding the superiority of stocks relative to other financial assets is unambiguous: stocks have outperformed bonds, commodities, real estate, and gold by a wide margin over the long term (Figure 13-2). Still, in adverse markets, many people give in to fear and abandon stocks for alternative investments. What are the relative returns from hard assets?

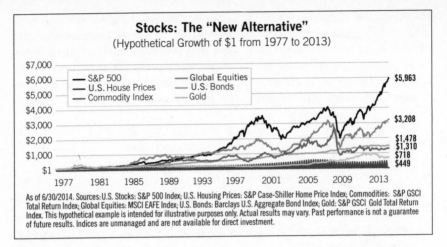

Stocks: The "New Alternative"
(Hypothetical Growth of $1 from 1977 to 2013)

As of 6/30/2014. Sources: U.S. Stocks: S&P 500 Index; U.S. Housing Prices: S&P Case-Shiller Home Price Index; Commodities: S&P GSCI Total Return Index; Global Equities: MSCI EAFE Index; U.S. Bonds: Barclays U.S. Aggregate Bond Index; Gold: S&P GSCI Gold Total Return Index. This hypothetical example is intended for illustrative purposes only. Actual results may vary. Past performance is not a guarantee of future results. Indices are unmanaged and are not available for direct investment.

Figure 13-2 Even compared with the dramatic spikes in the prices of gold, real estate, commodities, and bonds at certain points in time, as well as the collapse in equities in the financial crisis of 2008–2009, stocks have outperformed over the 36-year period ending in 2013.

Gold

Gold has been touted as a reliable inflation hedge, but take a closer look. From 1900 to 2000, the yellow metal appreciated by a mere 2.6 percent annually.[4] U.S. inflation averaged 3.2 percent per year between 1900 and 2000.[5] Some inflation hedge! Even if you were fortunate enough to bail out at the top of the metal's spectacular run in 1980, your returns would still have been subpar relative to those of equities over the same period. Between 1926 and 1981— gold's first glittering period—its price rose by just 5.8 percent per year, or barely half the annualized return of the S&P 500 Index. Despite another peak in 2011, gold prices went mostly nowhere after that relatively brief spike, especially compared to stocks.

Investing takes on a different sheen in non-U.S. countries such as Canada, which is home to five of the world's top-10 gold mining companies, all of which issue public shares.[6] Many value investors there prefer to invest in these companies rather than actual bullion to exploit pricing inefficiencies, which is something that you just can't do with an inanimate precious metal. Gold's price is always its value, but businesses tied to gold can often be priced much lower than what they are actually worth.

Commodities

Many investors pick commodities as their ticket to instant wealth. In reality, a lottery ticket might provide better odds. Even professional investors armed with sophisticated trading techniques and the latest software programs have difficulty consistently making money in commodities and their derivatives.

Commodities are also sought as inflation hedges and alternatives to equities. They certainly provide diversification opportunities, but they don't pay dividends or interest. They can also be extremely vulnerable, as witnessed by the steady three-year decline in the Dow Jones Commodity Index that ended with a 9.3 percent drop in 2013 alone. Given the speed, volatility, leverage, and pressure inherent in the commodities business, this asset class offers no margin of safety advantage to bank on.

Fine Art

Fine art may provide enjoyment, but it falls short as an investment asset. A study based on an auction database showed an average annual return of 6.5 percent from 1972 to 2010. The study also suggested a higher level of risk on fine art because of selection bias. In fact, the Sharpe Ratio, which measures returns on a risk-adjusted basis, was 0.04 for fine art, versus 0.18, 0.33, and 0.26 for commodities, corporate bonds, and equities, respectively, during the period.[7]

Real Estate

Property seems to be everyone's favorite investment topic. "They're just not making any more of it, so it's always a good investment," goes the saying. If you haven't already, please turn to Chapter 11 to review the harsh realities that speculating in real estate can create. Even during the post–World War II period—a time considered by many to be the golden age for U.S. land values—unleveraged real estate was generally only a mediocre long-term investment.

Unlike businesses, real estate does not *create* wealth. Values are based on whatever real estate revenue streams can be generated, and those cash flows are a direct result of overall business health. For example, the cost of owning a single-family home is covered by money earned through a business. Consequently, businesses have to be more profitable than real estate (as an investment), or else rents couldn't be paid or houses purchased.

If real estate has been a relatively pedestrian performer over time, why do many people believe it to be so profitable? The answer is simple: leveraging, that is, the potential to make money with borrowed money. Most excess real estate profits are the result of extreme leveraging, especially when real estate prices are rising rapidly. The downside, of course, is that while paper profits often go up as a result of borrowing, so do potential losses. Many investors forget that real estate prices also tend to be cyclical.

Whenever you are tempted to see real estate as an investment panacea, remember the U.S. real estate market in Texas in the 1980s, in California in the 1990s, and nationwide in 2008! If businesses don't do well, neither does real estate. And if businesses are doing well, I believe there is no better way to build wealth than by owning a diversified portfolio of stocks.

New *New* Is Really Same *Old*

Comedian George Carlin once quipped, "If you can nail two old things together that have never been nailed together before, someone will buy it from you."[8] I think of that line every time I see the new *new* offerings from Wall Street. So much of what's produced and positioned as unique and different is just cobbled together from old ideas that most likely didn't work before, and probably won't again for any length of time.

We frequently hear from advisors and institutional fiduciaries about how they often feel that their hand is being forced, and they need to delve into the complicated new arrivals just to make it appear that they're doing something for their constituents. But most of them know deep down that traditional allocations to equities are what really help their clients in any meaningful way. It's just that when their clients get sucked into other things, so do they.

Value investing really has to go out of its way to get caught up in overcomplicating itself. We save the tough stuff for the individual company analysis. But out there, in the arena, we tend to stay grounded in what we know works, while the rush of fads and trends and shiny new things flows by around us. Unfortunately, the glitz distracts investors from what we feel are the important things, like building wealth through long-term investment in businesses around the world. Sometimes investor distractions disappear, but it's only a matter of time before the same familiar tune starts all over again.

STAYING ACTIVE:
THE STOCK PICKER'S EDGE IN A PASSIVE WORLD

You can't use the value approach without patience. And patience isn't something you find on the floor of the New York Stock Exchange.

—Charles Brandes, in an interview with the *Robb Report*, September 1986

It's an understatement to say that indexing has become an extremely popular way to invest. However, if assets under management are a worthy gauge, indexing still hasn't caught up with active strategies by any stretch of the imagination. At year-end 2013, index equity mutual funds held just an 18 percent share of the $17 trillion in assets under management throughout the industry.[1]

Indexing got its start in August of 1976, when John Bogle inaugurated his Vanguard 500 Index mutual fund. You may be surprised to learn that its early reception by the investment community was tepid. Ironically, many observers reacted to the approach as "un-American," while in the background, the nation was famously celebrating its bicentennial.

Indexing today encompasses a wide range of *passive investing* styles, all of which take the general approach of replicating the performance of a particular index, such as the MSCI EAFE (Europe, Australasia, and Far East), the MSCI World, or (the most popular) the S&P 500. Index portfolio managers tend to purchase only those companies that are in their corresponding benchmark—or at least enough of them to try to mimic its performance. This approach is considered *passive* because the buying and selling decisions are distantly dictated by the composition of the index, not by an active walk around the investment landscape. Index managers' decisions are typically guided by the need to slightly rebalance the portfolio as the markets shift or listings are added to or removed from the index for reasons unrelated to the value of the security itself.

Mass Management

In terms of stock selection, index fund managers aren't making reasoned choices by evaluating the value of individual businesses in relation to their stock price. Instead, they buy and sell massive baskets of stocks to match the performance of their broad-based index. Some of them try a few roundabout maneuvers to beat the index or bet against it, but generally, when the index rises, the portfolio does too, and vice versa.

As a result, index fund portfolio managers have no need to conduct extensive, company-specific fundamental analysis; instead, they simply buy whichever stocks are in the index they are tracking. In the late 1990s, the markets began to inflate rapidly because of the tech bubble. As a result, index funds delivered solid gains during the run-up, raising interesting new questions about the usefulness of hiring active managers. Given their obsession with the overheated market, investors' thinking began to coalesce around the idea that indexing was all you needed. A new mindset emerged that if you hitched your portfolio to the S&P, you could just float upward along with the index.

It's never this simple. There are important considerations that investors need to recognize when they are investing in index funds—namely, these funds' contribution to irrational pricing. If you reflect on what I've been saying throughout this book, you can understand the importance of evaluating the difference between business value and stock price for *every* holding in your portfolio. Managers of index funds don't go through this process. They simply buy what an index holds. This is because proponents of passive investing simply believe that active managers are unable to consistently exploit price and value gaps to generate returns that justify their fees.

Weighting Is the Hardest Part

That indexing turns a blind eye to relative prices is a top problem for me. It's why I believe that indexing isn't the most effective strategy—especially if your goal is outperformance over the long term. The pricing problem starts with the indexing process itself. Most index funds, like the benchmarks they try to mirror, are weighted by the size of the companies' capitalization. Thus, the money invested in an index fund is not equally distributed among all the fund's holdings. For example, if you invested $100 in an index fund that held 100 stocks, it is unlikely that the fund would hold $1 worth of each of 100 stocks. You might have $5 invested in each of 10 companies and only 55.5 cents invested in each of the 90 others based on market cap. The stocks with the greatest weight in the portfolio have the greatest influence on returns. If their price climbs, they make up a larger percentage of the portfolio and therefore have a greater effect on overall results—in either direction.

Furthermore, if you *add* money to an index fund that's appreciating, your investments will probably be further tilted toward the prior winners. The companies with the greatest weighting receive the biggest allocation. This aspect of how index funds are structured reflects their irrational approach to investing, because investors end up buying more of the stocks that have already experienced significant price increases. That could make them overvalued! Not surprisingly, this approach has worked magnificently during bull markets, when escalating share prices create a short-term, self-fulfilling prophecy (as in the tech bubble). But when the market reverses and stock prices fall with it, the same lockstep methods just exacerbate the losses.

Indexing's Good Side

To be fair, there are many benefits to the indexing approach when it comes to meeting various investor goals. The most touted is the inherently lower average costs compared to *active* strategies, where managers' fees and expenses have to cover the costs of research, stock-selection skills, and leadership in creating and managing portfolios. Fees and expenses are a factor in gauging returns, so the lower they are, the better the net returns for the investor. Tax efficiency comes into the picture as well, but we'll come back to these larger points later.

Indexing tends to be relatively straightforward and is designed for low maintenance, which attracts investors who prefer a "set-it-and-forget-it" approach. Indexing also serves those who like to take shortcuts, as it offers "one-stop shopping" diversification. With most passive strategies, you get everything that's in the index, and you get them all at once. Whether you want them all is of no consequence. Finally, there is a variety of choices. In the 40 years since John Bogle developed Vanguard 500, the index world has grown a lot more complicated. I'm not convinced that so much variation is a benefit to either investors or the industry, especially when you add to the mix the most popular spur of the indexing movement: exchange-traded funds.

Passive Gets Aggressive

In the early 1990s, a new indexing product was introduced that changed the investing landscape, probably forever. Exchange-traded funds (ETFs) were launched first in the United States and soon after in Canada and Europe. ETFs combine the features of an index mutual fund with the ability to do intraday trading on the major stock exchanges. In other words, they trade like stocks. Some ETF shares are also exchanged on the secondary markets.

At first, ETFs were limited to passive strategies, but by 2008 an actively managed variation had been launched to suit the more ambitious indexers. In no time, the number of ETFs grew to keep pace with the broad spectrum of bond, U.S. Treasuries, precious metals, commodities, and other indexes, as well as single or small groups of stocks. One variety, leveraged ETFs, is designed to double or even *triple* the daily index return. You read that right: the *daily* return. Yet another type, called *inverse ETFs*, tries to capture the exact opposite of the market's performance for the day; it is essentially geared toward short sellers.

By mid-2014, the ETF rush had reached a record $2.3 trillion in assets worldwide.[2] Like those of index funds, the basic attractions of ETFs for many investors are relatively low costs, easy diversification, tax efficiencies, and simplistic design. With ETFs, however, there is an added allure from their behaving like a stock, so that you can trade them all day long.

Is Liquidity All *That*?

The easy liquidity component of ETFs may not be all good, of course, especially when investor behavior takes over, as it usually does. When the index struggles, it's easier to pull out than to ride it out, especially if you're sensitive to the daily movement of the market, as most ETF investors tend to be. Though ETFs can be traded throughout the day, minute-to-minute liquidity is not a concern for the long-term investor.

ETFs may provide low annual expenses and increased tax efficiency, but keep in mind that they are rebalanced from time to time, usually semiannually or once a year. Some types of ETFs—active ETFs, global ETFs, and so on—may be rebalanced more frequently because of the nature of their holdings. The point is, rebalancing can incur costs. Such "slippage" is marginal on a per transaction basis, but it can really add up for large ETFs, particularly those that significantly trade beyond the index—a strategy called *optimizing*.

When it comes to the garden variety of nontraditional ETFs, I urge caution. As I shared in Chapter 13, shorting is not a strategy for effective long-term investing, and inverse ETFs fall into the trap of playing a zero-sum game. Double- and triple-leveraged ETFs are no different. They use mechanical processes that decouple them from meaningful investing in their race for short-term goals. They are also pricier than is usually suggested. I'm not alone in my opinion on how these work against investors' best interests. Many brokerage firms forbid their advisors to sell many types of them. "Average long-term investors should avoid these like the plague," said one Morningstar analyst.[3]

What's in It?

The old saying, "It tastes great until you read the list of ingredients," couldn't be more fitting for some ETFs. Transparency is supposed to be their strong suit, but it gets lost in the convoluted financial engineering. Indexing in its purest form is a simple concept, but this isn't necessarily true of all ETFs, many of which have started to include commodities, futures, swaps, currencies, derivatives, shorting, and many more of my favorite "new fish in old wrappings."

Not only do these underlying alternative securities and products make these ETFs complicated, but they also add costs. These ETFs have to be adjusted constantly, especially when shorting strategies are involved, so that they can do what they're supposed to and get on with their day. All this activity fosters exponential levels of daily arbitrage, which sparks trading activity and all the costs associated with it. Costs include not only brokerage commissions and spreads, but also another potentially expensive layer of intermediary known as *high-frequency traders*.

High-frequency trading (HFT) is the crossroads of speed-of-light computing and stock speculation. HFT firms use proprietary algorithms to intercept and trade short-term bulk equities positions wherever they can find them. And in this case, *short term* means that they may hold the stocks for one millionth of a second—briefer than the blink of an eye. Naturally, these firms keep a microfraction of a percentage of the trade for their efforts. This sounds simple, and even helpful, because they're bringing together buyers and sellers in a free market, or, as they call it, "providing liquidity." But their unneeded additional costs and their disruptive nature (for example, the Flash Crash of 2010 and forcing banks to start "dark pools" to avoid them) are potential contributors to intense market fragility. For this reason, my firm stepped up to help jump-start the efforts of a new firm, IEX, that was founded to help address this problem, which is discussed in Chapter 17.

Where Is the Company Research?

My philosophy, which is also that of my firm, is based on the premise that through fundamental research and the application of value investing principles, it is possible to achieve superior long-term performance. Indexing is in direct conflict with this. Value investors try to buy what they can measure today at a discount from its *current* worth. The only thing riskier than predicting the near-term economic outlook for a company is predicting the near-term economic outlook for an entire market, index, country, region, or sector.

Active Management Can Add Value—Overseas Example

Many international fund managers base their investments on the market capitalization weighting of the world's stock market indexes, such as the MSCI

EAFE Index. For example, if Japanese stocks make up 30 percent of the MSCI EAFE Index, some managers will make sure that their portfolios have about a 30 percent weighting in Japanese stocks. This style of investing ignores the value of individual businesses within the chosen countries. In addition, it ignores the possibility that the markets with the most compelling values may be underrepresented because of recent losses in equity value.

With the growth of international markets in the 1980s, the EAFE Index and other non-U.S. benchmarks outperformed the S&P 500 substantially, with much of that outperformance coming from the Japanese economic boom. By the end of that decade, fund managers with top-down index styles willingly "bought" the EAFE Index, which included a large exposure to Japan, even though it meant buying Japanese stocks at high valuations: roughly 60 times earnings. As I discussed in Chapter 11, by 1992, the Tokyo market had fallen to a mere 50 percent of its former value and Japan represented roughly 43 percent of the capitalization-weighted EAFE Index.[4] In this situation, adherence to an indexing philosophy resulted in significant losses.

Unintended Concentration Risk in Emerging Markets

With expanding GDPs and a rising wave of consumers, emerging markets (EM) countries provide a vast opportunity set for stocks, especially as companies that are either based in EM countries or just do business with them prosper. As a result, inflows into EM strategies have remained consistently strong, and these inflows have been channeled primarily into passive index strategies.

Emerging markets also provide a backdrop for another interesting phenomenon that can occur with passive indexing: concentration risk. In other words, for a long period of time, indexing in EM strategies wasn't giving investors the wide exposure that they were expecting (Figure 14-1).

The number of companies available for investment in emerging markets is greater than that in developed markets, reflecting a vast opportunity. However, the indexes (and the ETFs tracking these indexes) that are designed to reflect emerging markets tend to be heavily concentrated in just a handful of companies. For investors who are seeking greater potential in emerging markets and enhanced diversification benefits, active managers offer a better alternative.

The inefficient nature of global markets places an even greater premium on active management. In an early 2000 article in *Pension Management*, authors Christopher Carabell and Elizabeth DeLalla describe the benefits that active management can deliver when applied in global markets: "None of the criteria used in assessing the relative merits of active vs. passive—viable indices, available information, management fees, and transaction costs—strongly favor indexation when investing abroad. Active international management has the additional advantage of multidimensional investment opportunities, including country and stock selection."[5]

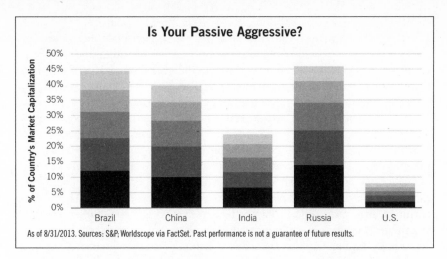

Is Your Passive Aggressive?

As of 8/31/2013. Sources: S&P; Worldscope via FactSet. Past performance is not a guarantee of future results.

Figure 14-1 By investing pro rata on a market cap basis, passive ETF strategies can become too aggressive at channeling money to a small number of large companies. Investors may end up with concentrated portfolios that they don't want. The most extreme example in this table is the Russia ETF, of which 45 percent was concentrated in just five companies.

On Value Index Funds

Can value investing and index investing ever share the same room? To put it differently, can indexing ever take individual company fundamentals into account? In theory, perhaps, but this doesn't mean that it would constitute pure Graham-and-Dodd value investing.

I commend the valiant entries in this space from Research Affiliates' Rob Arnott and a few others. The great majority of value indexing strategies, however, lean more toward value-*weighted* indexing approaches. That is, their strategies overweight those stocks in the index that *appear* to be the cheapest of the lot. Their relative "value" is determined by their price-to-earnings, price-to-book, and price-to-cash flow ratios. As we've reviewed, there's more to value investing than these three fundamentals. And, in an index of 100 to 500 stocks, there is little chance that a manager can even begin to get much deeper into other areas of a company's intrinsic value, let alone its all-important margin of safety. What about management, accounting practices, headline risk, and competitive and market pressures? How are these metrics involved in a company's potential for a takeover? I could go on, but you get my point.

You also still run the risk of overconcentrating your holdings among countries, industries, or sectors, as in the EM example in Figure 14-1. A company's market price could simply be reacting to

(continued)

something that is affecting these larger categories, so all the related companies, regardless of their quality, may be just riding the same downward wave. If you can successfully corral companies in an index based on discovering more than just their cheapness, where is the threshold between passive and active investing?

I think indexing in all its forms becomes no longer *passive* once you start reaching outside the benchmark. Call it what you will—optimization; smart beta; or fundamental, enhanced, or synthetic indexing—but if you don't stick to the index, how is that still indexing? "Because fundamental indices are primarily designed for simplicity and appeal, they are unlikely to be the most efficient way of benefiting from the value premium," concluded one 2008 study. "Value indexing products more resemble active investment strategies than classic passive indices." I think that if you're going to follow an index only in part, stand up and be seen as the active manager you're trying to be.

Active or Passive?

Which side of the active-passive fence you want to stand on should depend on your goals. Astute financial advisors remind us that the basic tenets of diversification do not force you to choose one or the other; you can perhaps take a little of both. This is where many investors have hung their hats, too, with about 42 percent holding combinations of active and passive mutual funds. The same survey also showed that 36 percent of investors own only active funds, while 22 percent own only passive (index funds and/or ETFs). Clearly, active investing is still a big part of the investor psyche.[6]

The two approaches can complement each other very well in many scenarios. In model portfolios and fund-of-fund designs like the allocation options in variable insurance and annuity products, I have seen them work side by side quite effectively. If the goal is to tone down volatility somewhat, adding a defensive active component, such as a value fund, alongside an indexing strategy can help. In those rare periods when markets are in high-concentration mode, index-oriented strategies can help counterbalance the short-term underperformance that active strategies tend to display during such conditions. But history shows that markets aren't all that efficient, when you consider their volatility over short-term periods (Figure 14-2). More arguments on portfolio strategies, particularly in the institutional world, are offered in Chapter 17.

The Returns Argument

A fair and balanced performance comparison between active and passive investing strategies can only conjure up the classic question, "Do you walk to school or do you take your lunch?" They each offer a wide swath of tools to help investors make money, but that's where any equal footing really ends.

I'm obviously biased, but I can't begin to say enough good things about how this approach has worked for my clients—quite well most of the time—especially within my chosen discipline of value investing. Big followers of John Bogle's *Little Book of Common Sense Investing* would certainly raise the question of active investing's fee drag on returns. In rebuttal, one could point to ETFs' renowned frictional costs from frequent trading in the daily grind for alpha. Likewise, Burton Malkiel's 1973 *Random Walk Down Wall Street*, which left muddy tracks on fundamental analysis, is easily countered by Buffett's nine featured value stars in his "Superinvestors of Graham and Doddsville" article a decade later. Going head to head is a zero-sum game, so I won't go there.

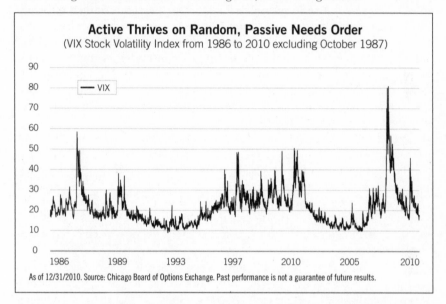

Active Thrives on Random, Passive Needs Order
(VIX Stock Volatility Index from 1986 to 2010 excluding October 1987)

As of 12/31/2010. Source: Chicago Board of Options Exchange. Past performance is not a guarantee of future results.

Figure 14-2 When markets are efficient, based on Harry Markowitz's theories, passive strategies tend to benefit because all asset classes do what they are "supposed to" do in relation to one another. Decades of volatility tell us that markets are *not* efficient, and their randomness is how active investors are able to find opportunities to outperform the market.

It really comes down to consistency and continuity, which are critical to investors' success in any investment approach. Like every type of investment at one time or another, active value investing has undergone periods of underperformance. Some of these periods were extended, lasting years, while at other times the rewards have been substantial for investors who stuck it out. Active value investing isn't for everyone. It takes a certain resolve and persistence to go the distance. Institutional and individual clients alike should agree with this active value strategy, seek advisors and professionals who can provide stewardship and continuity in management, and, most important, have the patience to withstand periods of underperformance.

Patience stems from knowing that active value is always working. It may not always *show* that it is, but its rhythm never stops. It doesn't "buy the market," so it doesn't have to show up every day to decide whether it needs to give it back or sell it short. Instead, active value investing commits to a handful of select, well-researched companies and is prepared to wait and watch.

Indexing is predicated on one primary idea: you just can't beat the market—ever. This mindset is self-defeating; the more it influences the average investor, the worse it stymies growth on many levels. Perhaps most troubling for me is indexing's tendency to divert capital from the places where it's needed most: undervalued businesses. By doing so, it throttles those companies that are most likely to succeed and that could contribute more to the larger economy. That said, there is a growing belief that passive investing works against the fundamentals of capitalism itself.

"If everyone does (indexing), there will be no allocation of capital to the great, high-potential projects that feed right into fixing our country's long-term problems," said Kim Shannon, founder of Toronto-based Sionna Investment Managers at a 2012 National Club debate on the topic. "The inbound capital just follows market cap, and this is counter to what investing is supposed to be about—taking on risk and getting paid for it in the long run." I agree with her sentiment. Index investing is a growing threat to our economic system, because investors and investment managers are abdicating their critical societal role of allocating capital most efficiently.

As ETFs have taken on new forms, passive investing has also become quite aggressive. ETF investors seem to have given up trying to beat the market, but they also soon fall for disguised indexing methods that try to do just that. Promises of passive investing's transparency also just aren't accurate, as new products grow more sophisticated and, in some cases, not really passive at all. Diversification is often missing, too, when the normal course of indexing chases the higher market caps right into a handful of concentrated industries or sectors.

If you want to invest in value effectively, you have to be active about it. It's the only way to get it right. You can't find margins of safety by piggybacking on an index. And when things inevitably grow volatile, you have to be confident that what you're holding will come out better on the other end. Such opportunities are best found in individual companies, fished for not through passive trolling, but with an actively and carefully baited hook.

VALUE IN AN EFFECTIVE PORTFOLIO

I n his book *Where Are the Customers' Yachts?*, Fred Schwed, Jr., challenged the elitist brokerage system of late 1920s Wall Street. Schwed's testament to "customer" mistreatment helps remind us of the long way we've come as an industry. Nearly a century and many sweeping regulations later, the modern system for fostering and enforcing financial professional integrity isn't perfect, but it's extremely effective.

The same client questions keep coming up, though: *Is owning more asset classes better? Are stocks smart investments anymore? Why are my so-called fixed-income investments losing money? What kind of risk should I be concerned about?* The answers to these questions are relatively simple, but they are frequently made more complicated than they need to be.

In the fourth and final part of the book, I offer my responses to these and other important investor questions. Pension leaders and fiduciaries can also be challenged in the struggle to meet both short- and long-term obligations. In both the individual and institutional worlds, the solutions don't have to be complicated, but they do need time, and in today's busy world, there is little of that to spare. With that in mind, I'll offer the quick and condensed version of my responses to these four key questions, in order of appearance: no, yes, inevitability, and paying too much for a stock. For the unabridged versions, please read on.

CHAPTER 15

ARE STOCKS AN INTELLIGENT INVESTMENT?

When you buy a share of stock, it's more than just a piece of paper; it's a piece of the business.

—Charles Brandes, in an interview with *Research* magazine, May 1988

I n the first three sections, this book highlighted the basics and the inner workings of value investing. By inner workings, I mean looking carefully inside a company, especially its balance sheet and income statement, to attach an intrinsic value to it. Value investors have a commitment to equities, but the value proposition includes the world of bonds, too. In the next two chapters, we'll examine both asset classes and show how—with a value investing mind-set—each has an important role in an effective long-term strategy.

The question stands: Are stocks an intelligent investment? Given *Business-Week*'s 1979 "obituary" for equities, have we merely been dancing with ghosts in the decades that followed? No. Despite the prediction, equities are alive and well in the modern age. Even with the dust still settling from economic turmoil in 2008, equities did not mourn for long and started their next rejuvenation in March of 2009. The Dow Jones Industrial Average racked up a 23.5 percent return (including dividends) that year.

Stocks Are Building Blocks

Of course there's more to stocks than just bull markets, which don't always reflect the *quality* of the stocks that are participating in the surge. Stocks can be viewed as the bricks that build strong economies. Individual businesses seek to raise money by selling shares or partial ownership in the company. The money they raise might help them build new factories, develop new products or technologies, create efficiencies, or expand their markets. In short, businesses seek to create wealth through providing valuable products or services that contribute to a healthy economy built on accessibility, opportunity, and exchange.

Individual businesses generate the wealth that fuels the capitalist economic system. Within this system, all assets—whether they are stocks, bonds, real estate, commodities, collectibles, or something else—maintain their value only if companies are viable. Many investors lose sight of the fact that asset values are interrelated. If businesses falter, many other areas of our economy, and, indeed, our well-being, will be affected negatively.

Modern economies face the same challenges that they did 50, 100, or 150 years ago: inflation, interest-rate fluctuations, unemployment, cyclical declines, conflict, and natural catastrophes. All these developments can cause economic uncertainty. When confidence wanes, some investors have looked to alternative products and markets, such as art, real estate, precious metals, bank deposits, and certain types of bonds. These assets may help preserve capital, but they may also lead to an irreparable loss of purchasing power over time. Over the long term, however, capitalism has endured, economies have survived, and stocks have continued to offer the most effective opportunities for substantial capital appreciation.

Stocks Are Wealth Creators

First, there is the obvious edge found through basic math. U.S. common stocks (as measured by the Standard & Poor's 500 Index) averaged a compounded annual return of 10.3 percent over the 25-year period through 2013, compared to 6.6 percent for U.S. government bonds and just 2.8 percent for cash equivalents (U.S. Treasury bills). Inflation averaged 2.7 percent for the period.

While those figures may not seem drastically different from one another, consider the ultimate difference in returns over time. Investors who put $100 into common stocks in 1989 would have seen their nest eggs grow to $1,151 by 2013; that same $100 invested in U.S. government bonds would have been worth just $489, much less than half the return on stocks during the largest stock market rally in history. The $100 invested in cash equivalents would have grown to even less: just $199.[1]

Jeremy Siegel, a professor at the Wharton School of Business at the University of Pennsylvania, once offered a timeless perspective on his research on the historical returns of U.S. asset classes. "The long-term stability of [stock] returns is all the more surprising when one reflects on the dramatic changes that have taken place in our society during the last two centuries. The U.S. evolved from an agricultural to an industrial, and now to a post-industrial, service- and technology-oriented economy. The world shifted from a gold-based standard to a paper money standard. . . . Yet despite mammoth changes in the basic factors generating wealth for shareholders, equity returns have shown an astounding persistence."[2] He is still right.

On the worldwide platform too, equities have proved resilient and rewarding for investors. As seen through the MSCI World Index, global equities have returned a compounded annual return of 9.4 percent over the past 40 years. As more emerging markets have grown stable and created reliable enterprises of all sizes, these countries have created busy avenues of equity opportunities as well.

What About Market Declines?

Just as people sometimes catch a cold, economies and markets also find themselves under the weather from time to time. If we use the height of the Great Depression (1934) as a starting point, there have been five such events through 2013. That's certainly not as frequent as we have been led to think, and in all cases, markets have recovered from their short-term illnesses. In fact, in the year following each of the four bear markets since 1934, the S&P 500 gained an average of 39.8 percent.[3] (So as not to appear disingenuous, I should also mention that the market regained its ground from a much lower starting point.)

While most investors appreciate evidence that markets recover, part of being human is a desire to want to see things coming before they happen. As a result, stock investing is also no stranger to superstition. The most renowned originated in 1894, when Mark Twain wrote in *Pudd'nhead Wilson*, "October. This is one of the peculiarly dangerous months to speculate in stocks. The others are July, January, September, April, November, May, March, June, December, August and February."[4] As the story goes, Twain was jaded from an "all in" bet he had placed on a start-up company that never got off the ground. Like a lot of Twain's witticisms, the "October effect" has had more than a few followers, especially after three of the worst downturns—1929, 1987, and 2008—struck in that very month. I think it's interesting, but nothing more than a coincidence.

Other questionable notions that are believed to portend market direction include:

- *The death cross.* This is a chart pattern in which the plotted points for the market's 50-day moving average intersect with the plotted points for its 200-day moving average on a downward trajectory to form an ominous cross.

- *The golden cross.* This involves even more data showing a stock's short-term moving average breaking above its longer-term moving average, suggesting that the market is bedazzled by its allure.

- *Hemline histogram.* The belief that women's fashion trends influence returns; the shorter the latest skirts are, the more attractive the… market's outlook.

- *Hindenburg omen.* Technical analysis of a zeppelin-size sampling of data weighs new high and low performers against the market's volume, all of which supposedly converge to predict another disaster in waiting.

- *Presidential effect.* Speculation that the political party that is taking office will determine the market direction for the next four years.

- *Skyscraper up drop.* The idea that the market in the country that builds the highest building will soon fall.

- *Super Bowl tickers.* If the AFC team wins the game, the market is more likely to fumble.

Some of these market "effects" are based on data, but none of them have a home in Graham and Doddsville. Although I will confess to a subdued penchant for harmless good luck symbols, they don't guide my stock picking or my investment outlook. "Luck happens when preparation meets opportunity," goes the saying, so crystal balls are not thrown into the cauldron with the other ingredients of value investing. What is certain, however, is that markets will rise and fall, and stocks along with them. When they fall, it presents investors with opportunities—especially those who lean toward value. Businesses bought at temporarily discounted prices then can benefit from a possible "rising tide lifts all boats" scenario. While bear markets can test one's discipline and patience, value investors recognize their impermanence and the opportunities that they can create. This is not a primary focus of value investing, but it is known to help the process now and then.

Bear Markets and the Value Within

While post–bear market recoveries have tended to be strong, astute investors may uncover and profit from equity investments even *during* bear markets. Although they may be indicative of sluggish returns among equities in general, index declines can mask strong performance by a large portion of the individual stocks in a given universe. This phenomenon was especially pronounced in 2002, when the S&P 500 Index dropped more than 30 percent over the two years ended June 30, 2002—a foray into bear market territory by almost any investor's standards. For the same period, though, S&P 500 constituents that registered gains actually outnumbered those that declined by a count of 279 to 210. In addition, 39 of these gainers posted returns of more than 100 percent during the period.

A key factor behind these seemingly contradictory numbers is the methodology used to construct the S&P 500. As I mentioned when addressing active and passive investment approaches in Chapter 14, a number of popular indexes are capitalization-weighted. This means that larger companies make up larger portions of the index than their smaller counterparts. As a result, bigger companies have a bigger influence on the index's returns just because they are big. When the S&P 500's larger members post declines, which was generally the case during the two years ended June 30, 2002, these declines overshadow the gains from smaller stocks.

I believe this evidence helps to highlight the hidden opportunities that bear markets can offer. Certain equities may deliver strong performance even when the major market indexes are posting declines. Similarly, active investment managers can earn solid returns for investors even when the broad market remains relatively flat. One study I did many years ago still validates this important point.

Actively Adding Value in Bear Markets

Between 1965 and 1982, the price level for the Dow Jones Industrial Average advanced at an annualized rate of 0.6 percent. This was not a bear market per se, but it wasn't a bull market either. If you include dividends, returns were better: the Dow gained an average of 5.7 percent per year. Over the same 18-year period, the S&P 500 Index climbed at an annualized rate of 7.1 percent. Could investors have done better with active managers during this tough stretch? To answer this question, I searched Morningstar for actively managed large-cap funds with track records that spanned the entire 1965–1982 period. These criteria yielded a sample of 47 funds. As shown in Figure 15-1, the funds tended to outperform the Dow and the S&P 500 by substantial margins.

Active Large Cap Sharpened Dull Market
(1965 to 1982)

	Annualized Performance	Growth of $100,000
Dow Jones Industrial Average	5.7%	$271,214
S&P 500	7.1%	$344,332
Average of 47 Mutual Funds	10.2%	$577,265

As of 12/31/1982. Source: FactSet. This is a hypothetical example and is not representative of any specific portfolio or mutual fund. Reinvestment of dividends and capital gains are assumed. All indices are unmanaged and are not available for direct investment. Past performance is not a guarantee of future results. Actual results will vary.

Figure 15-1 To put these annualized return figures into perspective, consider that a $100,000 investment in the Dow or the S&P 500 would have grown to $271,214 or $344,332, respectively. The same investment in the average fund would have appreciated to $577,265 over the same 18-year period.[5] Because this study excluded funds that ceased operating between 1965 and 1982, the results may be biased. At the same time, I believe it demonstrates that, even when the overall market is not charging upward, some active managers can deliver strong returns.

Entry Made Easy

One of the best things that helped the average investor potentially benefit from the stock market was the advent of qualified retirement plans. Starting in the 1980s, the tremendous growth in the number of 401(k) plans, individual retirement accounts, 403(b) programs, and the like opened an ever-widening window that allowed millions of investors to plan for their futures. As the new crop of "participant" investors sought solutions to their long-term planning needs, investment firms answered with innovative asset allocation programs and advisory services for the expanding retirement planning business. I'm pretty sure the mutual fund industry would be a shadow of its modern-day self without the 401(k) plan.

Insurers and other financial firms are always on the scene, too, with equity-sensitive products that are designed for similar long-term growth potential, yet that have unique twists in the form of guaranteed benefits and income payouts. Tax-deferred, tax-free, taxable now but not later, guaranteed floors, step-ups in value, lifetime payouts: name your general need, and there is a product for you. Of course, you could ask 10 advisors and get 21 opinions on whether all the complicated variable insurance products were helping or hurting investors, especially during the period leading up to the big drop in 2008. Almost everyone agrees that plowing the roads to enable prudent investing in the stock market was a win-win, but many people saw the vehicle that the client chose to drive as being of little importance. Products and approaches to retirement investing strategies in the institutional world are another discussion altogether, which I save for Chapter 17.

Whether investors purchase stocks directly or through one of many equity-type products, they will typically sway with the markets. Qualified retirement plans have certainly been no exception, especially since the trouble started in 2008. While most 401(k) plan investors who stuck it out lost assets, a closer look reveals some interesting facts. According to the Employee Benefit Research Institute (EBRI), from January 2008 to January 2009, the largest participants (those with $200,000 or more in balances) lost an average of just over 25 percent, while the smallest accounts (those with $10,000 or less) *gained* an average of 40 percent for the period. This seems counterintuitive, but it's a very believable outcome. It occurred because growth is a function of both account balances and annual contributions. The owners of the smaller accounts in EBRI's sample probably were making contributions during this time frame. Holders of larger accounts were more likely to be near or at retirement, and probably were not contributing. In its 2013 follow-up study, EBRI showed an average two-year gain of 56 percent through 2012 among the sampled 401(k) participants who continued to contribute.[6]

This is a great example of how dollar cost averaging can sometimes be very effective for investors, particularly when it's done during a down market that is beginning to recover. This also shows us the importance of the most powerful commodity in the equity investor's toolbox: time.

The Importance of Time

Time may heal all wounds, but it also helps investment strategies in a big way. Figure 15-2 shows how a hypothetical $100,000 investment grows over various time periods at different compounding rates. Over a typical 45-year career span, the difference between a $100,000 investment compounding at 5 percent and at 10 percent (the long-term average for common stocks) is $6.4 million. And the difference between earning 10 and 15 percent—an ambitious target for value investors—is *$46.5 million* over those 45 years. Yes, equity prices will fluctuate, but tolerating short-term uncertainty can be well worth the long-term results. It also helps to begin saving and investing early in life, because the compounding rate is less of a key driver than simply getting a very early start.

The Power of Compounding
(Growth of $100,000)

Years	Compounding Rate 5%	Compounding Rate 10%	Compounding Rate 15%
5	$127,628	$161,051	$201,136
15	$207,893	$417,725	$813,706
30	$432,194	$1,744,940	$6,621,177
45	$898,501	$7,289,048	$53,876,927

Note: This is a hypothetical example of mathematical compounding and is not representative of any specific investment.

Figure 15-2

Timing the Market: Speculative Ground

Trying to time one's exposure to the stock market is futile in the long run, regardless of the theory or indicator employed. Bear market low points are impossible to predict, and spending time trying to identify them distracts one from prudent financial decisions.

Charles Dow, cofounder of the *Wall Street Journal*, expressed a similar sentiment in 1902. "In dealing with the stock market," Dow said, "there is no way of telling when the top of an advance or the bottom of a decline has been reached until sometime after such a top or bottom has been made."[7]

Trying to time the market presents two dangers to an equity investor. First, any time spent out of stocks presents the risk of missing out on appreciation. As shown in Figure 15-3, $100,000 invested in the S&P 500 Index over the 6,554 trading days from the beginning of 1988 through 2013 grew to $1,341,910.

However, missing just the 15 best days of those 6,554—that is, the 15 biggest daily gains in the S&P 500 over the 26-year stretch—would reduce the final value of that $100,000 investment to $523,983, a difference of more than $820,000.

And as the number of days missed increases, so does the value erosion. With the index's 40 best days excluded, for example, a $100,000 investment in the S&P 500 over the 26 years ending in 2013 would grow to only $187,395—an annualized return of just 2.4 percent.

Timing the Market Can Have Consequences
(S&P 500 Index from 1988 to 2013)

	All, 6554	Less 10 Best	Less 20 Best	Less 30 Best	Less 40 Best
Cumulative Gain	1242%	570%	317%	176%	87%
Annualized Gain	10.5%	7.6%	5.7%	4.0%	2.4%
Growth of $100,000	$1,341,910	$669,695	$417,295	$275,678	$187,395

Note: This is a hypothetical example, assuming a $100,000 initial investment mirroring the S&P 500 Index. It is not representative of any specific investment. Reinvestment of dividends and capital gains are assumed. All indices are unmanaged and are not available for direct investment. Past performance is not a guarantee of future results. Actual results will vary.

Figure 15-3

Second, by moving out of equities, you're sacrificing the advantage of business ownership and investing in asset classes that have lower historical returns, a disadvantage to those who are seeking *long-term* appreciation. Also, based on historical evidence, the longer you stay invested in stocks, the more you diminish your potential for relative losses.

Utilizing the S&P 500 Index, we looked at quarterly returns for stocks between 1936 and 2013. During that time frame, there were 308 one-year periods (4/36 to 4/37, 7/36 to 7/37, 10/36 to 10/37, and so on). Of those 308 one-year periods, stocks registered gains 76 percent of the time. If the investment period was stretched to five years, (1936 to 1941, 1937 to 1942, 1938 to 1943, and so on), stocks posted gains during 90 percent of the 292 five-year periods between 1936 and 2013. And during the 252 fifteen-year periods over the same time, stocks never failed to appreciate. Patience—rather than attempting to time the market—has proved beneficial.

The Effects of Inflation

In 1982, U.S. economists assured us that Paul Volcker had killed the inflation dragon once and for all. That belief proved greatly exaggerated as we moved through the 1980s. Although the United States experienced a steady period of relatively moderate inflation, as long as governments borrow and spend excessively, inflation and high interest rates remain threats.

Inflation, as measured by price increases for consumer goods, has remained benign from the 1990s onward in many developed nations, but the potential threat hasn't disappeared entirely. Inflation has always been present, although at certain points in the business cycle, it usually remains discreetly out of sight. And I believe that investing in stocks may help people maintain their living standards or help them meet long-term investment objectives, such as making a down payment on a home or covering years of retirement living expenses despite the effects of inflation. Generally, companies' revenues increase with inflation, and margins have been fairly stable. Therefore, investing in companies can be an effective inflation hedge.

Jeremy Siegel examined the effects of inflation in his 1994 bestseller *Stocks for the Long Run*. "It is clear that the growth of purchasing power in equities not only dominates all other assets but is remarkable for its long-term stability. . . . In contrast to the remarkable stability of stock returns, real returns on fixed-income assets have declined markedly over time . . . since 1926, and especially after World War II, fixed income assets have returned little after inflation."[8]

All Aboard for Equities

I had an enriching conversation with a veteran financial advisor in 2009. She had seen her fair share of bull and bear markets, and our chat turned to the topic of investor behavior. I asked her how she directs her client conversations toward equities during long periods of bad headlines and negative market sentiment. It was an especially good time for investors to buy, and I expressed my frustration with trying to get clients to add funds to their portfolios.

"I start by showing them two immutable truths," she said, reaching into her valise. "Truth one is that *stuff* always happens. Truth two is that the market has *always* gone back up despite it." She unfolded a colorful marketing piece that depicted miniature *Time* magazine covers along a 40-year timeline. Each cover proclaimed a piece of gloomy economic history, such as "Can Capitalism Survive?" (1975), "The Crash" (1987), and "Will You Ever Be Able to Retire?" (2002). However, all the magazine covers were nested within a larger-than-life chart showing the unmistakable upward slope of the Dow's most recent 40-year track record. This said it all at one glance. All investors should see this thing, I thought, not just her clients.

As a long-term investment vehicle, common stocks have clearly been superior. Stocks represent businesses, which create the wealth of an advanced economy. And all other values flow from that wealth. Even in the bond world, stocks have a purpose. Interest on corporate bonds is paid by the cash flow of businesses, and interest on government bonds is paid by taxes on the wealth of businesses and individuals. Real estate rents are paid by businesses' cash flow. Art, commodities, and precious metals are all purchased with wealth produced by businesses. So it follows that businesses, over the long term, should produce higher returns than all other asset classes.

The superior returns record of stocks is well documented. Such data have long proved that stocks should have a permanent place at the investor's table. Unless something unimaginable happens to upset the natural course of global enterprise, equities will always be the most effective conduit for benefiting from—and supporting—the success of all businesses.

Investors will always change their minds about what they want from time to time as the market and their own behavior create distractions. Real estate, bonds, gold, cash instruments, commodities, more real estate, another round of bonds—you get the pattern. But they always come back to equities. It's a naturally occurring cycle that is perpetuated by the simple fact that owning stocks feeds business growth, which helps the economy, which in turn sparks increased wealth for all individuals. Equities are empowering—to the investor, the business, and the system.

That's why some of the greatest opportunities await diligent and patient investors, and they don't rely on timing the market. They depend on investigative acumen and a long-term investment horizon. The value investor constantly keeps these in mind when mingling with Wall Street, especially because "stuff" happens and stocks have always gone up.

CHAPTER 16

VALUE INVESTING IN THE BOND WORLD

All experienced investors recognize that the margin-of-safety concept is essential to the choice of sound bonds and preferred stocks.

—Benjamin Graham[1]

When PIMCO's Mohamed El-Erian abruptly left his post as second in command in 2014, it raised more than a few eyebrows. It wasn't just the fact that the heir apparent to Bill Gross, the company's founder and president, had walked away from the $2 trillion house that bonds built. After all, financial leaders seek new challenges all the time. But El-Erian's unexpected and no-excuses departure—and Bill Gross' abrupt resignation and move to a competitor a few months later—couldn't help but be taken the wrong way. That is, if the stewards of the largest bond mutual fund in the world are hinting at unseen problems in their wheelhouse, the market tends to borrow its worry.[2]

This ended up being only a speed bump in PIMCO's otherwise long and successful history, but at the time it was a clear snapshot of how hypersensitive the fixed-income landscape can be. It wasn't always this way. Bond investing was once blasé—the softer-spoken Dean Martin to equities' more animated Jerry Lewis. But this changed quickly as the fund industry expanded its fixed-income offerings and the individual and institutional world took a big liking to their convenience and diversification benefits.

Bonds and bond strategies today are hardly plain vanilla, and they can actually provide exciting insights into company fundamentals, depending on where you look. For my firm and our approach to fixed income, this points us in one direction: intrinsic value. The majority of fixed-income strategies direct their attention toward volume, and managers basically are content to generate a wave of small returns by trading among the hundreds, or sometimes even thousands, of holdings in their portfolios. But value fixed income is an entirely different animal because it seeks discounts to intrinsic value on a select number of holdings to ultimately gain from their capital appreciation.

Despite subtle differences, value investing applies equally to the stock and bond worlds. In their different ways, both of them deliver income and the potential for capital appreciation. Both offer plentiful value opportunity sets, too. Bonds are typically the first go-to for businesses that need money, because debt, unlike stock, lets them retain ownership and recognize the bonds as an expense on their balance sheets. So, just as for equities, the direction of the overall fixed-income market will have little bearing on the value opportunities that present themselves on a company-by-company basis.

Bonds . . . Ben's Bonds

You are probably wondering why a book devoted to picking undervalued stocks includes a chapter on fixed income. But bonds are actually what started it all; they were at the core of value investing right alongside the principles of value-oriented equities in Ben Graham's 1934 *Security Analysis*.

Graham devotes nine full chapters to fixed-income investing, cementing his school of thought that a company's intrinsic value can move separately from the prices of its bonds, just as it can from its share price. One of his first brushes with this concept was a Northern Pacific Railway 100-year plus issue maturing in 2047. In 1920, the company's bonds were trading below the $50 level based on concerns about their safety. The concerns abated, and by the mid-1940s, the bonds were trading for more than $90.[3]

Graham's most important caveat was that searching for value among bonds was not easy. In *Security Analysis*, he argued that the right approach to bond investing depended on the investor's first choosing between the defensive (passive) and the aggressive (enterprising) role. "The aggressive investor must have considerable knowledge of security values." He felt that many, if not most, investors placed themselves right in the middle, which he believed was "a compromise that is more likely to produce disappointment than achievement."[4] Graham suggested that many investors didn't have the time or the intellectual resources to take the aggressive bond investor role, but that bargain issues were out there for those who did.

Coupons are fixed, but the businesses that issue them are not. The market's perception of a company can change, and this affects the perceived value of its bond issues, just like its stock. Investors who can see when this happens—who examine the company's balance sheet from all angles—can find opportunities on both sides. And the only discipline that can do this with any consistency and patience is value investing.

Before examining why value investing works in the fixed-income world, we need to take a step back to get a sense of the bigger challenges it can address in its unique way.

Solve One Problem, Get Another

Although bonds festered in the early 2000s, trouble for them was really stirred up just after the financial crisis of 2008–2009. Trying to fix one problem, economic malaise, the Federal Reserve Board helped to create another, a bond rush. Keeping the federal funds target rate at near zero (0.25 percent) for more than five years was part of the Fed's effort to help stimulate growth. U.S. Treasuries felt the most pain, and the stubbornly flat U.S. Treasury yield curve did not help matters. So, even if they were willing to go to longer maturities (30 years rather than just 5 years, for example), fixed-income investors weren't getting paid enough additional interest to make it worth their trouble. Naturally, as interest rates fell, corporate bond prices rose, and this added to their attraction for investors who were searching for yields and a "safe haven" from equities.[5]

Also working in the background was a series of money injections called "quantitative easing." At one point, the Fed was buying an astounding $85 billion in U.S. Treasuries every month for years. While this was considered highly unusual, such measures had been used in the 1990s to jump-start Japan's struggling economy, discussed in Chapter 11.[6] Although quantitative easing isn't designed to have a direct impact on future short-term interest rates, all that cash entering the system and its inherent sour message stymie them anyway.

Bond Rush Begins

All this led to an extended flurry of bond buying, either through direct purchases or through investment companies, for the better part of a decade. Now everyone was scrambling even more to get the maximum yield wherever they could find it.

In the process, investors slowly and steadily began replacing interest-rate risk with credit risk. It got so disconcerting for policy makers that Richard Fisher, president of the Federal Reserve Bank of Dallas, echoed one bond analyst's reference to investors seeing the world through "beer goggles."

"Things often look better when one is under the influence of free-flowing liquidity."[7]

Credit Quality Woes

When things get this excited, investors are usually forced not only to pay up for their yield, but to take on additional risk by accepting lower credit quality. This means that they're sacrificing liquidity, extending maturities, or a combination of these. Industrywide insights showed an alarming level of junk bonds within the 10 largest U.S. bond mutual funds in 2013. Among the four funds that grew fastest from 2008 to 2013, an average of 20 percent of their bond holdings were rated below investment grade.[8]

Investors' willingness to accept higher credit risk doesn't always mean that they get paid for it. By mid-2014, the risk premium for all the major fixed-income asset classes was the tightest in more than a decade (Figure 16-1).

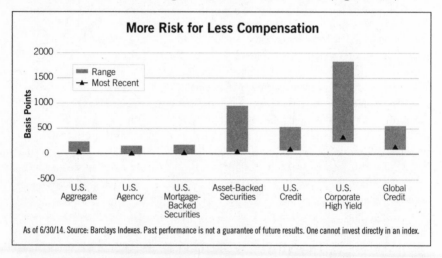

As of 6/30/14. Source: Barclays Indexes. Past performance is not a guarantee of future results. One cannot invest directly in an index.

Figure 16-1 The yield difference between a bond and a low-risk U.S. Treasury security with a similar maturity is the *option-adjusted spread* (OAS). It measures the risk premium that investors demand for taking on harmful bond risks such as credit, default, and prepayment risk. The lower the OAS, the less return investors are getting in exchange for taking on risk, also called "paying up." At June 30, 2014, OAS levels for virtually every taxable fixed-income asset class were their tightest in a decade. Investors were paying up, but not getting much gain in return.

The Good, the Bad, and the Ugly of Bonds

U.S. Treasuries and corporate bonds are an important part of the financial ecosystem. But like any asset class, their complexity can make them dynamic and not for everyone. Here's a brief summary of just a few of the benefits and limitations of bond investing.

Upsides:

- *Diversification.* Bonds are a distinct asset class with many subcategories that generally follows a different path from stocks. (This is a big draw for pension plans, too, discussed in Chapter 17.)

- *Capital preservation.* Bond principal, the investor's stake, is generally to be returned at a later date.

- *Risk mitigation.* Bond owners are typically first in line if companies become insolvent.

- *Economic contribution.* Bonds provide long-term loans to help businesses grow, thus supporting the building blocks of a sound economy.

Downsides:

- *Inflation risk.* The relative value of a bond's coupon (the interest rate it pays) can be eaten up if inflation rates increase. This is especially true of short-term bonds.

- *Credit risk.* The quality of the company issuing the bond determines whether it makes its payments and returns investors' principal.

- *Interest-rate risk.* As long as you own the bond, the rate you get is the one you signed up for (except for floating-rate bonds, discussed later), even if interest rates rise and you would rather get a better rate somewhere else, or even from the same company. Bond prices for existing issues move inversely with rates. When rates rise, the prices of bonds tend to fall.

- *Limited growth potential.* The long-term historical returns pale in comparison to those from stocks.

Like any investment, bonds have on-again off-again relationships with the market, usually based on constant white-knuckle bracing for the next interest-rate change. Like a confirmed bachelor who convinces himself that he's keeping his options open, bond investors just couldn't settle down for many years. From what I've seen, this worry is often all for naught. Interest-rate increases don't always spell as much trouble for bond prices as we've been led to believe, as shown in Figure 16-2.

Meanwhile, years of monetary easing kept money cheap for good companies, which really benefited from it. With their debt being in high demand and yields averaging about 1.21 percent for high-grade bonds by year-end 2013, the volume of new issues reached a record $1.1 trillion that year. A highlight of 2013 was Apple, Inc.'s $17 billion new issue, followed four months later

Rate Hikes Not Always Bad for Bonds

10-Year U.S. Treasury Yield Rise	Annual Yield Move (%)	Change in 10-Year U.S. Treasury Yield (%) in the Following Year	Barclays U.S. Aggregate Bond Index — Annual Total Return (%)* in the Following Year
12/31/1978	1.37	1.18	1.40
12/31/1979**	1.18	2.10	1.92
12/31/1980**	2.10	1.55	2.71
12/31/1981	1.55	-3.59	6.26
12/31/1983	1.41	-0.29	8.37
12/31/1987	1.64	0.28	2.76
12/31/1994	2.03	-2.25	-2.92
12/31/1999	1.79	-1.33	-0.82
12/31/2009	1.62	-0.54	5.93

As of 12/31/2013. Source: Sources: Bloomberg and Barclays.

*The Barclays U.S. Aggregate Bond Index was created in 1986 with history backfilled to January 1, 1976

**Periods with large moves in subsequent years (end of 1977-1980) were accompanied by rapidly rising inflation; the Consumer Price Index rose from 6.7% at yearend 1977 to 12.5% at yearend 1980.

Past performance is not a guarantee of future results. One cannot invest directly in an index.

Figure 16-2 Falling bond prices are a bond investor's major concern, because this means that interest rates are rising. Historically, however, big increases in interest rates have not been that rough on bond returns. Since 1978, most fixed-income returns held steady following large rises (more than 1 percent) in 10-year U.S. Treasury yields. Only twice were they hit hard (1994 and 1999). *Note:* The declines analyzed here are only for 10-year maturities; longer maturities can have very large declines.

by Verizon Communications Inc.'s $49 billion offering, the largest ever at the time. These were all great deals for the issuing companies, but I'm not sure how well investors made out. However, at the time, they had little choice. If they wanted high-quality debt, they had to either put up with the deals being offered or search for a higher-paying offering that had a lower rating.

As bond investors stretched for yield over the years, the proliferation of fixed-income products used for fuel was almost overwhelming to them. At one point or another, any and all of these debt-based offerings took investors ever further from the basic fundamentals of effective long-term portfolio strategies, with varying results:

- *U.S. Treasuries.* The three basic types of government-issued and reliable standbys (bills, notes, and bonds) have maturities ranging from months to 30 years; in addition, there are also Treasury Inflation-Protected Securities (TIPS).

- *Foreign debt.* These are a growing allocation in institutional pension plans; they entail additional risks, including political and currency considerations.

- *Intermediate-term debt.* This is the most popular choice among fixed-income investors, which suggests a normal investor preference for average but doesn't mean that they're effective.

- *Short-term or limited-duration debt.* This is the bond investing equivalent of a "pillow mint" and doesn't fill the hunger for real growth.

- *Multisector debt.* This is closer to the better idea of not limiting your investment, but top-down investing doesn't get you value.

- *High-yield debt.* Just be sure that your larger strategy can support the additional credit risk that comes with these bonds, and be very familiar with the companies that issue them.

- *Floating-rate bonds.* These aren't really fixed income at all; for most of them, their rates vary in tandem with the London Interbank Offered Rate (LIBOR), plus a spread. Rates don't reset as quickly as investors think, which exposes them not only to more credit risk, but to interest-rate risk as well—perhaps more than they bargained for.

- *Leveraged closed-end funds.* Generally, these ETFs borrow at a lower rate than they expect to get in returns, with the possibility of large losses in the mix.

- *Municipal bonds.* They have some tax-efficient benefits, but they usually come with tricky call features and have very long maturities that subject them to interest-rate risk.

- *Subordinated debt.* These bonds offer higher rates in exchange for placing the investor on a much lower rung in the repayment ladder, often even after some stock owners.

- *Unconstrained.* Also called "go anywhere," these have a constantly moving holding composition that makes it hard to know what you own if you want to diversify effectively.

- *Commercial paper.* This is very liquid, but not regulated, so buyer beware.

- *Bond derivatives.* There is an array of synthetic products available that make investing very intimidating for the very investors the industry is supposed to be helping.

- *2008 residuals.* The fallout from 2008 has created some new entries:

  - Credits supported by *rental payments on foreclosed homes.* Even the rating agencies vacillate on how to rate these.

  - Fannie Mae *risk-sharing* certificates. Investors cover losses on defaults of loans that Fannie guarantees. The early-generation offerings were well received.

Value Investing in Bonds

Investors may struggle to make money in corporate bonds, but this doesn't mean that there aren't opportunities out there. Most investors tend to focus on index averages, but there are literally thousands of opportunities in the corporate bond world. If you're going to find the hidden gems, however, you need to look beyond the index average. And if you believe that lower credit always means higher return, then you're fishing in the wrong place.

Taking on more actual risk isn't always necessary in order to get higher returns, especially in the non-investment-grade bond pool. Whereas value stocks are those of companies whose value is greater than their stock price suggests, value bonds are those of companies whose quality is found by the manager to be better than that implied by the higher interest rates they're forced to pay. It takes some searching to recognize these inefficiencies, but they do happen, and sometimes in striking patterns. In fact, U.S. high-yield bonds rated Ba significantly outperformed B-rated bonds from 1984 through 2012.[9] This more than suggests that there is an area on the ratings-return spectrum that offers a beneficial blend of growth potential with credit ratings that are a little higher on the non-investment-grade scale.

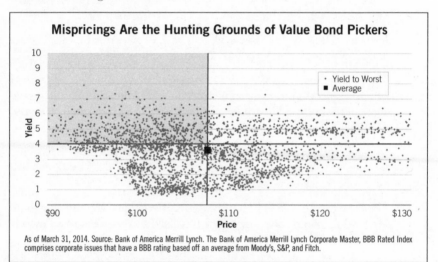

Mispricings Are the Hunting Grounds of Value Bond Pickers

- Yield to Worst
- Average

As of March 31, 2014. Source: Bank of America Merrill Lynch. The Bank of America Merrill Lynch Corporate Master, BBB Rated Index comprises corporate issues that have a BBB rating based off an average from Moody's, S&P, and Fitch.

Figure 16-3 Because of the vast number of corporate bonds, a disciplined process for evaluating their individual merits is needed. The top left quadrant is the "sweet spot" where value bond investors search. It represents a combination of below-average prices and above-average yields compared to the even larger sampling of bonds rated BBB when the data were plotted.

Regulations and Transparency—Leveling the Field

As I've said throughout this book, value investing is always working, and when given the chance and patience, it has always come through sooner or later.

Sometimes happenstance can work in your favor too, which was true for us in 2005 when the rules about how bonds showed their true colors started changing. Also, after the financial crisis of 2008–2009, structural and regulatory changes motivated larger bond dealers to scale back their capital commitments—with big implications for fixed-income managers. In 2005, the Financial Industry Regulatory Authority (FINRA) imposed rules concerning bond trade reporting that leveled the pricing playing field between the big and smaller players in the market. It was called Trade Reporting and Compliance Engine (TRACE), and it essentially required all bond dealers to report prices and whether they were buying or selling, which hadn't been required before.

"Before TRACE, there was no centralized exchange where you could view that information," said a delighted Tim Doyle, one of our veteran bond fund managers. "This opened the gates wide for us, because we could now calculate the bid/offer spread and see what the big firms were charging for retail trades." This was a huge game changer. We had access to prices, whereas before, only the select few who were involved with the transactions were privy to this information. And, obviously, when you have the price, you can see its relationship to value more clearly.

Inventory Trends Aid the Search

Another huge shot in the arm for value fixed-income investing was the Dodd-Frank Wall Street Reform and Consumer Protection Act (Dodd-Frank). Banks—including those that served as corporate bond dealers—were forced to strengthen their capital requirements.[10] As a result, many dealers reined in their risk profiles by selling much of their corporate bond inventory to avoid charges for keeping those bonds on their books. Inventories had shrunk to 25 percent of their former levels by March 31, 2013, based on New York Federal Reserve data.

This flooded the market with corporate bonds, but dealers didn't want them. Under Dodd-Frank, there was little incentive for the dealers to rebuild their inventories. How did this changing environment foster value fixed-income success? Shrinking inventory as a result of Dodd-Frank created pricing volatility. And now we had a full view of that world thanks to TRACE. When prices dip and yields spike in the short term, this creates buying opportunities for long-term managers who are focused on fundamentals. As the market gets even more distorted, value bond pickers can take full advantage of that. As a bond fund manager, even the smaller hand now had a good stake in the very large jar.

Banking on a Value Bond

One example of a value bond opportunity was JPMorgan Chase, a Ba1/BBB/BBB-rated issue with a callable feature. The bond fell a bit lower in the capital structure, meaning that we would have to

(continued)

wait our turn to be paid. The bond was not an exotic structure, but we felt that it offered excess yield relative to other JPMorgan Chase bonds, especially the bank's straight year maturity senior unsecured bullet bonds. In other words, it was mispriced compared to what we believed it was worth.

This disconnect was also fostered by the fact that JPMorgan Chase had been in the news a lot at the time. Losses from the "London Whale" derivative trades, the push to strip Jamie Dimon of his dual role of chairman and CEO, and the government's stiff fines for mortgage lending practices all didn't look good for the bank. The irony was that most of the mortgage lending practices in question emanated from Bear Stearns and Washington Mutual—two entities that the U.S. government had pushed JPMorgan Chase to purchase. We believed that the market wasn't seeing through this. JPMorgan Chase was as strong as ever, and was not going away any time soon.

Value Bonds Play Nice

Fixed income has its place in a diversified investment portfolio, and there is no shortage of choices. Value bond investing, however, is not something that you'll see everywhere. Although it dates back to 1930s Graham-and-Dodd principles, value fixed income is not your conventional bond fund strategy.

It's nimble in its holdings and more transparent than most fixed-income strategies. You always know what you're getting with value bonds. It's not a dart-throwing contest with an array of 5,000 bonds, swaps, currencies, and other alternatives. Rather, it carries out its mandate with a carefully chosen group of about 70 to 90 undervalued corporate bonds, sprinkled with varying levels of U.S. Treasuries to serve as dry powder for the next big target. So, at times, cash-like levels may appear a little higher than average for a value bond portfolio.

Adding alpha through individual security selection also means that value fixed income doesn't make macro calls or bets. So, like its value equities cousin, value fixed income will take on its own appearance relative to the index. Moreover, it's highly selective and constantly working within the "sweet spot" of mispriced BBB and Ba bonds, so that investors aren't necessarily forced to trade a lot of credit quality for return enhancements.

The process is repeatable: searching for and evaluating overlooked issues of sound companies that are paying steady coupons, but that the market thinks are either struggling or priced more efficiently than their valuations truly reveal. "Individual strength may compensate for an inherent weakness of a class," wrote Graham in 1934.[11]

Malcolm Gladwell's 2008 book *Outliers* posits that in order to understand highly successful people, you also have to look at the surroundings that help them to excel. I believe this extends to organizations too and is especially valid for our value fixed-income discipline. Not only is its success rooted in the process, but the environment has been nurturing as well.

Bond value investing needs an undisturbed perch from which it can survey, brace, and strike. Since 1996, our management team's vantage point has been Milwaukee, the perfect blend of proximity to the nation's financial centers without the superfluous noise and potential distractions of Wall Street. Moreover, the larger playing field is being leveled through TRACE, which empowers our managers with vital bond pricing intelligence—the linchpin of patient and persistent value investing. Just as enriching is the banking industry's general abhorrence of any hint of risk under Dodd-Frank, which keeps most bonds other than investment grade off their books and in the waiting hands of the market. That's great for value bond hunters, who are more than happy to take a look and, while they're at it, look at the other side of the balance sheet too.

CHAPTER 17

MANAGING RISK AND DIVERSIFYING A PORTFOLIO

The markets are very inefficient, manic depressive and wrong a lot of the time.

—Charles Brandes, interview with *BusinessWeek*, 1995

I n 2014, I had the privilege of addressing the Niagara Institutional Dialogue, an annual gathering of top Canada-based retirement plan leaders to exchange research, best practices, and new ideas.[1] In the audience were some of the smartest institutional pension minds in North America, who are well aware of difficult markets and the challenges of delivering payment certainty. So I wasn't surprised by the wave of fidgets I saw when I told them that they should add more risk to their portfolios.

"We need to embrace risk and not avoid it, particularly if we want to meet increasing longevity and long-term funding obligations," I said. "The biggest hurdle is that many investors are confusing short-term volatility risk with risk of capital loss, and they are not—and never were—the same thing."

Stocks may be the top-performing asset class historically, but there is always some risk involved with investing in them. Some of this risk is associated with a stock's going up and down in the short term—that's volatility, and it can be managed by holding a stock and waiting for it to revert to its mean and appreciate. But there are other risk dynamics that may not work out over time.

What *Are* the Risks?

Financial academics and theorists often define risk in terms of volatility, standard deviation, beta, and other mathematical quantities. These concepts of risk dominate because they are the only measures that can use hard numbers. However, these numerical conclusions are very limiting and greatly flawed. Analysts are preoccupied with these concepts, but for most investors, risk means only one thing: Will I lose money?

Loss of Capital Risk

In the four decades I've worked in the industry, I've seen a basic pattern of why investors generally lose money:

- *Overpaying.* The investor's cost was more than the underlying value of the company.

- *Selling at a loss.* For any of a number of reasons, the investor exited before the stock went up.

- *Company deterioration.* Something went wrong at the business level.

- *Lack of focus.* The investor strayed from fundamental investing disciplines.

Overpaying

In Part II of this book, we reviewed what value investors should look for before purchasing the shares of a company. The essence of value investing is weighing the *value* of a business against the *price* of owning a piece of it. As Benjamin Graham pointed out, paying too high a price for a stock—a price that is greater than the company's underlying worth—eliminates the margin of safety and thus can be very risky.

This fair warning supports my first point, the danger of paying too much. Expanding on this notion, Graham wrote, "The risk of paying too high a price for good-quality stocks—while a real one—is not the chief hazard confronting the average buyer of securities. Observation over many years has taught us that the chief losses to investors come from the purchase of *low-quality* securities at times of favorable business conditions. The purchasers . . . assume that prosperity is synonymous with safety."[2]

Selling at a Loss

Obviously, investors lose money when they sell shares at prices below what they paid for them initially. So why would an investor do such a thing? Why would anyone buy a stock at $25 per share, for example, and later sell it for $15? There are two general reasons. First, the business fundamentals underpinning the purchase decision might change, in which case taking a loss reflects a prudent, long-term decision. Second, the investor succumbs to the lure of Mr. Market. Introduced in Chapter 1, Mr. Market now helps to warn of the potential risks for value investors if they succumb to the temptation to stray from their disciplines.

Company Deterioration

Let's say that a company's products or services are shown to be inferior, management guides the company down an unwise path, or technology renders its products obsolete. In these cases, value investors may reevaluate the company and revise their estimate of its intrinsic value. If developments at a company prompt a revision of the company's underlying worth, value investors may wish to sell their shares if they are trading *above* the revised estimate of the company's intrinsic value.

The company may initially have had some pull, but sometimes the investment no longer offers a margin of safety. You may lose money by selling the shares, but it's nevertheless wiser to recognize the occasional loss and reallocate the proceeds of the sale to another, more attractively valued opportunity. At the same time, if the share price is still significantly *below* the revised estimate of the business's intrinsic value, and thus continues to offer a significant margin of safety, you should hold it. Again, the relationship between business value and stock price should be the primary factor in your decision to buy, sell, or hold.

Lack of Focus

This fourth point is the most important and sets up the bulk of this chapter's content. Focus requires discipline, and for most investors, any path toward consistency begins with understanding the various notions of risk and a common way to mitigate each of them—*diversification*.

Volatility Risk

Short-term volatility gets all the attention, but it's actually not that harmful if you're focused and can actively manage through it. All volatility is simply the tendency of a security's market value to fluctuate sharply up or down in the short term. For short-term investors who want to sell their positions at a moment's notice, volatility and risk are roughly equivalent. But for value investors, who don't have the urge or the need to liquidate their portfolios any time soon, volatility isn't an accurate measure of real risk. It's much less significant than the values of the businesses in your portfolio and the prices you paid for them.

Despite my reservations about the usefulness of volatility as a risk measure, I think it merits addressing, because:

- Many investors are volatility-averse and cannot tolerate significant short-term price fluctuations in their portfolios.

- In the academic community, volatility is the only quantifiable measure of risk, and therefore it is extensively cited in studies of risk analysis.

- Empirical studies also use *beta* as a yardstick for risk to compare a portfolio's volatility against the overall market movement rather than against its own historical returns.

Beta Measures

Let's look first at the risk measure beta, which is just a measurement of volatility relative to the market. For example, a beta of 1.0 means that a stock has about the same volatility as the overall market. A beta of 1.7 indicates that when the market has risen 1 percent, the stock has historically climbed 1.7 percent on average. Conversely, when the market has fallen 1 percent, the stock has historically declined 1.7 percent. According to the academic theory of capital markets, the higher the beta, the greater the risk and the greater the potential reward. Conversely, the lower the beta, the lower the risk and the lower the potential reward. Risk-averse investors have contributed to the Wall Street myth that supports avoiding high-beta stocks.

Many people believe that this notion has oversimplified good investment practice, including author John Train. In *Midas Touch*, Train takes beta theory to task and provides considerable insight into the investing philosophy of Warren Buffett.[3]

In the book, Buffett described being able to buy $1 worth of stock in the market for 75 cents. Suppose the price declined so that the same $1 worth of stock could be had for 50 cents. At the same time, prices for the general market remained unchanged. In this case, because the price of the $1 worth of stock fell while prices for the broader market remained flat, the stock's beta increased. Beta theorists see this as a negative development. However, the price drop usually creates an opportunity and provides a larger margin of safety. Avoiding the stock now because beta says so would be absurd.

Beta really helps only when you're looking at the whole market (or large numbers of stocks within it) and don't drill down to the fundamentals of specific companies. Short-term volatility may be reduced by purchasing only low-beta stocks, but long-term returns are likely to be diminished, and investors may fall short of their goals. Not having enough money to fund a college education or enjoy the lifestyle that you aspired to in retirement are far greater risks than the bumps of short-term volatility. For long-term investors, short-term price fluctuations are of little importance. As Warren Buffett wrote in the chairman's letter in the 1996 annual report to shareholders of Berkshire Hathaway, "I would much rather earn a lumpy 15% over time than a smooth 12%."[4]

Standard Deviation

When discussing how to measure the volatility of returns, you'll often hear the phrase *standard deviation*. You may recall that standard deviation is the dispersion of returns around an average return. So what does *that* mean? Generally, it suggests that the *greater* the standard deviation, the *greater* the volatility of a particular investment, portfolio, or market. That's good to know, but can standard deviation tell you whether the companies have the potential for long-term growth? I don't think so, and I think standard deviation can actually put you on the wrong track if you're not careful. I'll give you an example.

Standard Deviation on Campus

Sometimes it helps to deconstruct standard deviation in a very simplistic setting to get a better view of its hidden dangers. That being said, let's go back to high school, and the often-dreaded report card, to illustrate why standard deviation can be a flawed method of identifying high-quality stocks.

Most of your high school classmates probably earned a mixture of Cs and Bs, which were indeed average grades before the onset of the trend toward grade inflation. For this example, consider such grades as being average returns as well.

Meanwhile, a smaller number of students might have received all Ds or all Bs. And at the extreme ends of the scale, an even smaller number of students probably earned all Fs or all As.

You can think of the range of grades your classmates earned as being similar to the range of returns for an investment such as stocks or bonds. And based on historical precedent, you might be able to draw a reasonable estimate of how a student might perform during a semester or a year. For example, you'd expect a typical C student to get Cs. Occasionally he might do really well and get an A in one class, or he might do poorly and get an F. But for the most part, you'd expect him to get Cs.

Applying this approach to each of your high school classmates, you could quantify how much their grades fluctuated from their historical average and come up with a standard deviation. This would measure the variability of their grades (returns), or to what degree they fluctuated around their average. Thus, a student with a high standard deviation of grades might have erratic performance—for example, he might get Cs one quarter, As the next, Bs the next, and Fs the next. His performance would be characterized as more unpredictable, and thus he might be considered a "higher-risk" student.

A student who got As virtually all the time would have a low standard deviation—there would be little variability in her performance. But a student who consistently got Fs would *also* have a low standard deviation. For a failing student who regularly got poor grades, a low standard deviation wouldn't necessarily mean that he was a "low-risk" student. It would simply mean that he was a consistently bad performer.

The same logic applies to investing. When the straight-A student and the straight-F student have the same standard deviation, which would *you* invest in? Which student is more likely to succeed in the future? A low standard deviation in and of itself isn't necessarily good or bad. You have to look at it within the context of actual performance, and that takes bottom-up research.

Liquidity Risk

If all the investors in a stock want out at the same time, is the door big enough to accommodate them? How quickly can they exit? Generally, *liquidity* represents the extent to which the market can accommodate purchases or sales of a stock without large price changes. If prices are affected by such moves, investors consider that to be a major risk. With some exceptions, concerns about liquidity are largely unfounded and may limit investment opportunity. In extreme cases, liquidity can become an issue for money management firms that hold large amounts of an individual company's shares. For the most part, however, institutional and individual value investors who buy high-quality, undervalued businesses and hold on to them for a while tend to downplay the significance of a stock's day-to-day trading capacity.

Keeping Liquidity Fair

Although my firm will always focus on value at the company level, getting the best execution when trading is a critical part of the investment process as well. In his 2014 book *Flash Boys*, Michael Lewis stirred controversy with an exposé of what he called the market's "rigged game" as a result of high-frequency trading (HFT). It was no surprise to my firm, because we were part of the story—and were glad to be.

My firm, thanks to a push from our director of trading, Joseph Scafidi, was one of a handful of buy-side asset managers that helped support the start-up of IEX Group, a broker-neutral trading platform that is designed to protect investor orders from predatory HFT firms. IEX was formed when a small group of technology and securities professionals became convinced that enough was enough. They shared our conviction that the very heart of the financial markets—the exchange system—had become flawed.

By the end of 2013, the U.S. stock market had become a fast and fragmented electronic network of some 11 official exchanges and more than 40 alternative trading systems, such as "dark pools."[5] Orders would enter the market through a broker-dealer, which would place them in one of several computer programs (algorithms). These programs then sliced the orders into smaller ones (child orders), and yet another layer of the program, called smart order routers, electronically determined where the orders would go in the myriad venues just described. As efficient as this

(continued)

sounds, the process actually increases the opportunity for "infor- mation leakage" about each trade. That is, a buyer or seller's inten- tion can be inferred to a sufficient extent that the trade price could be affected. In this environment, a new class of short-term-oriented traders evolved, high-frequency traders (HFTs).

"HFT firms go home every night flat," said IEX founder Brad Katsuyama. "They don't take positions. They are bridging an amount of time that is so small that no one even knows it exists."[6]

Although it is completely legal, some HFTs weighed on market cost efficiencies, integrity, and, equally important, liquidity issues. There are many theories behind the Flash Crash on May 6, 2010, but most observers agree that HFTs had a big role in it, not to men- tion subsequent electronic market glitches.

Flash Boys, which showcases IEX and its founding members, basically shed new light on many HFT-related challenges. Regu- lators and Congress wanted answers, and new rules and regula- tions are being considered with some banks rethinking their private exchange dark pools ownership.

Brad and his young team at IEX took a major risk in doing something that they truly believed in, and most of them left very lucrative jobs to start the new venture. My firm's alliance with IEX is an extension of our shared vision of efficient, positive change in the marketplace that helps to serve the investor's long-term finan- cial interests.

Sometimes, hypersensitivity to liquidity concerns can get in the way of opportunity, and even be costly. Here's a classic example.

Delaware Trust Company, a small bank, was just one of many companies that Wall Street consistently overlooked in the late 1970s, perhaps because ana- lysts considered the stock to be illiquid. Yet the company was clearly underval- ued. In 1978, the company had $500 million in total assets and the following fundamental traits:

- P/E ratio: 4

- Price/book: 35 percent

- Return on equity: 8 percent

- Return on assets: 0.5 percent

- Loan loss, as a percent of reserves: 15 percent

At the time, Delaware Trust's book value was over $120 per share, and the stock, which traded by appointment only, was priced at $45. After investigating every aspect of the company's financial health, an astute value investor could have acquired shares of Delaware Trust, even though it traded by appointment only. In other words, shares sometimes would not trade for three months at a time. Note in Figure 17-1 that for the first few years after this hypothetical purchase, the investor would have made very little progress. In 1984, however, the stock price surged dramatically.

Delaware Trust Company's Share Price History	
End of February	Share Price
1979	$56
1980	$61
1981	$66
1982	$79
1983	$92
1984	$128
1985	$200
1986	$260
1987	$475
1987*	$854

*Buyout (May).
Source: Brandes Investment Partners. Past performance is not a guarantee of future results.

Figure 17-1

In 1987, Delaware Trust Company was purchased by Meridien Bank, which paid shareholders $854 per share. This equated to a 33 percent annualized rate of return on the initial investment. Clearly, liquidity is not always important for long-term value investors. But it *is* important for short-term speculators.

Diversifying Away from Risk

If you focus on just one company, sector, or industry and stop there, you're more than suggesting that the area you have focused on will outperform everything else. This is more uncertain than prudent investing, and, while your decision may prove to be correct, it probably represents excessive risk for most investors. Even in a well-structured portfolio, risks can't be eliminated, but they can be dealt with through diversification.

However, while diversification is important, some investors believe that it not only limits risk, but also *enhances* returns over the long term. This may or may not be true, especially when it comes to diversifying a portfolio across different asset classes. A portfolio that is diversified among stocks, bonds, and cash, for example, can indeed reduce short-term volatility, but it may also reduce long-term results relative to an all-stock portfolio.

Recalling the discussion from Chapter 15, stocks have delivered the greatest returns over the long term. But mixing in bonds and cash (which tended to lag stocks) with an all-stock portfolio can have a diminishing effect. Keep in mind that there is no "proper" portfolio mix. A portfolio made up wholly of stocks may not be appropriate for you. It largely depends upon your individual goals.

Is Risk Predictable or Efficient?

In Chapter 4, I argued against the efficient market theory—the notion that stock prices always accurately reflect everything that is known about a company and its prospects. Here, we'll outline a similar concept focused on risk: modern portfolio theory (MPT). Introduced by Dr. Harry Markowitz in the 1950s, MPT asserts that risk can be reduced through asset allocation: building a portfolio composed of different asset classes (such as stocks, bonds, and cash) with low correlations. In Chapter 8, I addressed correlation as referring to how closely returns for one asset class (large-cap U.S. stocks, for example) mirror returns for another asset class (such as small-cap non-U.S. stocks). In short, if part of your portfolio is "zigging" when another part is "zagging," the gains in one part help offset the losses in another.

While Markowitz's theory seems logical (and helped earn him the Nobel Prize), you have to understand how risk is defined within it. Over the years, investors have adopted MPT's mantra, "risk reduction through asset allocation," without perhaps giving more thought to what risks are being reduced by following this strategy.

MPT redefined risk as solely share price fluctuation, or price volatility. But value investors find this definition unacceptable. Value investors do not lose money just because share prices decline, even if those prices temporarily drop below the original purchase price. Commenting on MPT's redefining risk as just volatility, Malcolm Mitchell, the managing director of the Center for Investment Policy Studies, wrote, "That unsupported and unexplained redefinition confounds what all investors previously thought of as risk—and what non-professionals still think it is—that is, the possibility of losing money."[7]

Mitchell adds, "Markowitz did not find a way to measure the risk that investors care about: the risk that arises from an uncertain future, the risk that things will turn out to be worse than we expect. He simply ignored that kind of risk and focused instead on variability—or, to take the term more commonly used today, volatility. Instead of measuring risk, Markowitz demonstrated how to measure volatility in a portfolio. Why volatility? One obvious reason is that volatility is measurable, whereas uncertainty is not. In summary, defining risk as volatility is irrelevant to investors' real experiences, and worse, it obscures the true definition of investment risk as the possibility of losing money."

Risk in the Institutional World

Although everything discussed so far is universal, pension fiduciaries, trustees, and large wealth managers have unique challenges that revolve around risk topics. With that, let's return to Niagara-on-the-Lake and my reminder to a ballroom of institutional pension leaders that they mustn't forget about generating alpha (the excess return of a portfolio compared to its benchmark) if they're ever going to meet their long-term obligations. Derisking is dangerous, I told them, because passive and low-volatility strategies bring new risks that could be just as harmful as those that they're trying to avoid.

Not only does the constant quest to control the downside limit the upside, but it changes the mindset of what investment management is supposed to be about. A derisking mentality soon becomes a psychological barrier that fosters an aversion to *any* loss. This quickly creates a *total* aversion to risk and leads to adverse behavior patterns. One such pattern is action avoidance: do nothing, and you're not criticized. The other is action bias: do something, or else you'll be criticized for not doing *anything*.

Do Something—Anything

A simple example of action bias occurs in many soccer games. In a penalty kick situation, goalkeepers jump right or left to anticipate the direction of the ball 94 percent of the time, naturally thinking that either direction will be a 50/50 bet. But they guess correctly only 40 percent of the time. Even if they do guess right, they make the save just one out of four times. They would do better by just standing still in the middle of the net, where 30 percent of all penalty kicks are actually placed. When they meet the ball at the center of the net, they make the save 60 percent of the time. Therefore, just by standing still, they increase their chances of blocking from about 13 percent to 33 percent.[8] So why do they jump left or right? Because it looks smarter, even though statistically the numbers support no movement at all. The keeper must "do something" or be severely criticized for standing pat.

This bias toward action is a big part of the investment world—the need to do something rather than nothing, even when the data say not to. It touches all investors, but it has an especially great impact in the institutional world. If it keeps up, it's going to create serious obstacles to retirement plans meeting their long-term obligations, especially if their strategies remain too wrapped around just short-term liabilities.

Keeping a sharp watch on volatility isn't all bad, especially when you're taking on a lot more *potential* risk and not getting much in return. One example is when the California Public Employees Retirement System (CalPERS) nearly halved its weighting in hedge funds in 2014. Although its decision was performance-based, I felt that it was a step in the right direction—back to the more conventional approach that large institutions need to revisit.[9]

Back to Transparency

One of the most beneficial features of conventional approaches is transparency. A portfolio can still be effective without being complicated. A study sponsored by the Brandes Institute, "Back to the Future," showed that complicated diversification strategies that included higher allocations to alternatives underperformed simple, "old-fashioned," but effective asset allocations that were strategically focused on stocks and bonds with occasional rebalancing. Robert Maynard, chief investment officer for the Public Employee Retirement System of Idaho, presented data against the so-called endowment model. First advocated by Yale's David Swensen, the endowment model was shown to be relying "too heavily on a false sense of diversification." Although it was one of the top-performing allocation strategies beginning in 2000, the endowment model's aggressive use of alternatives led to problems beginning in 2008.

I Herd That

When everyone adopts the same diversification and passive strategies to "immunize" their portfolios from risk, this creates an alarming pattern of herding and correlation that makes things even more risky. In 2014, the chief economist of the Bank of England, Andrew Haldane, gave a speech about the self-inflicted dangers of wealth managers all herding to the same concentration of asset classes. "The behavior of unlevered asset managers may have the potential to induce pro-cyclical swings in portfolio allocation and in risk premia, with damaging consequences for systemic and economic activity . . . undergoing cycles of feast or famine."[10]

In his eloquent style, Haldane was talking about the dangers of irrational investor behavior and bubbles—two things that we already know have dire implications for the markets and systemwide risk. Furthermore, Haldane predicted that the long-term implications of the herding effect will land especially hard on institutions that have diversified away from equities. He called this the "deequitization" of portfolios, a trend that can have tragic consequences in terms of these institutions' ability to meet their future payout obligations.

What's *Your* Risk?

Beauty is in the eyes of the beholder, they say. I feel the same way about risk.

If you are a volatility-averse investor, overreacting to a short-term period of dismal stock prices can be hazardous to your long-term financial health. If your fear of fluctuating market values or your need for short-term cash could push you into selling at low prices, it might make sense for you to dampen the volatility in your portfolio.

Diversification can help to mitigate some risk by spreading your investments across multiple asset classes so that you can supposedly benefit from the ones that are up when others are down. But overdiversification can cost you, not only through potential growth constraints, but in terms of commissions, spreads, and taxes. For some investors, that equates to losing money—the worst of all possible risks.

Too often we hear the golden rule that if everyone is doing something, it must be good. This rarely applies to investments, particularly when it comes to managing risk and diversification. If everyone adopts a passive approach and chases the same asset class, it creates bubbles that become self-fulfilling and eventually pop. Equally troubling, it complicates the investor's world. Simplicity is always better.

Working with equities is not about reading the beta or standard deviation and diversifying away the alpha potential. It means doing some homework, stepping up, and taking on some additional volatility risk that could turn out to be an excellent value opportunity.

Consider the purchase of stock in McDonald's in the mid-1980s, when its market capitalization was about $4 billion and the fast-food giant was undergoing a major menu overhaul and international expansion strategy. At the time, what if the company's market value had dropped further as forecasters worried about the peak of the fast-food market—say from $4 to $3 billion? The additional downside volatility would have increased the stock's standard deviation, but it also clearly would have made it a better value. Should investors have been frightened by the high standard deviation? Not really. By 2013, McDonald's had a market capitalization of nearly $100 billion, up nearly 25-fold since 1984.

A well-chosen selection of stocks, some bonds, and an appropriate measure of rebalancing go a lot further than complicated risk measurements and alternative investments that can come back to bite you. Nobody knows what the future holds, and there is always the risk that tomorrow may not live up to our expectations. However, by carefully choosing and maintaining a diversified portfolio of value stocks, you can pursue your long-term investment goals with the confidence that comes from knowing what these risks really represent.

CHAPTER 18

WHICH WAY TO
THE MARKET?

In the long run, we shape our lives and we shape ourselves. And the choices we make are ultimately our own responsibility.

—Eleanor Roosevelt

After one of the most costly securities run-ups in U.S. history, the financial elite of New York City grew fed up with it. So, 24 of the most influential brokers in town met under a buttonwood tree near 68 Wall Street and cut a deal to bring order to the fledgling system of exchanging stocks and bonds.

The Buttonwood Agreement of 1792 laid the foundation for the New York Stock Exchange. Its goal was to prevent further bubble-causing speculation by removing the peripheral "auctioneers" from the process and transacting only among each other for a standard commission. Basically, they wanted to *restrict* entry.

Centuries later, the doors to a significantly more dynamic market are wide open to practically anyone who is willing to step up. The plethora of discount and full-service brokers, online trading firms, financial advisory services, and asset managers offers no shortage of entries. The challenge for investors is to choose the entry method that makes the most sense, given their needs.

Whether you decide to manage things yourself or hire a professional advisor, value investing can be approached in a variety of ways, none of which necessarily is the best. Your method of operation simply reflects your inclinations, your interest level, and your financial needs. Although I outline a handful of the more common approaches, it's prudent to be sure that the direction you choose is right for you.

"Know Thyself"

The Greek philosopher Socrates probably wasn't talking about global stock markets when he shared his self-awareness advice around 400 BC, but his words are particularly relevant for investors and deceptively complex. People have inherent biases and tendencies to act irrationally. Ben Graham described the individual investor as his own worst enemy. How can we protect ourselves from ourselves?

Who Are You?

Following Socrates' advice, let's get a better handle on who we are—by making toast.

Author Rich Tennant has developed a humorous test to help assess your risk tolerance when investing:[1]

Which one of these phrases best describes how you retrieve toast?

1. Wait for toast to pop up, even though it's burning.

2. Go after toast with wooden toast prongs.

3. Go after toast with an all-metal butter knife.

4. Go after toast with a metal butter knife wearing a wet swimsuit and stainless-steel colander on head.

Match the number of your answer to the following risk profile:

1. Low risk

2. Moderate risk

3. High risk

4. Ultra-high risk

While your toast-gathering technique may not necessarily provide an exact script for how you will act when you are managing a portfolio of value stocks, this fun quiz may provide some insight into who you are. Namely, how aggressive are you? How patient are you?

Successful value investors are patient investors. How patient are you? How willing are you to trust your judgment and swim against the often irrational current of the market? To gain clearer insight into what motivates you, I suggest searching the Internet for different tests that can help you assess your investment profile; key words such as "risk tolerance quiz" or "risk tolerance profile" will help narrow your results.

Keep in mind that the objective is to help you gain a better understanding of yourself so that you can build the necessary defenses against your own potentially self-defeating tendencies. Often, it's difficult to be objective. It's difficult to look at our behaviors for what they really are. This is why we're often our own worst enemies. The most important question is: Can you hold on for the long term when prices decline? Most people answer yes, until price declines actually happen.

Daily Chats with a Manic-Depressive Partner

Get used to having daily chats with Mr. Market. Benjamin Graham developed the parable of Mr. Market to help explain the stock market's often irrational behavior when it comes to pricing individual stocks. He also helps to explain the risks that value investors invite when they fail to *remain* value investors.

Graham suggested imagining that you own a $1,000 stake in a business. Think of Mr. Market as one of your business partners. Every day, "He tells you what he thinks your interest is worth and furthermore offers either to buy you out or to sell you an additional interest on that basis."[2] Be warned, however: Mr. Market has a personality quirk. Years ago, we might have described his condition as manic-depressive or bipolar. So, Mr. Market often does not act rationally. At times, he is extremely optimistic and puts a very high price on the business. Other days, he can be extremely pessimistic, putting a very low price on the business because he is convinced that it will fall to zero. The important thing to remember about Mr. Market is that *you choose how to interact with him.*

As Graham wrote, "You may be happy to sell out to him when he quotes you a ridiculously high price, and equally happy to buy from him when his price is low. But the rest of the time you will be wiser to form your own ideas of the value of your holdings."[3] Graham wrote that investors who hold shares of common stock share a similar relationship with the broader market. An investor "can take advantage of the daily market price or leave it alone, as dictated by his own judgment and inclination."

The fickleness of Mr. Market underscores yet again *the* fundamental tenet of value investing. Value investing works by capitalizing on the difference between business values and share prices. The fluctuating share prices that Mr. Market presents you with each day have very little or nothing to do with the underlying value of businesses. Always be vigilant and guard against confusing business value with stock price.

Remember, despite any market swings, you remain in control. *You* decide the true value of the companies you hold, not Mr. Market. *You* decide when, and at what price, you want to purchase or sell shares. Because of his irrational mood swings, Mr. Market can tempt you to sell your holdings at a loss or to purchase businesses at high prices. Trust *your* judgment. Trust *your* research. Don't be swayed by the siren song of an overly emotional marketplace. Being aware of Mr. Market and his mood swings can help you to be patient and help you make rational investment decisions.

With Mr. Market bending your ear, the trend toward more volatile markets may or may not continue. Either way, you need to be prepared mentally and emotionally for swings in share prices. Let's look at some specific means of preparation.

Regret

How often have you given someone a lottery ticket as a gift? If you said never or rarely, you're in good company. Most people don't want to give away a ticket that turns out to be a winner and have to regret it.

This mindset also influences how we manage portfolios. If developments at a company lower its intrinsic value to less than what we paid to purchase the shares, effectively eliminating our margin of safety, selling that stock at a loss is not a bad decision. Our aversion to regret, however, may prevent us from executing a trade on which we will lose money. We don't like to lose, and we may hope that the stock will rally. We don't want to "give away" what could turn out to be a "winning" investment. But our hopes, likes, and dislikes have no place in an investment process. Stay focused on value investing disciplines. Strive to manage your portfolio without emotion. Stick to analyzing business fundamentals and comparing the relationship between business value and stock price.

Framing

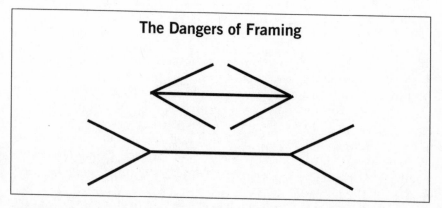

Figure 18-1

Look at the lines in Figure 18-1.

Which horizontal line is longer? Look closely. Things are not always what they *appear* to be. As shown in Figure 18-2, the lines are actually equal in length.

These illustrations underscore a key point for investors: we cannot always trust our perceptions. As shown in Chapter 5, there are differences between a good *company* and a good *investment*, so value investors need to be diligent. We need to be skeptical. And most important in this context, we need tools and rules to help us distinguish opportunities from empty promises.

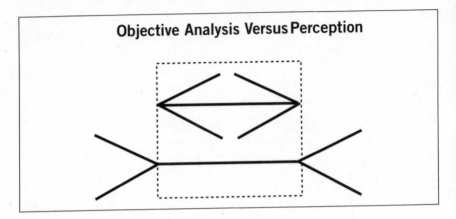

Figure 18-2

Think of the lines in Figure 18-2 as stocks in which you could invest. Imagine your eyesight as the evaluation tool that most investors use when they are analyzing stocks. Then picture the ruler as your value investment discipline. By applying a disciplined approach to evaluating opportunities, you limit guesswork, emotional influence, and cognitive errors. You force yourself to trust objective analysis, not your emotions or the opinions of others. The goal is to make more informed decisions based on facts.

Managing Your Own Portfolio

If you decide to manage your own value portfolio, be aware that this could be a time-consuming process. It also means that you will need to stay objective about your money, which can be challenging because we often don't see our own situations as they really are. There's a lot of work to it, too, and you'll have to conduct your own research, handle your trades, and evaluate your investment performance. Ideally, do-it-yourself value investors should have considerable experience in finance and accounting. Several chapters in Part II of this book provide insights into what to look for and how to interpret the data.

While managing money requires a high level of dedication and commitment, a value investor with sufficient time and expertise could realistically expect to improve on the returns earned by many professional managers. As we've addressed, many larger institutional managers can fall prey to irrational behavior. So whether you're managing a large account or a personal "rainy day" fund, I believe that staying focused and evenhanded can give you quite an edge over many professionals. The value investor who is acting independently should plan to spend a good deal of time on managing a portfolio and becoming familiar with some of the resources shown in Chapters 5 and 6.

Investment Clubs

Sometimes do-it-yourself investors join with others to form investment clubs. In general, I don't think this is a good idea. As with casino gambling, there is a social aspect to investment clubs that can prove detrimental. Like gamblers, investment club members may feel that they are united as a team against a common foe—the house or the market. This team mentality can lead to overconfidence, illusions of control, and decisions that reflect a follow-the-herd mentality.

"Investment clubs serve many useful functions," according to research by Brad Barber and Terrance Odean, professors at the University of California–Davis. "They encourage savings. They educate their members about financial markets. They foster friendships and social ties. They entertain. Unfortunately, their investments do not beat the market."[4] Many of these clubs had to be disbanded during the financial crisis of 2008–2009.

Doing what everyone else is doing—even everyone else in your investment club—means that you'll probably also get the same returns as everyone else. Based on my experience, if you want to achieve solid results over the long term, you often have to go against the grain. Conduct your own research and act upon it.

Establishing a Course

If you want to go it alone in your value approach, I offer four suggestions:

1. Draft an investment policy statement.
2. Rebalance your portfolio.
3. Pause to reflect.
4. Follow a structure.

Developing a Personal Investment Policy Statement

Institutional investors have *investment policy statements* (IPSs). I think individual investors should have them as well. Given that only 61 percent of financial advisors create them, it's important that you ask for one.[5] This statement is a detailed plan that outlines your specific objectives. It may include guidelines for asset allocation, time horizons, and how you will work with a financial advisor if you want one. Your IPS also may include more specifics, such as restrictions on certain stocks that you don't want to own. Regardless of the level of detail that is included in it, your plan should help you do at least three things:

- Set realistic objectives.

- Outline your asset allocation strategy.

- Establish procedures for managing your portfolio.

If you are working with a financial advisor, the IPS is your constitution. It will outline how your investment process and objectives will be communicated to all parties that are involved with your investments—for example, advisors, beneficiaries, and current and future fiduciaries—and who is responsible for implementing what aspects of the plan.

Setting objectives can help you avoid the tendency to constantly compare the short-term returns on your portfolio against an index or against your brother-in-law, who likes to brag about how much money he's making in stocks. Having owned the best-performing stock each quarter might make you feel better, but it is far more important that you evaluate periodically how your overall portfolio is doing compared to the specific goals you have set.

In addition to assessing your risk tolerance and gauging your time horizon, there are other factors to consider when you are creating your objectives, including return requirements, income and liquidity needs, and tax considerations.

Here's a sample investment objective for a doctor: "To make his job optional by the age of 55; to have an annual income from his investments of at least $100,000 (after taxes and in today's dollars, with an inflation factor of 4 percent beginning at 55); to leave a substantial legacy to his two daughters; and to minimize potential tax liabilities."

Working with a Financial Advisor

Because of the highly specialized nature of portfolio management, many investors might do well to consider using the services of a professional financial advisor to carry out the day-to-day work.

If you decide to partner with a financial advisor, I echo the advice offered by the CFA Institute, a nonprofit group that promotes high standards of ethics, education, and professional excellence in the industry. It administers the Chartered Financial Analyst designation, a widely accepted professional qualification, and provides leadership in "investment education, professional standards and advocacy." The institute recommends that investors look for five things in selecting a financial advisor:

1. Preparation

2. Professionalism

3. Philosophy

4. Performance

5. Professional designations

In essence, you should follow these steps to prepare questions for potential advisors and interview them as if you were selecting an employee for your own business.

- *Ask for referrals.* Research candidates' backgrounds: their employment history, education, and professional affiliations. Ask about advisors' investment philosophies, how they intend to work with you, and their frequency of communication.

- *Ask to see samples of reports you would receive.* Analyze the long-term performance of the advisor's recommendations.

- *Ask how the advisor gets paid.*

- *Ask about the advisor's investment process.* What can you expect in working with him or her? For more guidance on selecting an advisor, you may want to search the Internet for online resources, using key words such as "selecting a broker," "choosing a financial advisor," or "advisor relationship."

Once you have selected a competent advisor, you still have a job to do. A good client can help an advisor function efficiently. How can a value investor become a good value client? Above all, understand how implementing the value investment philosophy will affect your returns over both the short and the long term.

For example, an initial value portfolio, whether it is created by the advisor or established through a mutual fund portfolio or a separately managed "wrap" account, may take time to show gains. Unpopular securities do not become market leaders overnight; often it can take as much as three years before a value portfolio begins to demonstrate its initial intrinsic worth. Being patient, however, doesn't mean being passive. While you are waiting for the more emotion-based segment of the marketplace to recognize your portfolio's intrinsic value, make certain that your advisor is sticking to the value approach. Do not, however, get caught up in such minutiae as short-term quotes. If questions arise about particular holdings, focus on how the company fits the chosen philosophy and whether the advisor is still on track.

The investor's second responsibility as a client is to communicate. Tell the advisor how much money you have available for equity investments, how much will be available in the future, and your time horizon. Keep the advisor informed of any changes that might affect your plans. Be aware that large and unexpected capital withdrawals can disturb investment strategies, especially during market lows. Finally, let the advisor know of any concerns or problems.

Doing your part to make an advisory relationship work can save you time, money, and frustration. Also, remember that changing advisors increases the amount of time required for an investment plan to prove itself. Furthermore, switching advisors usually results in significant transaction costs as one advisor's positions are sold and another's purchased.

Retirement Planning Is Front and Center

As the wave of baby boomers reaches retirement age, their influence has altered trends in investment strategies from putting money in to taking it back out. Naturally, investors want to be sure that their retirement nest eggs will last longer than they do, and this is not unique to baby boomers. Helping investors of any age accumulate assets and plan ways to generate income later in life is one of the largest value adds that financial professionals can offer.

Income engineering is a growing strategy that represents a combination of payout guarantee products and asset classes with growth potential. The paradigm of retirement planning used to be that you worked for one company throughout your career, raised a family, saved a little, and drew a company pension for as long as you and your spouse lived. Unfortunately, those days are gone, and financial advisors should be able to help you invest to fill the gaps.

The biggest challenge is the result of the best news: you may live a long time—so plan on that. Knowing this, advisors strive to design portfolios that provide a steady stream of income, but also have a growth component to increase your chances of not running out of money. We're living longer, averaging about 25 to 35 years after retirement. So, putting all your assets into fixed income and cash is *not* the right way to go.

Financial planning veteran and author Nick Murray likens fixed income to a rattlesnake, which always warns before it strikes. "Just by its name alone," says Murray, "fixed income tells you how it's going to behave. Why would you put your clients there, especially in retirement when they need income the most?" I agree, and while many folks are starting to come around, I think we're still among a small minority who think this way.

In a white paper called "Boomers Behaving Badly," the Brandes Institute argues against the conventional wisdom of matching the percentage of a portfolio's fixed-income holdings to the person's age. A widely held belief is that a 65-year-old should have just 35 percent in equities, and that this should drop with age as more fixed income is added. Instead, the goal should be to maximize postretirement investment returns to accommodate the fact that we will need income well into our nineties and probably won't have a pension to supplement our savings.[6]

Following a Structure

When it comes to procedures for managing your portfolio, you might want to follow specific, step-by-step guides for purchasing or selling shares and rebalancing. Having a written game plan for buying or selling a stock greatly reduces the likelihood of your making emotional decisions and can be an excellent defense against the kinds of psychological pitfalls addressed here and in Chapter 4. A written action plan also brings greater consistency to your approach.

Careful monitoring is critical too, because there is more to value investing than buying cheap stocks, holding them, and selling them when they're up. It's also about keeping a close watch on your target margin of safety, testing it, possibly adjusting it, and certainly applying it to your ongoing decisions. So, instead of winging it or wondering whether you've considered all the angles before making a decision, you have a mental checklist to guide you. Think of this as a recipe that's designed to bring success. You can build a portfolio from scratch and maintain it with each ingredient along the way.

With respect to developing your asset allocation strategy, balance your long-term goals with any short-term needs. Consider your tolerance for volatility and your time horizon. Again, a financial advisor may be able to assist you in coming up with a mix of different asset classes.

As for reviewing your progress toward your goals, establish how often you plan to do this. You may want to examine your portfolio every six months or once a year. I suggest that you put a lot of time into *developing* your plan and far less time into tinkering with it. Unless your long-term goals or objectives change, you will probably make few adjustments to your IPS once you nail it down.

Fees Are Earned, Not Just Charged

Fees and charges that are attached to the management and maintenance of a relationship with a financial advisor or asset manager are always a key consideration in selection. Fees are certainly a factor in long-term returns. However, fees are earned, not just charged. Active value investing in particular takes a considerable amount of resources, talent, and time to get it right. So it's important that you look beyond the bottom-line fee structure and evaluate what exactly the manager is providing in terms of value added for those charges.

Thoughts on Dollar Cost Averaging

One investment approach that I think is often misrepresented is dollar cost averaging (DCA). DCA is designed to build wealth over the long term by continuously investing a fixed amount in securities regardless of fluctuations in their prices. It is most often associated with mutual fund investing, but it also applies to systematic payments into the underlying fund options for variable annuities and the like.

In theory, this appears to be a sound approach: getting shares at a good price while regularly investing a fixed amount of money to build long-term wealth. Benjamin Graham also extolled the virtues of DCA. "The monthly amount may be small, but the results after 20 or more years can be impressive and important to the saver," he wrote in his book *The Intelligent Investor*.[7]

Certainly, a long-term bull market can make DCA successful. But what about applying this tactic during a *declining* market? Investors should consider their ability to continue purchasing through periods when prices are low.

The emotional pressure can escalate if they feel that they are "throwing good money after bad" when prices decline for a protracted period.

When stock prices fall over a long period, the average *cost* per share may *not* prove to be less than the average *price* per share. In fact, DCA strategies can never assure a profit or protect against loss in declining markets. Yet, I believe that it is often precisely at the moment when investors are tempted to abandon DCA that maintaining a commitment to such a plan is essential.

Graham addressed DCA in commenting on business executive John J. Raskob's article "Everybody Ought to Be Rich," published in the *Ladies Home Journal* in 1929. Extrapolating the stock market's rise during the 1920s two decades into the future, Raskob had contended that a $15 investment each month in good common stocks (with dividends reinvested) would grow to $80,000 in 20 years. How did his theory pan out in reality?

Based on Graham's calculations—assuming investment in the Dow Jones Industrial Average (DJIA) between 1929 and 1948—an investor's holdings 20 years after embarking on the program would have been worth about $8,500. "This is a far cry from the great man's promise of $80,000, and it shows how little reliance can be placed on such optimistic forecasts and assurances."[8] However, Graham makes an important counterargument: "The return actually realized by the 20-year operation would have been better than 8% compounded annually—and this despite the fact that the investor would have begun his purchases with the DJIA at 300 and ended with a valuation based on the 1948 closing level of 177."[9] (That's a decline of 41 percent.)

While DCA may deliver benefits for some people (namely, establishing a disciplined method for investing), long-term investors should be aware that this strategy makes impossible the core tenet of value investing: consideration of *price*. Systematic investing programs eliminate any comparison between business value and stock price when making purchase decisions. Perhaps money can be made in this way, but the strategy doesn't qualify as value investing. True value investors buy only when the price is right.

Rebalancing Your Portfolio

When you examine your portfolio periodically, one aspect that you need to consider is rebalancing. This is a fancy word for making any necessary adjustments to keep your portfolio's asset allocation in line with your goals. Adhering to a sound rebalancing strategy often forces you to make decisions about your portfolio that run counter to the crowd. For example, when stocks surge, you may sell a portion of your holdings to prevent them from becoming too large a piece of your portfolio. Conversely, when stock prices fall, you may purchase *more* shares to bolster their diminished allocation.

"Rebalancing and the free lunch of diversification go hand in hand," argues Robert Maynard, chief investment officer of the Public Employee Retirement System of Idaho. "Rebalancing benefits increase as volatility rises. If you don't rebalance, you get no diversification benefits."[10]

Many investors add to their stock positions when the market climbs and sell shares when the market declines. Effective value investors go the other way.

They see market declines as short-term events that create opportunities to purchase attractive businesses at bargain prices. Keeping a long-term perspective and rebalancing your portfolio periodically can deliver important benefits down the road.

Pause to Reflect

Often, we tend to get swept up in our day-to-day activities. Responsibilities for work, family, and friends may divert our attention from the longer-term goals we have set for ourselves or for the people we care about. The same can be true of investing. I encourage you to pause periodically to reflect on your investment approach, to review your goals and how you've set about achieving them, and to refresh your convictions concerning the value approach. In addition to the book you're holding, I suggest purchasing *The Intelligent Investor* by Benjamin Graham and reading a chapter or two at least once each year. You may not learn anything new in reading excerpts from Graham's book, but hopefully you will fortify your defenses against making irrational investment decisions.

As you construct your portfolio and manage the stocks in it, focus on your margins of safety and follow your IPS. Graham's insights from Chapter 8, "The Investor and Market Fluctuations," and Chapter 20, "'Margin of Safety' as the Central Concept of Investment," are particularly timeless.

There are few guarantees in any form of investing, and if you strictly adhere to value investing principles, you are very likely to question the merits of this approach at some point. You will probably also second-guess your decisions and raise self-doubts. By investing in out-of-favor stocks, you may appear to others to be foolish in the short term. Your portfolio may languish when the rest of the market is surging. You'll see and hear negative news about your portfolio holdings and wonder why you ever purchased them. I'm telling you all of this now not to frighten you, but to prepare you. I saved the encouragement for the last chapter, where I tell you to stick to your value disciplines, trust your independent analysis, avoid the temptation to abandon value principles and, above all, be a very patient harvester of toast.

CHAPTER 19

STAYING THE COURSE

The market has taught me many important lessons, an important one being to ignore the market most of the time.

—Charles Brandes, in an interview with the *Globe and Mail*, Toronto, September 2013

They said that Paul Allen was throwing his money away when he bought the struggling Seattle Seahawks in 1997 for nearly $200 million. The team's outlook was dismal, as was its crumbling stadium. The franchise was such a money loser that the league very briefly moved it to Los Angeles. Did Allen pay too much?[1] Over the next 18 seasons, the Seahawks made the playoffs nine times, including two trips to the Super Bowl and a resounding win in 2014, the same year that the team's estimated value topped $1 billion.[2] Was it still too overpriced?

In 1919, Babe Ruth hit 29 home runs for the Boston Red Sox—a league record—but he had never hit more than 11 in any prior year. To everyone's shock, he was sold to the Yankees the following season for the astronomical sum of $125,000. Was Ruth overvalued?[3] His first year in New York, he nearly doubled his home run count, and he fell below the 29 mark just three times in his next sixteen seasons.[4] How overvalued was he after that?

In some ways, stocks can behave like football teams and baseball players—they have some good years and some bad ones. Yet, if leadership, vision, management, and competitive focus are all intact, they tend to follow the right course over the long run to make their owners proud. Serious value investing is no game, but investors and sports fans can agree that stock picking and team loyalty share one important truth—the need for patience to stay the course.

As I close this book, I will appear to repeat myself. This is deliberate and necessary. After all, history continues to show us that things repeat: the markets, irrational behavior, "new" investment products, and sundry investor distractions. But if you follow the principles of value investing, keep focused, and stay rational, this repetition can work in your favor.

Find Your Patience Zone

Don't expect to achieve financial success overnight. There will be periods when your stocks or your portfolio are not performing well. This is when patience becomes especially important for your long-term success. Find your zone. Don't fidget, fuss, bail out, let your emotions get the better of you, or be concerned with day-to-day market fluctuations. Remember that basic value principles aren't effective without the willingness to stay the course.

Be a Good Driver

My career began at the swan song of the "Go-Go Era," but it wasn't long before the "Nifty Fifty" swooped in to impress upon me the cyclical dangers of investor behavior. The hazards of speculating loom everywhere. Bubbles are caused by nothing more than irrational thinking and will always pop under the strain, only to start right up again somewhere else. If you can avoid such short-term thinking and speculative impulses, you're more likely to succeed in the long run. But you have to catch yourself, and it's not always easy. Think back to the book's sections on investor psychology and how everyone believes that he or she is one of the "best drivers." But the reality is that most people can't or won't understand how very normal behavioral flaws work against them and their long-term plan. Rise above it, and take the high road.

Benjamin Graham made the argument for restraint in *The Intelligent Investor*: "We have seen much more money made and *kept* by 'ordinary people' who were temperamentally well suited for the investment process than by those who lacked this quality, even though they had an extensive knowledge of finance, accounting, and stock-market lore."[5]

Know Your *Real* Risks

Short-term volatility and so-called sideways metrics like standard deviation and beta are *not* your enemy. Losing capital is the real threat in investing, and this particular risk starts when you pay too much for a company. Investors don't suffer a loss because a stock price declines. They lose by deciding to sell a falling security. Long-term objectives, not short-term price fluctuations, should determine investment decisions.

Diversification has its risk mitigation benefits, but don't go overboard with it. Too much of it can work against you by limiting your upside growth opportunities while costing you more than it's worth in the long run. A phrase that is frequently heard is, "The more colorful your pie chart, the worse you did this year."

The pursuit of alpha should never be totally ignored, especially when the real risks are greater than the imagined ones. All the evidence shows that equities should be a larger portion of one's nest egg, even *during* retirement—to a degree that challenges the status quo's "minimal" exposure. This means adding undervalued stocks of solid businesses, which are the only vehicles that provide meaningful, consistent growth over time. Life spans are lengthening, not shrinking. If deequitization swings your allocation to fixed income, that's exactly what you'll get—until your assets are depleted much too early. *This* is a serious risk.

Stand Up for Simple

While the rest of the world is rushing to buy great concepts or the latest high flyer, the successful value investor must hang tough and stick to the basics. A fundamental value approach and the courage of your convictions will do more to land you undervalued businesses throughout the world than a quant formula or the like. The key is to always be looking for companies to invest in, monitor and test your holdings, and adjust your portfolio accordingly. Don't let the dry spells push you in the more complicated directions. Most important, beware of the new *new* products that are just like retreaded tires—previously used and maybe even a little more dangerous now.

Claim Your Independence

The consequences of following the market's orientation toward short-term results and instant gratification can be detrimental to your plan. Successful value investors need to stand apart and defy group thinking.

If you follow the crowd, you'll perform with the pack. You're also likely to get trampled, or, worse, you'll become part of the problem. That is, the asset you're flocking to balloons to such an extent that even if it doesn't necessarily pop, it causes serious damage to the system. Recall the unsettling reality of how pension managers are treading on thin ice—they are mentally conditioned to "derisk" their plans away from the one asset class that can help them grow the most—equities.

Feel Free to Wander

Margins of safety pay little attention to coordinates on a map. It's smart to read about the political, economic, social, and other macro elements of the environment, but always start with the company first. Then multiply that all over the world. And it's OK if this leaves some countries behind or puts you inside some that most investors are avoiding. Location is a by-product of the process. Remember, you may be wandering, but you're not drifting. The value journey has purpose.

Remain Studious

Contrary to public opinion, the value style is not a "set-it-and-forget-it" strategy. The work never really stops, and neither do the questions. Valuations of price-to-earnings, price-to-cash flow, and price-to-book will get you to first base, but the golden nuggets are found inside the ledger. Profits, depreciation, goodwill, revaluations, taxation, inventories, and restatements will keep you busy.

You may also feel obliged to go head-to-head with management. Value investing sometimes means that you have to dig deeper than just the books. Influencing change through shareholder activism can be an option, but it should be used sparingly. Infinitely more effective, and what Warren Buffett swears by, are amicable discussions behind the scenes rather than boardroom showdowns. The post-Enron world of "what else can go wrong" malfeasance and scandals will also keep you on a constant governance watch. Companies are organic and led by people, whose occasional faults and weaknesses can lead to some interesting angles, especially in a company's value and outlook.

Don't Be Misled

Financial media and investment advertisements may lead investors astray and often in circles, constantly offering stock and investment recommendations and predictions. Investment ads often show affluent investors making trades or checking stock prices while they're on the ski slopes, in a cab, or at the airport. All of these imply that knowledge is power, convenience is essential, and rapid trading is investing. Unfortunately, these messages can undermine an investor's patience and selectivity. The only thing that frequent trading and price monitoring are likely to guarantee the investor is increased trading costs.

When authors Thomas Stanley and William Danko surveyed millionaires for their book *The Millionaire Next Door*, they found that fewer than 1 in 10 millionaires are what they termed "active investors." In fact, 42 percent of the millionaires they interviewed had made *no* trades whatsoever in their stock portfolios in the year prior to the interview.[6] So much for the media's portrayal of "the real investors of Wall Street."

Dismiss Predictions

Another fallacy that the financial media promote is the illusion that markets can be predicted. Once anyone gets the idea that he or she can recognize a pattern, watch out. It's hard to suppress those speculative instincts. This hind-sight bias is rampant in the financial media. Within minutes after the closing bell, market analysts are busy explaining the exact reasons why the Dow was up 90 points or why the Nasdaq was down 2 percent. Events that even the best-informed experts did not predict seem to have been inevitable immediately after they occurred. The truth is that people can rarely reconstruct, after the fact, what they thought about the probability of an event before it occurred.

Test Your Approach

To be successful, you have to know that what you're doing is worth it. Value in-vesting is no different, so it's a good idea to keep testing its effectiveness. Ask the tough questions that only a careful study of human behavior and invest-ment trends can answer. Why do investors bet against themselves? How are pension managers responding to bond rates? You just have to keep asking. And if you uncover something new, thought-provoking, or validating, share it with the world. A free enterprise system should also include free-flowing ideas and thought leadership to benefit all. That's the larger goal of the Brandes Institute, and I always encourage the public to peruse its online library.

Tune Out

Patience is certainly a tall order when you consider the dominance of the finan-cial media that provide apocalyptic headlines, inconsistent recommendations, suggestions for short-term market trades, superficial explanations, and a fixa-tion on short-term market performance.

Investors will find their patience tested by the media, whose messages are produced for mass consumption. Practicing patience and discipline demand tuning out the media's incessant prattle.

In early 2009, the world was hip-deep in the Great Recession, and the markets never stopped reminding us every minute that the bottom could be anywhere. It was hard for anyone to ignore. So, my firm placed "caution signs" throughout the office to remind everyone to settle down and look past the media distractions no matter what. "Caution: media hyperbole can be conta-gious, inflammatory, hazardous, corrosive, and irritating to our clients' long-term value focus," was the gist of the message.

Most Important, Stay Safe

Nothing is more important in value investing than purchasing shares of a busi-ness that offer a decent margin of safety—a difference between the price of the stock and the value of the underlying business.

And don't stop at a slight discount. Look for solid companies whose stock is selling at a *substantial* discount to the intrinsic value of the businesses they represent. The bigger the margin of safety, the safer you are from the real risk that you should be worried about—paying too much.

Ben Graham and I talked about margin of safety in many contexts. This was one of the few constants in our discussions of everything that was going on around us. He never seemed to look back, and he enjoyed every new opportunity to apply and test his principles as the market became ever more dynamic and fragmented in the early 1970s. Value held up then and still does. Even more immovable are the facts that value investing is often challenging, never glamorous, and has always outperformed in the long run.

As a committed value investor, I never make predictions. It's not what I do. But I will make an exception now and predict that times will certainly change, but the superiority of value investing never will—not unless they find a cure for irrational human behavior.

The investment world is light-years from what it was when I joined it in 1968, and yet it's the same in many ways. Market complexity has evolved to create new and challenging environments. But the natural law of price and value has not changed, and neither has human behavior. This is why value investing will always exist and Ben Graham will always remain relevant. Ben's value principles will be his lasting gift to me and to generations of investors who embrace their superior logic and apply them in their unique ways.

Notes

Chapter 1

1. The Dow Jones Industrial Average was down 22.61 percent on Monday, October 19, 1987.
2. Jay R. Ritter, "Initial Public Offerings," in Dennis E. Logue, *Handbook of Modern Finance* (Boston: Warren, Gorham & Lamont, 1984), reprinted in *Contemporary Finance Digest* 2, no. 1 (Spring 1998), pp. 5–30.
3. Federal Reserve Board Flow of Funds.
4. There is no formal list of the Nifty Fifty. Kidder Peabody's monthly list of the top 50 Big Board (New York Stock Exchange) stocks based on price-to-earnings ratios is sometimes cited. Fifty company names compiled by Morgan Guaranty Trust and footnoted in a 1977 *Forbes* article is considered by many to be the closest thing to an official list.
5. The Dow Jones Industrial Average dropped from 1051 on January 11, 1973, to 577 on December 6, 1974.
6. The FTSE 100 was down 31.35 percent in 1973 and 55.34 percent in 1974.
7. Mark Carlson, "A Brief History of the 1987 Stock Market Crash with a Discussion of the Federal Reserve Response," Board of Governors of the Federal Reserve, November 2006.
8. Ibid.
9. Timothy Curry and Lynn Shibut, "The Cost of the Savings and Loan Crisis: Truth and Consequences," FDIC, December 2000.
10. Lars Jonung, "The Swedish Model for Resolving the Banking Crisis of 1991–93: Why It Was Successful," European Commission, Directorate-General for Economic and Financial Affairs, February 2009.
11. Charles Mackay, *Extraordinary Popular Delusions and the Madness of Crowds*, London, 1841.
12. The S&P 500 Index had a 34.5 percent weighting in technology stocks on March 1, 2000.
13. Bill Gross, PIMCO Investment Outlook, August 2012.
14. According to the Investment Company Institute, there were $73 billion in outflows from fixed-income mutual funds in 2013.

Chapter 2

1. Benjamin Graham, *The Intelligent Investor: A Book of Practical Counsel*, 4th rev. ed. (New York: Harper & Row, 1973), p. 277.
2. DALBAR frequently updates information and data from its "Quantitative Analysis of Investor Behavior Report." Although overall results are available at DALBAR's website, www.dalbarinc.com, methodologies and data usually must be purchased.
3. Graham, *Intelligent Investor*, p. 1.

Chapter 3

1. James Montier, "No Silver Bullets in Investing (Just Old Snake Oil in New Bottles)," white paper, December 2013.
2. Benjamin Graham, *The Intelligent Investor: A Book of Practical Counsel*, 4th rev. ed. (New York: Harper & Row, 1973), p. xvi.

3. Josef Lakonishok, Andrei Shleifer, and Robert W. Vishny, "Contrarian Investment, Extrapolation, and Risk," *Journal of Finance* 49, no. 5 (December 1994).
4. Ibid.
5. As of December 31, 2013. Source: FactSet. This is a hypothetical example and is not representative of any specific portfolio or mutual fund. Reinvestment of dividends and capital gains is assumed. All indexes are unmanaged and are not available for direct investment. Your actual results will vary.
6. mba.tuck.dartmouth.edu/pages/faculty/ken.french/.
7. David Dreman, *Contrarian Investment Strategies: The Next Generation* (New York: Simon & Schuster, 1998), p. 257.
8. Lakonishok et al., "Contrarian Investment, Extrapolation, and Risk."
9. The Nasdaq market capitalization of Microsoft (MSFT) was $354.04 billion as of August 1, 2014.
10. The price of Microsoft went from 15.28 on March 2, 2009, to 37.29 on December 30, 2013; it went from 26.55 on December 28, 2012, to 37.29 on December 30, 2013.

Chapter 4

1. Michael Lewis, *Moneyball: The Art of Winning an Unfair Game* (New York: W. W. Norton & Company, 2003), p. 90.
2. Daniel Kahneman, "The Psychology of the Non-Professional Investor," article presented at Harvard seminar on behavioral finance, November 1998.
3. There are many other cognitive illusions and biases. For a more exhaustive list, see publications by David Dreman, Daniel Kahneman, and Amos Tversky.
4. The Nasdaq price of Netflix (NFLX) went from 50.95 on January 11, 2010, to 295.14 on July 4, 2011.
5. The price of Netflix on July 30, 2012, was 53.91.
6. The price of Netflix on July 30, 2014, was 472.35.
7. Harrison Hong and Jeffrey Kubik, "Analyzing the Analysts: Career Concerns and Biased Earnings Forecasts," *Financial Times*, February 2002.
8. Amos Tversky and Daniel Kahneman, "Judgment Under Uncertainty: Heuristics and Biases," *Science* 185, September 27, 1974, pp. 1124–1131.
9. Benjamin Graham, *The Intelligent Investor: A Book of Practical Counsel*, 4th rev. ed. (New York: Harper & Row, 1973), p. 287.
10. The DAX price of BMW on July 30, 2014, was 87.63.
11. Cliff Pratten, *The Stock Market* (Cambridge, U.K.: Cambridge University Press, 1993), p. 174.
12. Robert A. Haugen, *The New Finance: The Case Against Efficient Markets* (Englewood Cliffs, NJ: Prentice Hall, 1995), p. 1.
13. Ibid.

Chapter 5

1. Nicholas Carr, *The Shallows: What the Internet Is Doing to Our Brains* (New York: W. W. Norton & Company, 2010), p. 7.
2. Bloomberg.com, December 12, 2011.

Chapter 6

1. Trevor Hastie, Robert Tibshirani, and Jerome Friedman, *The Elements of Statistical Learning*, 2nd ed. (New York: Springer, 2009). The book's authors also note that, while this quote is popularly attributed to Deming, "ironically, we could find no 'data' confirming that Deming actually said this."
2. Berkshire Hathaway annual meeting of shareholders, Q&A session, May 7, 2007.

Chapter 7

1. Callan Associates, Inc., "Going Global," 2013. Data as of September 2011.
2. Based on the MSCI EAFE Index as of December 31, 2013.
3. Dave Kovaleski, "Bear's Eye View," *Pensions & Investments*, December 23, 2001, p. 34.
4. International Monetary Fund, as of June 30, 2014.
5. Ibid.
6. Ibid.

7. American Institute of Certified Public Accountants, "International Financial Reporting Standards (IFRS)," 2011, p. 1

Chapter 8

1. Price, income (earnings), and cash flow.
2. Data from the International Monetary Fund, as of December 31, 2013.
3. Bank for International Settlements, "Triennial Central Bank Survey," as of December 31, 2013.
4. Newley Purnell and Nopparat Chaichalearmmongkol, "Thai Confidence Improves After Coup," *Wall Street Journal*, June 3, 2014.

Chapter 9

1. Andrew Ross Sorkin, *Too Big to Fail* (New York: Penguin Group, 2009), p. 295.
2. Financial Accounting Standards Board, "Facts About FASB," www.fasb.org/facts.
3. Fitch Ratings; cited in Daniel Inman, Fiona Law, and Enda Curran, "China Commodity Loans Add to Surge in Offshore Borrowing," *online.WSJ.com*, June 12, 2014.
4. Securities and Exchange Commission, "Review of the Proxy Process Regarding the Nomination and Election of Directors," www.SEC.gov., November 19, 2003.
5. International Finance Corporation, "Corporate Governance Development Framework," www.ifc.org.
6. Benjamin Graham, *The Memoirs of the Dean of Wall Street* (New York: McGraw-Hill, 1996), p. 200.
7. Ibid., p. 201.
8. Ibid., p. 204.
9. David Benoit, "Clash Over Darden Board Will Be Measure of Activist Clout," *Wall Street Journal*, May 22, 2014.
10. David Benoit and Ben Lefebre, "Dow Chemical Lands in Hedge Fund's Sights," *Wall Street Journal*, January 21, 2014.
11. David Benoit, "In Rarity, Credit Suisse Aids Activist," *Wall Street Journal*, July 2, 2014.
12. Liz Hoffman, "Bitter Medicine in Store for Activists," *Wall Street Journal*, January 28, 2014.
13. Ibid.
14. CalPERS, "CalPERS Moves Motion for Majority Voting Standards at Apple Annual Meeting, Shareholders Approve," www.Calpers.ca.gov, February 28, 2014.
15. Anupreeta Das and Erik Holm, "Warren Buffett Defends Coca-Cola Abstention at Berkshire Meeting," *online.WSJ.com*, May 3, 2014.
16. Charles Dickens, *A Christmas Carol: A Ghost Story of Christmas* (New York: Chapman & Hall, 1847), p. 23.
17. Smithsonian Institution, "Gulf Oil Spill," www.ocean.si.edu.

Chapter 10

1. U.S. Census Bureau, 2007.
2. Yalman Onaran, "Bear Stearns Tells Hedge Fund Investors 'No Value Left,'" *Bloomberg*, July 18, 2007.
3. Bradley Keoun, Bloomberg, "Countrywide Taps $11.5 Billion Credit Line from Banks," *Bloomberg*, August 16, 2007.
4. David Ellis, "Countrywide Rescue: $4 Billion," *CNNMoney.com*, January 11, 2008.
5. Andrew Ross Sorkin, "JP Morgan Pays $2 a Share for Bear Stearns," *New York Times*, March 17, 2008.
6. David Gaffen, "Robert Steel Really Likes His New Company," *MarketBeat, Wall Street Journal*, July 25, 2008.
7. Joseph E. Stiglitz, "Capitalists Fools," *Vanity Fair.com*, January 2009.
8. Bill Vlasic and David M. Herszenhorn, "Detroit Chiefs Plead for Aid," *New York Times*, November 18, 2008.
9. "U.S. Exits GM stake, Taxpayers Lose About $10 Billion," *CBS/AP*, December 9, 2013.
10. "JPMorgan 'Agrees' to Tentative $13 Billion Penalty for Role in 2008 Financial Crisis," *RT.com*, October 20, 2013.

11. Chris Wright, "Citi: Where a $7 Billion Fine Makes Your Shares Go Up 4%," *Forbes*, July 14, 2014.
12. Sharon Terlep and Randall Smith, "GM Stock Rises in First-Day Trading," *Wall Street Journal*, November 18, 2010.
13. Benjamin Graham, *The Rediscovered Benjamin Graham Lectures*, (New York: John Wiley & Sons, 1999); http://www.wiley.com/legacy/products/subject/finance/bgraham/benlec1.html.

Chapter 11

1. OECD.org., 1945–1979.
2. Robert Lindsey, "Japanese Riding Hawaii's Real Estate Boom," *New York Times*, March 18, 1988.
3. Land Economy and Construction and Engineering Industry Bureau, Ministry of Land, Infrastructure, Transport and Tourism, 2004; Urban Land Price Index, Japan Real Estate Institute, 2004.
4. Tokyo Stock Exchange (TSE), Morgan Stanley Research, as of March 2014.
5. "Japan Earthquake Shakes World Economy; Stock Market Drops," Associated Press, March 15, 2011.

Chapter 12

1. Benjamin Graham and David L. Dodd, *Security Analysis*, 3rd rev. ed. (New York: McGraw-Hill, 1951), p. 646.
2. Benjamin Graham, *The Intelligent Investor: A Book of Practical Counsel*, 1st ed. (New York: HarperCollins, 1949), p. 4.
3. Charles Munger, "The Psychology of Human Misjudgment," speech at Harvard University, June 1995; http://buffettmungerwisdom.files.wordpress.com.
4. Robert J. Shiller, *Irrational Exuberance* (Princeton, NJ: Princeton University Press, 2000), p. 162.
5. Ibid., p. 56.
6. Matti Huuhtanen, "Two Americans Win Nobel Prize for Economics," *Seattle Times*, October 9, 2002.
7. Richard L. Peterson, *Inside the Investor's Brain: The Power of Mind Over Money* (Hoboken, NJ: John Wiley & Sons., Inc. 2007), pp. 289, 290.
8. Josef Lakonishok, Andrei Shleifer, and Robert W. Vishny, "Contrarian Investment, Extrapolation, and Risk," *Journal of Finance* 49, no. 5 (December 1994).
9. Warren Buffett, "Berkshire Hathaway Chairman's Letter to Shareholders," February 28, 2001.
10. Warren Buffett, "Berkshire Hathaway Chairman's Letter to Shareholders," February 28, 2005.

Chapter 13

1. In his review of Van Halen's premier album, *Rolling Stone* music critic Charles Young wrote, "They are likely to be a big deal. Their cover of the Kinks' 'You Really Got Me' does everything right, and they have three or four other cuts capable of jumping out of the radio," *Rolling Stone*, May 4, 1978.
2. Mark Carlson, "A Brief History of the 1987 Stock Market Crash with a Discussion of the Federal Reserve Response," Board of Governors of the Federal Reserve, November 2006.
3. Robert Maynard, "Conventional Investing in a Complex World," *Journal of Investing* 22, no. 1 (Spring 2013), pp. 57–73.
4. Gold Information Network, www.goldinfo.net.
5. Elroy Dimson, Paul Marsh, and Mike Staunton, *Triumph of the Optimists: 101 Years of Global Investment Returns* (Princeton, NJ: Princeton University Press, 2002), p. 63.
6. www.24hgold.com, as of July 31, 2014.
7. Arthur G. Korteweg, Roman Kräussi, and Patrick Verwijmeren, "Does It Pay to Invest in Art? A Selection-Corrected Returns Perspective," October 15, 2013.
8. George Carlin, *Class Clown*, LP recording (New York: Little David, September 29, 1972).

Chapter 14

1. Investment Company Institute, *2014 Investment Company Fact Book*, 54th ed. (Washington, DC: Investment Company Institute, 2014), p. 44.
2. Ibid., p. 55.
3. Anna Prior, "Leveraged ETFs for Retirees?," *Wall Street Journal*, March 4, 2013.
4. Japanese stocks made up 20 percent of the EAFE Index at December 31, 2013.
5. Christopher C. Carabell and Elizabeth L. DeLalla, "Index vs. Active Investment," *Pension Management*, April 1995, pp. 11 and 38.
6. Michael A. Pollock, "Actively Managed or Index Funds? Why Not Both," *Wall Street Journal*, March 3, 2014.

Chapter 15

1. Of course, U.S. government bonds and bills are backed by the full faith and credit of the U.S. government. Common stocks have no such backing and have tended to exhibit greater short-term price volatility. This is a hypothetical example and is not representative of any specific portfolio. Reinvestment of dividends and capital gains are assumed. Taxes and other expenses are not applied. Past performance is no guarantee of future results. Your actual results will vary.
2. Jeremy J. Siegel, *Stocks for the Long Run* (New York: McGraw-Hill, 1998), p. 13.
3. S&P 500 Index, using annualized quarterly returns on a rolling basis.
4. Mark Twain, *The Tragedy of Pudd'nhead Wilson* (New York: Charles L. Webster & Company, 1894), p. 166.
5. This is a hypothetical example and is not representative of any specific portfolio or mutual fund. Reinvestment of dividends and capital gains are assumed. Taxes and other expenses are not applied. Past performance is no guarantee of future results. Your actual results will vary.
6. Employee Benefit Research Institute, "The Impact of the Financial Crisis on 401(k) Account Balances," Issue Brief No. 326, February 2009, p. 1.
7. Janet Lowe, *Value Investing Made Easy* (New York: McGraw-Hill, 1996), p. 118.
8. Siegel, *Stocks for the Long Run*, pp. 11–12.

Chapter 16

1. Benjamin Graham, *The Intelligent Investor: A Book of Practical Counsel*, 4th rev. ed. (New York: Harper & Row, 1973), p. 277.
2. Jennifer Ablan and Liciana Lopez, "Damage Control at Pimco After Gross, El-Erian Clash," Reuters, March 17, 2014.
3. Benjamin Graham and David L. Dodd, *Security Analysis*, 3d rev. ed. (New York: McGraw-Hill, 1951), p. 82.
4. Ibid., p. 175.
5. According to the Investment Company Institute, "The decline in interest rates in 2009 pushed annual returns on corporate bonds to 19 percent for non-prime investment grade bonds and to 58 percent for speculative bonds. In addition, low short-term interest rates and the relatively steep yield curve likely enticed some investors to shift out of money market funds—whose yields hovered just above zero—and into short-term bond mutual funds." Investment Company Institute, "Frequently Asked Questions," April 2010; www.ici.org.
6. Agustino Fontevecchia, "QE4 Is Here: Bernanke Delivers $85B-a-Month Until Unemployment Falls Below 6.5%," *Forbes*, December 12, 2012.
7. "Fed's Richard Fisher: Liquidity Causing 'Beer Goggles,'" *CNBC*, January 14, 2014.
8. According to Morningstar, Templeton Global Bond A, Lord Abbett Short Duration Income A, DoubleLine Return Bond I, and Pimco Income A Morningstar were in this category as of December 31, 2013.
9. Barclays, as of June 30, 2013. Past performance is not a guarantee of future results.
10. Anjan V. Thakor, "The Economic Consequences of the Volcker Rule," U.S. Chamber of Commerce, Center for Capital Markets Competitiveness, Summer 2012.
11. Benjamin Graham and David Dodd, *Security Analysis*, 3rd rev. ed., New York: McGraw-Hill, 1951, p. 299.

Chapter 17

1. Niagara Institutional Dialogue, Niagara-on-the-Lake, Ontario, June 9–11, 2014; http://www.institutionaldialogue.com.
2. Benjamin Graham, *The Intelligent Investor: A Book of Practical Counsel*, 4th rev. ed. (New York: Harper & Row, 1973), p. 280.
3. John Train, *The Midas Touch* (New York: Harper & Row, 1987), p. 55.
4. Warren Buffett, "Berkshire Hathaway Chairman's Letter to Shareholders," February 28, 1997.
5. Laura Tuttle, "Alternative Trading Systems: Description of ATS Trading in National Market System Stocks," Securities and Exchange Commission, October 2013, p. 2.
6. Michael Lewis, *Flash Boys: A Wall Street Revolt* (New York: W.W. Norton & Company, Inc., 2014), pp. 108–109.
7. Malcolm Mitchell, "Is MPT the Solution—or the Problem?" *Investment Policy*, July 2002.
8. Michael Bar-Eli, Ofer H. Azar, Ilana Ritov, Yael Keidar-Levin, and Galit Schein, "Action Bias Among Elite Soccer Goalkeepers: The Case of Penalty Kicks," *Journal of Economic Psychology* 28, no. 5 (October 2007), pp. 606–621.
9. Dan Fitzpatrick, "Pensions Pull Back from Hedge Funds," *Wall Street Journal*, July 24, 2014.
10. Andrew G. Haldane, "The Age of Asset Management?," speech given at the London Business School, April 4, 2014.

Chapter 18

1. From Andrew Bell, *Mutual Funds for Canadians for Dummies*, 2nd ed. (Toronto: CDG Books Canada, 2000).
2. Benjamin Graham, *The Intelligent Investor: A Book of Practical Counsel*, 4th rev. ed. (New York: Harper & Row, 1973), p. 108.
3. Ibid.
4. Brad M. Barber and Terrance Odean, "Too Many Cooks Spoil the Profits: Investment Club Performance," *Financial Analysts Journal* 56, no. 1 (January/February 2000), p. 24.
5. Blaine F. Aiken, "Fiduciary Corner: The Importance of the Investment Policy Statement," *Investment News*, report of survey of advisors by Russell Investments, October 27, 2013.
6. "Boomers Behaving Badly," Brandes Institute, January 2012; www.brandes.com/institute.
7. Graham, *The Intelligent Investor*, p. 57.
8. Ibid., p. 1.
9. Ibid., p. 2.
10. Robert Maynard, "Conventional Investing in a Complex World," *Journal of Investing* 22, no. 1 (Spring 2013), pp. 57–73.

Chapter 19

1. Sam Farmer, "Seattle's Savior Is a Silent Partner," *Los Angeles Times*, January 26, 2014.
2. The team's value was estimated by *Forbes* at $1.08 billion as of December 31, 2013.
3. Dayn Perry, "This Day in 1919," December 26, 2013.
4. Baseball-Almanac.com.
5. Benjamin Graham, *The Intelligent Investor: A Book of Practical Counsel*, 4th rev. ed. (New York: Harper & Row, 1973), p. xv.
6. Thomas J. Stanley and William D. Danko, *The Millionaire Next Door: The Surprising Secrets of America's Wealthy*, Atlanta, CA: Longstreet Press, 1996, p. 100.

Acknowledgments

As in my previous books and value investing, my acknowledgments tend to have great staying power. I again recognize my colleagues at Brandes Investment Partners for their support, knowledge, and contributions to the insights of this book.

I am greatly indebted to my mentor, the father of security analysis and value investing, Benjamin Graham. His personal guidance formed the solid foundation for my investment success.

One person who needs to be individually named is Rick Ryan. As our product and program manager at Brandes Investment Partners, Rick's research, writing ability, and hard work were vital to the production of this book. Thank you, Rick.

Index

assets
  hidden, 78
  intangible, 78
  and liabilities, 77–78
  undervalued, 78
AT&T, Inc., 85
Atwater, Lee, 120
Australian Financial Digest interview, 154
Austria, return and U.S. market, 99
automakers
  assistance received by, 137–138
  Chrysler, 137–138
  Ford, 137–139
  GM, 137–139
  receipt of TARP assistance, 137

B

baby boomers, retirement planning
  for, 226
"Back to the Future" study, 215–216
balance sheet debt, 68–69
balance sheets
  assets, 77–78
  liabilities, 77
  shareholders' equity, 77
The Bank of New York Mellon Corp., 63
banks, attractiveness in 2007, 133
Barber, Brad, 223
bargain-hunting techniques
  safety, 71
  value, 70
bear markets
  adding value in, 189
  value within, 188–189
Bear Stearns funds, 133–134
behavioral biases, 43, 48. *See also* bias
behavioral finance, 43, 155–156, 160–161.
      See also investor behavior
Belgium, return and U.S. market, 99
Berkshire Hathaway, 155
Berlin Wall razing, 82
bias, influence of, 36. *See also* behavioral biases
Black Monday, 10
  amount of losses, 11
  causes of, 4
Bloomberg Radio interview, 18
BMW, 53
board appointments, controlling, 119
Bogle, John, 173, 181
bond fixed-income products. *See also* debt
  2008 residuals, 201
  commercial paper, 201
  derivatives, 201
  floating-rate bonds, 201
  foreign debt, 201
  high-yield debt, 201
  intermediate-term debt, 201
  leveraged closed-end funds, 201
  limited-term debt, 201
  multisector debt, 201
  municipal bonds, 201
  short-term debt, 201
  subordinated debt, 201
  unconstrained, 201
  U.S. Treasuries, 200
bond investing, 195–197

bond mutual funds, 17. *See also* mutual funds
bond returns, impact of interest rates on, 200
bond rush, 197
bonds. *See also* value bonds
  capital preservation, 199
  credit risk, 199
  diversification, 199
  downsides, 199
  duration-managed, 169
  economic contribution, 199
  floating rate, 169
  foreign, 169
  growth potential, 199
  high-yield, 169
  inflation risk, 199
  interest-rate risk, 199
  inventory trends, 203
  regulations, 202–203
  risk mitigation, 199
  versus stocks, 186
  transparency, 202–203
  upsides, 199
  versus U.S. Treasuries, 198–199
  value investing in, 202
  volatility, 199
boomer behavior, 160
"Boomers Behaving Badly," 226
Boonsongpaisan, Niwattumrong, 103
Botox, 119
brand names, embracing, 106
Brandes Institute
  behavioral finance, 160
  body of work, 159–160
  boomer behavior, 160
  expectations, 160
  FRBs (floating-rate bonds), 161
  launch of, 157
  and LSV study, 159
  passive investing, 160
  private versus public equity, 161
  risk parity, 161
  short-term underperformance, 161
Brazil
  economic crisis of 2002, 103
  investment in 2014, 104–105
Bretton Woods system, 7
Bristol-Myers scandal (2002), 114
British Sky Broadcasting Group
      PLC, 63
Brown, Jim, 110
bubble. *See also* Internet bubble; tech bubble
  causes of, 231
  extent of, 129
  signs of trouble, 131–132
"buffer" of opportunity, 20
Buffett, Warren, 72
Bunning, Jim, 139
Burroughs Corporation, 6
Bush, George H. W., 82–83
Business Times, Singapore interview, 55
businesses. *See* companies
BusinessWeek
  cover story in 1979, 8–9
  interview, 206
Buttonwood Agreement (1792), 218
buy low, sell high, 19
buy-and-hold strategy, lack of, 25

K

Kahn, Irving, 36
Kahneman, Daniel, 155–156
kaizen, 143–144
keiretsu, 146–147
Kinks, The, 163
Kiplinger website, 76
"know thyself," 219–220
Kozlowski, Dennis, 115
Kubik, Jeffrey, 46

L

Ladies Home Journal, 228
Lakonishok, Josef. *See* LSV (Likonishok Shleifer, Vishny), 33
leverage
  as behavior pattern, 16
  concerns, 134–135
  Countrywide Financial, 134
  as debt, 133–134
  Federal Reserve actions, 134
  IndyMac, 134
  "lending facilities," 134
  "quantitative easing" program, 134
leveraged closed-end funds, 201
Lewis, Michael, 41–42, 211–212
Lewis, Ray, 151
liabilities and assets, 77–78
LIBOR (London Interbank Offered Rate), 201
LIFO (last-in, first-out) technique, 77
Lincoln Savings and Loan, 11–12
liquidity
  explained, 211
  keeping fair, 211–212
liquidity risk, 211–213. *See also* risks
Little Book of Common Sense, 181
Loeb, Daniel, 119
long-term investing, 27
long-term performance, achieving, 177
losing capital, 231–232
losing money
  company deterioration, 208
  lack of focus, 208
  overpaying, 207
  selling at a loss, 208
Louvre Accord, 144
LSV (Likonishok Shleifer, Vishny), 30–31, 33, 37, 157–159

M

macro hedge funds, 164. *See also* hedge funds
Malkiel, Burton, 181
Manhattan Fund, 5
March 2000 tech bubble, 14–15, 23
margin of safety, 19–20, 195, 232–235
market behavior, exploiting, 49–51
market declines
  death cross, 187
  golden cross, 188
  hemline histogram, 188
  Hindenburg omen, 188
  presidential effect, 188
  skyscraper up drop, 188
  Super Bowl tickets, 188
market leaders, change from 1993–2001, 98
market prices, rising, 25–26

market sentiment, vetting, 156–157
market swings, 27, 220–221
Markowitz, Harry, 181, 214
Marks & Spencer Group PLC, 63
Marshall Plan, 13
Maryland's Old Court Savings, 11
Maynard, Robert, 165, 216, 228
McDonald's, 6, 217
media impact, 59–60
The Memoirs of the Dean of Wall Street, 118
Merck, 6, 115
Mexican investing, 13–14, 94
MGT (Morgan Guaranty Trust), 5–6
Microsoft Corporation, 37–38
The Millionaire Next Door, 233
misleading, avoiding, 233
money
  investing in, 101–102
  reasons for losing, 207
money management. *See* portfolio management
money market funds, 11
Moneyball, 41–42
Montier, James, 29
Morgan Stanley, 139
MPT (modern portfolio theory), 214
"Mr. Market," 5
Mr. Market parable, 220–221
MSCI EAFE Index, 178
MSCI Emerging Markets Index, 88, 96
MSCI Japan Index, 111. *See also* Japanese stocks
Munger, Charles, 155
municipal bonds, 168, 201
mutual funds. *See also* bond mutual funds
  ESG strategies, 122
  short-term perspective, 25

N

Nasdaq 100, 22
Nasdaq Composite, 22
Netflix streaming extrapolation, 45–46
net-net method
  explained, 69
  profitability, 69–70
"new economy" companies, 21–22
New Zealand, return and U.S. market, 98–99
Niagara Institutional Dialogue, 206
Nifty Fifty, 5–7, 231
Nikkei 225, 144–145, 151
Nissan Motor Co. Ltd., 63
Nixon, Richard, 122
"Nixon shock," 7
Northern Pipeline shares (1925), 118
Norway, return and U.S. market, 99

O

objectives, setting, 224
October 19, 1987, 3–4, 9–10
Odean, Terrance, 223
Oklahoma, hard times in 1980s, 58
"old economy" companies, 22
Omura, Shingo, 151
Ono Pharmaceutical Co., Ltd., 149–150
OPEC oil embargo of 1973, 7
optimism
  excess of, 53
  pitfall of, 46

About the Author

Charles Brandes is the founder and chairman of Brandes Investment Partners, L.P. and also a member of the firm's Investment Oversight Committee.

After starting his career in 1968 as a broker trainee, Mr. Brandes decided to dedicate his practice to value investing soon after a chance, yet inspiring, meeting with the man who had pioneered this time-tested investment philosophy, Benjamin (Ben) Graham. Considered the father of value investing, Graham is the author of such books as *Security Analysis* and *The Intelligent Investor*—groundbreaking insights that, as Mr. Brandes often puts it, "changed my life."

Following this sage advice, Mr. Brandes, with the enthusiastic support of Ben Graham, founded Brandes Investment Partners in 1974 based on the Graham-and-Dodd value investment tenets.

Since he founded his eponymous firm, Brandes has never wavered from this straightforward Graham-and-Dodd approach, building portfolios one company at a time through the firm's equity and fixed-income strategies to help clients pursue their long-term investment goals.